# Anatomy of Failure

**Also available from Bloomsbury:**

*Alain Badiou: Live Theory*, Oliver Feltham
*Being and Event,* Alain Badiou, translated by Oliver Feltham
*Libertarian Anarchy*, Gerard Casey

# Anatomy of Failure

Philosophy and Political Action

OLIVER FELTHAM

BLOOMSBURY
LONDON • NEW DELHI • NEW YORK • SYDNEY

**Bloomsbury Academic**
An imprint of Bloomsbury Publishing Plc

| 50 Bedford Square | 175 Fifth Avenue |
| London | New York |
| WC1B 3DP | NY 10010 |
| UK | USA |

www.bloomsbury.com

First published 2013

© Oliver Feltham, 2013

All rights reserved. No part of this publication may be reproduced or transmitted in any form or by any means, electronic or mechanical, including photocopying, recording, or any information storage or retrieval system, without prior permission in writing from the publishers.

Oliver Feltham has asserted his right under the Copyright, Designs and Patents Act, 1988, to be identified as Author of this work.

No responsibility for loss caused to any individual or organization acting on or refraining from action as a result of the material in this publication can be accepted by Bloomsbury Academic or the author.

**British Library Cataloguing-in-Publication Data**
A catalogue record for this book is available from the British Library.

ISBN: HB: 978-1-4411-6088-1
PB: 978-1-4411-5864-2
ePub: 978-1-4411-6512-1
ePDF: 978-1-4411-9954-6

**Library of Congress Cataloging-in-Publication Data**
Feltham, Oliver.
 Anatomy of failure : philosophy and political action / Oliver Feltham.
   p. cm.
 Includes bibliographical references (p.   ) and index.
 ISBN 978-1-4411-5864-2 (pbk.) – ISBN 978-1-4411-6088-1 (hardcover) – ISBN 978-1-4411-6512-1 (epub) – ISBN 978-1-4411-9954-6 (ebook pdf)
 1. Political science–Philosophy.  I. Title.
 JA71.F46 2013
 320.01–dc23
 2012030173

Typeset by Newgen Imaging Systems Pvt Ltd, Chennai, India

# CONTENTS

*Acknowledgements* vi
*List of abbreviations* vii

1 Thrasymachus versus Socrates on philosophy and political action  1
2 1647 – The history of the Leveller-agitators and the New Model Army  29
3 Hobbes' and Locke's metaphysics: Substances no longer act, institutions act  87
4 Hobbes and Locke on religious conflict: When institutions act, subjects act  131
5 Hobbes and Locke on politics: Sovereign action and contractual action  181
6 Unveiling the forgotten model: The Leveller-agitators on joint action  251

*Notes* 271
*Bibliography* 283
*Index* 287

# ACKNOWLEDGEMENTS

This book is dedicated to Alma and Giulio, fruit of joint action, partners who join new to old.

Many friends and colleagues have aided me in the long gestation of this book, whether it was in a brief exchange at a conference or through continual collegial support. Some of them have probably forgotten what they said when I unveiled this project to them, but all contributions were valuable, and kept me going at different points of the voyage. Having said that, the result is no one's fault but my own. In particular I would like to thank Bernard Aspe, Bruno Besana, Vanessa Brito, Andrew Buchanan, Lorenzo Chiesa, Justin Clemens, Mladen Dolar, Duncan Fairfax, Alexis Feltham, Bryony Feltham, Chris Feltham and Val Feltham, Tony Fry, Geoffrey Gilbert, Peter Hallward, Quentin Meillassoux, Alberto Toscano, Steven Sawyer, Jelica Sumic Riha, Frank Ruda, Cameron Tonkinwise, Tzuchien Tho and Ben Tunstall. The American University of Paris supported me by means of a research course release in the fall of 2010, and by providing a diligent research assistant, Sophia Ben-Achour, for one semester. Sally Murray, my librarian, did not give up on securing access to the Early English Books Online database. Bloomsbury have demonstrated inestimable patience and good will. Finally I thank my first reader, Barbara Formis – if it had not been for that first conversation about praxis in the café at the Bibliothèque Nationale Française, there would be neither book, nor children, nor us.

# LIST OF ABBREVIATIONS

Leveller-agitator tracts from the Thomason Tracts collection

| | |
|---|---|
| AP | *An Agreement of the People* |
| CA | *The Case of the Army Truly Stated* |
| SE | *Ahe Solemn Engagement* |
| PP | *Putney Projects* |

Books

| | |
|---|---|
| B | Thomas Hobbes, *Behemoth or the Long Parliament* |
| C | Thomas Hobbes, *On the Citizen* |
| E | Baruch Spinoza, *Ethics* |
| EHU | John Locke, *An Essay Concerning Human Understanding* |
| L | Thomas Hobbes, *Leviathan* |
| LT | John Locke, *A Letter Concerning Toleration* |
| ML | Martin Luther, *Martin Luther: Selections from His Writings* |
| PL | A. S. P. Woodhouse, *Puritanism & Liberty* (the Putney Debates) |
| R | Plato, *The Republic* |
| ST | John Locke, *Second Treatise on Government* |

# CHAPTER ONE

# Thrasymachus versus Socrates on philosophy and political action

## Origins

Thrasymachus is angry. He was allowed to figure in one of the grand opening scenes of philosophy only to disappear into the wings, a mere extra, yet he had come to declare a truth: that there is no justice, no Idea of the good that might direct action. What is called 'justice' is always what suits the stronger: 'in all cities the same thing is just, namely what is good for the ruling authority'.[1] Power determines what is said to be right. Two millennia before Hobbes or Marx, Thrasymachus insists that a theory of action has to take into account political power and the possibility of justice being fiction. But Socrates and his acolytes are not ready; for them this would result in a space of action without any orientation, which is absurd. They overwhelm him with reproaches of incivility and arguments that beg the question, presuming the truth of the very theory he is attacking. He gives ground reluctantly not able to fully articulate and defend what is actually the germ of an entirely different philosophy of action. And on the way he offers the only complete diagnosis of Socrates' tactics to be found in the Platonic opus: Socrates is not an ironist, but a trickster. Athens' self-appointed moral critic is stung by the attack; in response, his sarcasm is violent, his rhetoric cheap and arguments rough and flawed. Yet Thrasymachus is reduced to sulking and then silence. After Book I of *The Republic*, we hear no more of him apart from a few brief references in the *Phaedrus*. Another madman has to leave the town square, his message undecipherable.

So before the construction begins in *The Republic*, before political philosophy is founded, one doctrine is dismissed. The voice of Thrasymachus: excluded. Or is his voice only silenced to stage a return centuries later under another guise? Hobbes opens political modernity with the statement 'there is no sovereign good'. Marx introduces a theory of false appearances of justice with his concept of ideology. But surely Thrasymachus would have no truck with any 'social contract' or 'class consciousness', pale avatars of his original message, the work of bad disciples who did not understand. For him it is the philosophical operation per se which is at fault – it perpetually generates concepts of justice by abstracting from what actually happens in society. Lets go back to the original scene.

Thrasymachus is not just angry with Socrates and his disciples, he is contemptuous: philosophy turns you into children. It tells you bedtime stories, lulling you to sleep by putting anxiety at bay. Wake up disciples! You are not asking the right questions of your master. He is always trying to trick you. Is this really supposed to be a dialogue or is it a monologue with a chorus of sycophants? And when you finally get your turn to speak, you as a disciple, you will tell bedtime stories in turn. Jacques Lacan channels Thrasymachus when he diagnoses philosophy as a discourse of the master.[2] Socrates uses force in his arguments: he exposes his novice interlocutors to intellectual puzzles he has already been through a thousand times, obliging them to accept his own premises and then his conclusions as if no other logical path were open for thought and then he holds their hand when they walk into a wall, all the while repeating those masters, your masters, they do not know that they do not know – I do, I am the only one who knows that he does not know. Thrasymachus laughs. Philosophy is thus just one more attempt at mastery; its stories about justice are nothing but a feint on the way. There is one phenomenon to be accounted for when it comes to action and that is how power generates the appearance of justice. No one acts but the master, and his action is always a kind of trick.

At the level of our taxpaying existence is this not what we all suspect – that there is no genuine political action, only masquerades and tricks pulled off by would-be masters? Opinion polls deliver a roller-coaster show of politicians' popularity while public relations specialists spin statistics into policy analysis, and yet the real deals are being made in the back rooms by the banking lobbies. If we were to characterize our epoch it would be one of mastery reduced to tricks – we no longer even have nostalgia for a real master. Our masters today show us how they perform their tricks in the very act of pulling them off, like a celebrity cook on a television show: see, this is how I boost optimism in the economy by talking up the quarterly figures.

But Thrasymachus is no cynic and the rest of *The Republic* does not paper over his questions. At first glance Plato takes up the position of his barefooted master and expands it: there are actions which have as their principle neither mastery nor illusion but the philosophical knowledge of the Good. These actions are carried out by persons whose souls are balanced; reason, spirit and appetite, each playing its proper role. In more concrete terms, within the construction of Callipolis, the hypothetical just city, one can identify each institution as a kind of long-term political action – the breeding program, the communal property program, the education program, the myth of origins. Each of these organizational arrangements acts insofar as it causes a massive change to take place in society. But the most evident political actions Plato describes, the ones *The Republic* is famous for, are far more punctual and spectacular: the exclusion of the tragedians and the crowning of the philosopher-king.

As generations of students have suspected, these two actions are very close to being tricks themselves. Tragic theatre is a public discourse that articulates the moral relationship of the individual to the city – in short it is a rival to philosophy and its pedagogy. By banishing the tragedians from the city the philosopher deals with his rivals by simply writing them out of the scene, guaranteeing himself exclusive control over the field of education and mythmaking. The young guardians will listen to no one but the philosopher because the competition has been eliminated. But what about the philosopher crowning himself king? We have already had quite enough of the philosopher taking a perfectly amusing conversation topic – 'what is the good life?' – weighing it down with technical terms and taking enormous detours only to end up claiming that the good life is actually his life and that it consists of nothing other than continually answering the question 'what is the good life?'

Not only does the good life turn out to be the philosopher's life, but also the philosopher's definition of the just city turns out to be a city ruled by a philosopher. Adeimantus and Glaucon laughed when Socrates first said this and my students laugh every year when I review the argument – but the laughter is not for the absurd impracticality of the solution. No, the laughter is neither contemptuous nor dismissive; it is full-bellied and appreciative – a wonderful sleight of hand has been performed. We have been treated to an entire pantomime featuring a cast of tyrants, oligarchs, drones, mechanicals, Thrasymachus himself and the democratic man – all masks for the philosopher-king. Philosophy promises answers to all the real questions, to the questions other disciplines cannot answer nor even ask, yet its answers always turn out to be 'philosophy'. Its dialogues, rich in arguments, ideas, distinctions, interpretable on myriads of levels, end up being one long tautology. And these tricks – the trick of clearing the field of competitors by banishing the poets, the trick of putting oneself in charge of applying one's own plan for the city – these tricks require some mastery. The very exercise of constructing an entire city in one's head, on the fly, in response to objections, complete with division of labour, class structure, myths, education and breeding programs, hairdressers and perfumers, demands an authoritative performance. In a certain sense, a city founder enjoys absolute mastery. And so Thrasymachus' accusation surrounds *The Republic* and lingers – and Plato's construction does not develop enough velocity to escape the gravity of mastery and deception.

But perhaps this is precisely the point. Socrates refutes Thrasymachus violently in Book I, but years later, when Plato composes the rest of *The Republic*, he has his character Socrates take on the sophist's challenge.[3] What does Socrates do in Books II through X? Instead of continuing his relentless destruction of other people's answers to his own questions he actually does what Thrasymachus asks him to do and develops his own answer, at great length, and at great peril, making himself extremely vulnerable to attack. For one that claims not to know, this is a very fragile and complicated construction filling in the answer to 'what is justice?' But not only does the Socrates of Books II–X change his entire approach, becoming someone who knows, he also develops a theory of false appearances, or simulacra, which could account for the generation of precisely those images of 'justice' that Thrasymachus speaks of, images which have little to do with any Idea of justice. And in a nice ironic turn, these images would be precisely those manipulated by the tragedians and by the sophists – false masters according to the philosopher's measure. Plato does not dismiss but encompasses elements of Thrasymachus' argument within the very construction of Callipolis. The final proof of this lies in him directly addressing the question of power. Thrasymachus insists on one question that must be asked when it is a matter of action and justice – who? For him the only valid argument is ad hominem: whose 'justice' is at stake? And he already disposes of an answer: it will be the 'justice' of the ruling power in the city. So to ask 'what is justice?' is to ask 'who is the ruling power in the city?' And he laughs because the barefoot philosopher claims to have nothing to do with power. Plato, on the other hand, has Socrates openly admit the philosopher's desire for mastery:

> GLAUCON: ... Try rather to persuade us that such a city is possible, in what manner it is possible, and leave any other question alone ...
>
> SOCRATES: ... I believe that it is with one sole change that actual cities would be completely transformed; it is true that this change is neither unimportant, nor easy, but it is possible ... As soon as I say this I will be covered with ridicule and shame ... As long as philosophers are not kings in the cities, or that those that are today called sovereigns and kings are not philosophers, political power and philosophy will not meet in the same subject, and the numerous individuals that pursue one or the other of these goals exclusively will not be placed in the impossibility of acting in such a manner, and there will be no end to the evils of cities, my dear Glaucon, nor to those of human beings, and the city that we have described will never be realized such as it could be, and will never see the light of day. (R, V, 472a, 473c)

The ruling power in Callipolis is the philosopher-king. Although his knowledge of justice is based on the Idea of justice and not on simulacra, this Idea cannot be detached from his person or his knowledge. And so Thrasymachus' question – who? – holds good. It is the philosopher who knows what is Justice; it is the philosopher-king who directs the education of the guardians and maintains the institutions of the city according to this knowledge. Plato calls Thrasymachus' bluff and exposes the philosopher's desire – to be king. But despite the dreams of psychoanalytic ideology critique, the exposure of desire does not bring the philosophical operation to a halt, it just complicates it.

To understand just how complicated the question of political action is in *The Republic*, at the inception of the tradition, we have to return to Socrates' three arguments against Thrasymachus: the argument from error, the argument from technique and the argument from collective enterprise.

If justice is what is good for the ruling authority, Socrates asks, what happens when the latter makes a mistake? What happens when a king gives an order that ends up causing him harm? You Thrasymachus, you claim whatever is just is what is good for the stronger. This implies it is just for inferiors to carry out their superiors' orders. Thrasymachus concedes this additional premise – and he should not have, because it is incoherent with his original position. There are no rules for justice for Thrasymachus, there is no action – such as carrying out orders – which is automatically just, independent of any reference to a person. His position is that justice is ad hominem. Justice consists solely of what the present ruling authority in the city-state decides to call just. A ruler may dictate that carrying out orders is just, but he could just as well change his mind the following day and dictate that automatically carrying out orders is not just.

Thrasymachus however does admit this additional premise that carrying out orders is just. Socrates can then immediately generate a contradiction – the ruling authority may issue an order that ends up resulting in harm to himself. On the one hand, the execution of the order is just because inferiors have obeyed their superiors; on the other hand, it is unjust because it results in harm for the stronger. Thrasymachus tries to slip out of this dilemma by arguing that strictly speaking a ruler is not a ruler *when* he makes a mistake; he is a ruler by virtue of his knowledge, and while making a mistake his knowledge fails him. Such a position provides everyone with a fail-safe excuse for failure – 'oh sorry', says the surgeon, 'I was not actually a surgeon when I took out your spleen. I should have taken out your appendix but my knowledge momentarily failed me.'

Regardless of whether Thrasymachus should accept the additional premise, the actual point Socrates makes is fundamental; and that is the ad hominem argument can never be exclusive. No one person can completely decide and control the appearance and occurrence of actions. Orders can be issued on the basis of false information and the execution of orders can also result in unforeseen consequences. Both in acting and in calling his actions just, the ruling authority can make mistakes. The ruler calls whatever actions that are supposed to be good for him 'just'; yet in the event, if one action goes haywire, these appearances of 'justice' will turn out to be incoherent. To understand political action – even from the standpoint of one single subject, the stronger – one has to take into account the possibility of failure. Failure undoes mastery. Failure opens up a gap between intention, or what one declares about one's action, and its actual consequences. Failure shows that no agent can completely control the actual results of their action, however all-powerful he might be. Socrates' crucial step is then to interpret success and failure in terms of truth and error. In his view, an action fails if its agent does not possess true knowledge. Consequently, to assure an action's success political power alone is not sufficient. In the interrogation of action Thrasymachus' ad hominem argument – *Who is acting? For whom is something done?* – cannot stand alone; one must always add the instance of judgement – *What is being done? According to which criteria?*

In Socrates' second argument against Thrasymachus, he identifies politics as a species of technical practice (*techne*). He then argues from the nature of practice to the nature of politics. Any practice, whether it be medicine or navigation, is directed by a reference to the good, the good of the thing of which it is an art. Horsemanship, for instance, is directed towards the good of horses. Each practice also has its object – horsemanship has horses, navigation has sailors, medicine has bodies. A practice is said to control or have authority over its object. The very need for technique originates in a defect in those objects: they are not self-sufficient or self-directed. Sailors cannot naturally find their way on the high seas and the body cannot cure itself of every disease. Nature, in its lack, is thus supplemented by technique. A technical practice is a form of knowledge that completes nature. Socrates concludes his argument by making a general claim about the nature of authority in all technical practices, and by implication in politics:

No-one in a position of authority thinks about or prescribes what is good for himself, but only about what is good for the person under his authority – for whose benefit he himself exercises his art or technique. (R, I, 342e)

Here politics is subsumed under the general category of technique, in which all ruling authority assumes the same form and function. Aristotle in contrast begins his *Politics* by distinguishing four kinds of authority – that of parents over their children, that of a husband over his wife, that of a master over his slave and political authority, quite different from the other three. In his argument against Thrasymachus, Socrates assumes that there is only one kind of authority, the kind involved in technical productions. Within Socrates' second argument against Thrasymachus we find a not-so-innocuous thesis, a thesis that has not been demonstrated: politics is a technique, a productive technique.

But Socrates is not done yet. He launches into a third argument about collective enterprise. Once Thrasymachus has admitted that the unjust man will attempt to outdo any other man in any situation, Socrates asks him the following question:

> Suppose a city, or an army, or pirates, or thieves, or any other group of people, are jointly setting about some unjust venture. Do you think they'd be able to get anywhere if they treated one another unjustly? (R, I, 351c)

Thrasymachus responds in the negative and Socrates pursues his argument by explaining that injustice causes hatred, faction and quarrels whereas justice produces cooperation and friendship. Hence 'whatever [injustice] appears in – whether city, nation, army, or anything else – it first renders incapable of concerted action, through faction and disagreements' (R, I, 351e–352a). This appears to be Socrates' strongest argument since it is based on common sense: you know this! I know this! If we do not agree we are never going to get anything done together – this is the brute fact, the rock around which the impossible staff meeting endlessly circulates, and yet this argument begs the question. It presumes that there is such a thing as joint action. Of course it is the case that there actions which involve collectives – cities go to war, bands of robbers hijack convoys, offices manage to process some documents – but it is far from evident that there is a collective agent of such actions. Rather it seems that there is one person in charge who takes decisions while the others merely execute orders. Moreover in such an organization an underling can disagree with an order, complain to their colleagues, and yet still execute it, and so contra Socrates there can be cooperation amidst disagreement. This leads us to Socrates' other unfounded assumption: the only possible glue for a collective is the moral quality of its actions, justice producing cooperation and friendship. But other philosophers have found alternative mechanisms that produce cooperation: Hobbes argues that collectives can also be soldered together by passions, such as religious enthusiasm, or fear, and Adam Smith sees individual self-interest guiding the peaceful fulfilment of an economic contract. Indeed Plato himself bans the tragedians because of the nefarious effects of imitation, another mechanism which binds collectives together – as Freud will explore in *Mass Psychology and the Ego*. No, the real question that Thrasymachus raises and Socrates does not even want to explore, is the following: is there any such thing as joint action in the first place, and if so, what are its conditions?

The original disagreement between Thrasymachus and Socrates contains decisions that will go on to shape much of Plato's thinking of political action, if not the thinking of the many philosophers to come, all the way up to this little book, which is intended to address the original wrong, and take Thrasymachus seriously. For Thrasymachus the fundamental question is *who*? Who acts, and in whose interest, and who determines the appearances, the names of action? The figure he creates and Glaucon perpetuates is that of the unjust master, the master who overreaches, outdoes, exploits and cheats other people yet is socially integrated: the ancestor of Freud's primitive father, the tyrant, the all-encompassing boss who has anticipated your every critique, your every move to independence and disqualified it from the outset. Thrasymachus' challenge is to think action in terms of power and the generation of appearances – if justice is what is good for the stronger then politics is no more than the ruling authority calling 'justice' whatever actions suit its interests. In short, there is no politics.

And the philosopher's retort? Any action can fail, even that of an all-powerful tyrant. The question of power is insufficient; one must add the question of knowledge, and truth. The kind of knowledge at stake in political action is that of productive art: politics is an art that cannot take place without justice. Furthermore no kind of collective enterprise would be possible without justice. In this manner the barefooted philosopher saves the existence of politics, a realm that cannot be reduced to the exercise of force and the manipulation of appearances.

## Angelic critique or servile apology

When the philosopher argues that there is such a thing as political action, and its quality is justice, it is a liberating affirmation, it gives hope. Yet in Plato's reenactment of the original dialogue the conceptual construction of the city-state is so elaborate and radical that it seems to bear no relation – not even as ideal – to politics as it is actually practised. The philosopher claims to be at grips with reality and yet this esoteric practice of linking ideas by argument is so very far from the force and fortune of actual political action. Glaucon calls Socrates on this gap between his prescriptions and existing politics:

> The fact is, Socrates, if you're allowed to go on talking about this kind of thing, I don't think you will ever come back to the question you originally postponed in order to go into all these details, the question of whether it is possible – and just *how* it is possible – for political arrangements of this kind to be introduced. (R, I, 471a)

Socrates responds that the philosopher must become king. But in the absence of this trick solution – or even in its misfiring, as when Plato went to Syracuse to convert the tyrant to philosophy – the gap remains between philosophy's angelic conception of politics and existing political practice. In fact, it is almost as though this very sequence of arguments and questions – 'politics does not exist'; 'what is politics?'; 'politics is *x*'; 'but *x* has little if no relation to the actual practice of politics' – is constitutive of a particular kind of political philosophy. Only the philosopher could start by negating what exists and then comes up with a vision of politics that has very little resemblance to politics as it is named and practised! And this is not a problem that affects Plato alone. Amartya Sen laments an unfortunate focus in enlightenment political philosophy on identifying perfectly just institutions and then 'requiring that people's behaviour comply entirely with the demands of the proper functioning of these institutions'.[4] This problem of idealism has beset the entire philosophical tradition in its thinking of politics. One of its clearest diagnoses can be found in the work of Machiavelli. In situating his own novel approach he argues that many political philosophies are vulnerable to the charge of being angelic:

> Because I want to write what will be useful to anyone who understands it seems to me better to concentrate on what really happens rather than on theories or speculations. For many have imagined republics and principalities that have never been seen nor known to exist.[5]

The problem with the angelic approach is that 'how men live is so different from how they should live that a ruler who does not do what is generally done, but persists in doing what ought to be done, will undermine his power rather than maintain it'.[6] Machiavelli then positions his own philosophy of politics as a realist alternative; he focuses on 'what really happens rather than on theories or speculations'.

But then with what brush is Machiavelli tarred? What is the alternative to 'theories and speculations'? In his attempt to redress the idealism of philosophers by speaking of politics as it is actually practised, in his attempt to avoid building yet one more castle in the air, does he not go too far? Does he not end up writing an apology for the status quo, and even worse, as thousands of his less patient readers have suspected, an apology for abuses of power? Especially when he continues by writing:

> If a ruler who wants always to act honourably is surrounded by many unscrupulous men his downfall is inevitable. Therefore, a ruler who wishes to maintain his power must be prepared to act immorally when this becomes necessary.[7]

And so Machiavelli is caught on the other horn of the dilemma that spears Socrates: servile apology. To write an apology for particular political actions is to do one of two things. One can explain how necessary they were, being the only possible option open to a ruling authority given the difficulty of the situation. Or one could allow that there were a variety of possible courses of action, but the one undertaken was unmistakably the best. Both of these explanations dismiss any split between what should have been done and what was done. In the eyes of an apologist it is all very well to criticize, but the critics are not aware of all the constraints of the situation, and for this simple reason their ideals will remain forever unrealized. For an apologist the only ideals or goals that count are those directing actions that can be realized in the present situation given all the constraints. If a ruler has acted immorally to maintain his rule, and if his rule is the greater good, then it was the right thing to do. An apology thus fuses what ought to be done with what is done. This is the apologist's first mistake. The second mistake is to erase the contingency of action under the supposition of necessity. The apologist always has to reduce the range of possibilities to a very few options, to be compared using brutally simple criteria. The horizon for action becomes very narrow indeed, and this is also unrealistic. So little would ever have been accomplished in political history if the apologists were always right. Athenian democracy would never have seen the day, never mind the Leveller-agitators in 1647.

In hindsight, the apologist is always suspected of bad faith, of having jerry-rigged a conceptual apparatus to justify *post factum* actions taken by agents who cared little for legitimation in the first place. Who are they trying to deceive, the critics retort. The apologist builds no castles in the air, but only to curry favour with the authorities, and that is a sure route to a very real dungeon, if the authorities should change.

## The philosopher's show trial

It appears that when philosophers conceptualize politics either they imagine actions that could never take place or they justify questionable actions that have already taken place. Either philosophy takes place in an ideal realm far from the cut and thrust of daily power struggles, or it gets too close to such struggles and hitches its wagon to one particular party, like Plato disastrously choosing Dionysius, the Sicilian tyrant's heir.

In an essay on the ills of political philosophy, Vincent Descombes gives us a list of philosophers who hitched their wagons to particular political parties.⁸ Each are guilty of writing apologies for the wrong kind of political power. Each has made what he calls a 'systematic error' of political judgement. Without further ado, arraigned in the dock in no particular order, the accused: Lukacs on Stalinism, Heidegger on Nazism, Sartre on the communists, Foucault on the Iranian Revolution. No surprises here. Let's see if we can add to the list – surely if our author is happy to co-sign a book entitled *Why We Are Not Nietzscheans*, one could add all those Nietzschean philosophers, such as Gilles Deleuze or Jacques Derrida, who ever mentioned anything to do with politics.⁹ But why stop with the French Nietzscheans? The pleasure to be had in drawing up a hit list of all those philosophers who got politics wrong – and by implication shaming their disciples – is endless. In fact, one wonders with whom the list might stop – which philosopher got politics right according to Descombes?

Elsewhere one of my favourite philosophers, Alain Badiou, is accused of having lost his way, betraying his early intellectual promise, by jumping on the French Maoism bandwagon – in his own terms one could say Badiou 'sutured' his philosophy to the wrong political condition and so ended up writing apologies for the Terror and for the Cultural Revolution in the name of truth and the event.¹⁰

But to take up Marxist arms, could not one accuse every liberal political philosopher of hitching their wagon to a capitalist oligarchy that calls its own actions 'justice' through the dog and pony show of parliamentary democracy? Are Rawls, Habermas, Sen and even Nozick not guilty of writing apologies for a particular political system themselves? We too can play Descombes' game and conduct show trials of apologists.

However, the absurd consequence of Descombes' exercise is that as soon as a philosopher exercises any political judgement he or she becomes guilty of making a systematic error, at least from the partisan standpoint of a politician. If disagreement, as Jacques Rancière argues, is fundamental to politics then any political judgement, whether issued by a politician or a philosopher, can be the subject of disagreement.¹¹ Consequently there is no political judgement, apart from tautologies and truisms, that everyone would recognize to be correct.

Until the philosopher identifies a universal criterion inherent to what he or she calls practical rationality, a criterion that will allow a political judgement to be classed as either correct or an error independently of any partisan standpoint, all philosophers are vulnerable to being accused of systematic error.

Unfortunately Descombes does not end up providing us with a guide for avoiding systematic error in political judgement (this is a great shame, for if he had managed to do this, the entire problem of politics would be solved and all the philosophers could go home). To suppose we can identify the criteria for systematic error and systematic correctness is to beg the question of the collective good. In Descombes' hands 'systematic error' refers to any political judgement that does not exclusively embrace a liberal understanding of parliamentary democracy. But in a proper philosophy of political action, the term 'systematic error' must be neutral. In my terms, it is what I call *failure*: the failure of all forms of political action to realize their declared ends, the failure of all kinds of philosophers to think the reality of political action.

All philosophers are guilty of error as soon as they make an affirmative political judgement. To affirm any politician's action, to hitch one's wagon to his train, is to abandon the distance of critique. The degree zero of apology is the exercise of *any* political choice. Faced with the ubiquity of error one can understand the philosopher who chooses to remain angelic and above the fray.

Angelic critique or servile apology are two ways in which the philosopher fails to think the actual reality of political action.

## Theodicy as angelized apology

Did Leibniz found a way out of this bind? He hitched his wagon to a particular party: God. Despite Voltaire's satire this does not seem to have been such a disastrous choice – it enabled the invention of an entire new genre of philosophical discourse, the theodicy. Perhaps theodicy offers philosophy an exit from the dilemma of angelic critique or servile apology, perhaps it offers another way of thinking the reality of political action.

A theodicy differs from a simple apology in that it does not justify just one set of events and actions – say King Charles I's exercise of royal prerogative, or Cromwell's subsequent execution of Charles – but rather seeks to justify absolutely everything that happens, to the point that 'whatever is, is right'.[12] In a theodicy every action and event that composes human history is part of God's providence. Here, at the maximum degree of apology, no selection occurs, no course of action is privileged or rendered more necessary than another. Every tyrant's action is justified and so is every rebel's action: all part of God's great plan. If an apology is realist, a maximum apology ought to be the most realistic of political philosophies.

However it turns out that theodicy does not open up a third way beyond apology and critique. Upon further analysis a theodicy can be shown to simply operate a short circuit between critique and apology, fusing the two genres. One of the longer and prettier theodicies we possess is Milton's *Paradise Lost*, in which the blind poet sets out to 'justify the ways of God to men'. If we closely read the passage in which he announces this project, we find an invocation of the muse:

> what in me is dark
> Illumine, what is low raise and support;
> That to the highth of this great argument
> I may assert Eternal providence
> And justify the ways of God to men. (Milton, Bk I, 22)

To justify the ways of God to men is to not simply to take sides but to transform the entire relationship that humans have to events. Usually we judge that some events are beneficial, some harmful, we feel that some actions should not have happened and we are grateful that other actions were accomplished, against the odds. But if every action and event is part of a vast unfolding plan whose infinite mechanism is beyond our human intellect, then these daily exercises of judgement need to be suspended and reorientated. I need to accept every little accident that occurs as part of God's plan. In its most developed form, an authentic attitude of accepting every single event as necessary is equivalent to having absolutely no regrets. At its extreme point this implies that if one could turn back time and live one's life again, one would wish for every single event that happened the first time round to happen again, the second time round, in exactly the same order. This is what Nietzsche's Zarathustra glimpsed: the terrifying thought of the eternal return. The thinking of the eternal return is the acceptance of every event to the point of desiring its repetition. For Nietzsche such a thought required a complete transformation of values.

The desired result of a theodicy is thus as utopian and angelic and transformational as the philosopher-king's construction of Callipolis: everything dark in me must be illumined, everything low raised and supported. The theodicy, a maximum apology, requires a transformation of the human spirit. Rather than a form of realism, it looks more like angelic idealism in its promise of liberation. Theodicy does not offer an escape route but short circuits the dilemma between apology and angelic critique. Theodicy is angelic apology. So still the bind remains.

## Action as theatrical fantasy

What if philosophy did not commit to the existence of a specifically political form of action? In our times some philosophers have slipped out of the critique–apology bind by reducing 'politics' to an economic or technological or administrative or even evolutionary activity. Under this approach the art of politics vanishes and one is left with either epochal shifts in discursive or technological regimes or a generalized natural automatism and a consequent obsession with the problem of agency. In this line of thought 'action' itself is an idealist category, and to even think politics in terms of actions is to be destined to disappointment. In fact action would not so much be an idealist as an *aesthetic* category, one that applies purely to the representation or appearance of politics, not to its being.

Aristotle, in his *Poetics*, claims that the material of tragedy is a unified action, it is the artform of tragedy that presents political intrigues that upset the fate of entire cities in the form of one inexorable action that completes itself in ruin. Indeed in the formalisation of Aristotle's poetics that occurred in the hands of seventeenth-century literary critics, the unity of action, along with time and location, is one of the infamous three unities that Corneille had so much trouble respecting – not to mention Shakespeare. Would it not be entertaining to argue that our entire habit of thinking politics in terms of men and their actions, politicians and what they do, is a historical sediment of tragedy? Our political imagination is tragic, and we need to finally leave the theatre. Or should we just swap genres, and think politics through the lens of comedy? But the unmasking of the politician's shameful desire is a show that we are already familiar with in the tabloid newspapers. No, we definitely need to leave the theatre.

But how do we get out? Where are the exits?

To exit the critique–apology bind by dismissing the existence of politics in the name of a higher encompassing automatism or epochal shifts in technology and knowledge either leads to an endless quest for individual agency, or to absurd declarations like 'only a God can save us'. However, if one dismisses concrete political actions as nothing but the operation of private interest and the struggle for power, one simply takes the first step in angelic critique and thus in constituting the bind. To truly exit the bind the first step must be to affirm the existence of political action – without, for all that, knowing what it is, just as Socrates affirms the existence of justice contra Thrasymachus without yet knowing what it is. And to know what political action is, to determine its nature without falling into angelism or apology, we must identify and avoid the first steps that constitute these traps.

Angelism, on the one hand, presupposes an initial moment of critique: existent political actions are critiqued as not living up to their own presuppositions or to the true nature of politics. For Socrates the unjust actions that Thrasymachus promotes may result in short-term material gain for one individual but can never secure a long-term project or a collective enterprise. To act politically is to create harmony between human beings and join them together in a collective whereas unjust actions divide people and create disharmony, tension and conflict. This moment of critique thus diagnoses the failure of a particular type of action which is assumed to be political. In turn the philosopher constructs another kind of political action, more authentically political, which will be successful, such as the philosopher-king's direction of the guardians' education in Plato's ideal city, Callipolis. But then when the philosopher attempts to put this new conception of action into practice, as Plato did in Syracuse by educating the tyrant's son, he meets with another kind of failure.

Apology, on the other hand, starts by explaining the success of certain political actions which have the merit of actually having taken place. These actions may not appear to be successful from certain critical perspectives, but the apologist is at pains to demonstrate that any other action would have met with instant failure, and that only these particular actions could have met with any kind of success. And so what happened as a result of these actions is the best anyone could have hoped for. In fact, it was necessary for these particular actions to occur. But this seems to be a very pale vision of success. If an action was necessary – as the apologist argues – then surely the criteria of success and failure do not apply. If the nature of a political situation demands a particular action, and if its execution is predetermined by the elements of that situation, then how could it fail? When an action's success is automatic it seems to be no success. Aristotle argues that one of the defining characteristics of action is that it takes place in a realm of contingency, where there are no guarantees and no rule books. The apologist would triumph over the angelic idealist, crowing 'at least I can think successful actions – your philosophy ends in failure!' But in erasing the contingency of action the apologist loses his very grip on success and failure.

To think political action beyond angelism or apology is thus first to think its full-blooded success and failure; and second it is to think the success and failure not of conceptions of political action but of existing political actions. So we have two signposts to follow, but given how deeply the angelism–apology dilemma is embedded in the history of philosophy we are going to need more directions to find the exit.

## The theoreticist sin of foundationalism

Two philosophers from widely different corners of the field, Vincent Descombes and Raymond Geuss, offer diagnoses of a historical stalemate in which their discipline finds itself. Descombes argues that the original error of political philosophy was to identify a foundation for political activity, thereby determining its origins, its principles and grounds of legitimation. But not only this, the foundation that is eventually chosen by the philosopher always turns out to belong to a realm that is slightly different from actual politics. For example, Plato does not found true political action in the policies of Pericles but rather in the philosopher's knowledge of the Idea of the Good. Jurgen Habermas founds political action in the horizon of communication between well-intentioned interlocutors. Descombes writes:

> As soon as we attempt to philosophically reflect on politics we are supposed to have already taken all sorts of decisions in favour of reason and the universal. On the basis of these 'commitments' to rationality that he attributes to us the philosopher is quite confident he can derive the framework of an equitable legal system and a legitimate political order. In this manner, before our enquiry has even begun, an entire ideal city has already been put in place.[13]

Sounds like our angelism. However, this is only one horn of a dilemma that Descombes identifies: if one rejects this foundationalist approach – as do those who advocate a relativist and 'post-metaphysical' or 'decisionist' philosophy – then one is condemned to thinking politics as an irrational affair. But why is this still part of the dilemma? For Descombes the central challenge for political philosophy is to dispose of criteria for determining whether or not a political judgement is correct or mistaken. If politics is not a rational affair 'in the manner of an axiomatic construction of deductive system' then it is going to be difficult to identify universal criteria for measuring judgements.[14] Descombes identifies the origin of this dilemma in 'the persistent tendency to characterize practical problems as if it were a question of a theoretical problem'. That is, philosophers on both sides of the dilemma are guilty of recognizing only one form of rationality: theoretical reason. Descombes argues that to stop reducing politics to a Harvard discussion club, to stop talking about 'reasoners' and start talking about 'actors', the philosopher needs to develop a robust account of what he calls 'practical rationality'. This means the kind of reasoning employed by 'actors' in complicated practical situations. This is certainly a promising line of investigation: to analyse the operations and effects of reasoning in practical situations. However, Descombes' project is to find a fail-safe method for identifying systematic error and correctness in political judgements. If he wishes to ground this method in the nature of practical rationality, he is going to need one sole form of practical rationality, not several (if there were several types of practical rationality, there would be several sets of criteria for determining error). But to admit one sole form of rationality in practice is to embrace yet another theoreticist ideal, yet another universal foundation.

Raymond Geuss, the second philosopher mentioned earlier, also targets the foundationalist approach to politics in his recent pamphlet *Philosophy and Real Politics*. After criticizing Robert Nozick for founding political thinking on subjective rights, Geuss argues:

> It is not that there is some *other* foundation for all thinking or even for all 'normative' thinking about human society, namely, some foundation that does not appeal to subjective rights. Rather, why assume that one can begin to think at all systematically and to any effect without being critical about the assumption that politics needs foundations of this kind?[15]

He then tars John Rawls with the same brush, charging him with founding politics on an abstract social virtue, justice, with no historical content for the term and no account of political power. Geuss, in contrast, advocates a historical, realist or 'contextualist' approach to political philosophy in which the question of power and ideology is central as well as the particular institutional forms in which collective action is embodied.

Vincent Descombes and Raymond Geuss – however different their philosophical sensibilities, one anathematizing Nietzsche, the other canonizing him – thus concur in identifying foundationalism as one of the original sins of political philosophy. For Descombes it programs the idealism or relativism dilemma and for Geuss it involves a 'pernicious' mystification of the role of power in shaping our understanding of politics.[16] For Descombes foundationalism is caused by mistaking theory for practice: we need a realist account of political practice. From his corner Geuss writes, 'Politics is a craft or skill and ought precisely *not* to be analyzed, as Plato's Socrates assumes, as the mastery of a set of principles or theories.'[17]

## The siren of 'practice'

However, we have to be wary of this call to exit foundationalism by returning to the reality of political practice: this very exit is programmed by yet another conceptual dichotomy, that between theory and practice. And theory and practice, for the political philosopher, form not so much another dilemma as a moebius strip: every time the theoretician tries to get closer to practice he or she ends up in more theory.

Nevertheless, let us try to get out of the theatre once more, using the 'practice' exit. Would it be possible to describe a particular political practice without attributing any necessity to it, and without attributing one kind of rationality to it. Can practice be thought while maintaining its contingency and its multiplicity? Could we exit the neokantianism Geuss execrates by subtracting the inchoate manifold of experience from the transcendental subject or any other universal schema? Can philosophy be faithful to a multiplicity of contingent events and still survive as a recognizably discourse, albeit fragmented, mobile, inchoate? Or is this not the most insidious trap of them all? Would this not reduce philosophy to being a pure indicator or index of the occurrence of political events? 'Look', the philosopher says, pointing, 'some political events are happening over there!' No concept of 'political' is presupposed because our realist philosopher merely collates those social events in which the term 'political' or one of its many cognates is mentioned. But this is none other than the mass media's dominant model of human subjectivity: the human reduced to an index, to monstration, signalling the existence of affect somewhere else. The most intensely foregrounded modes and forms of communication in contemporary society follow this model, from the Twitter comment or Facebook update with embedded link – click this! – to the reality television host's 'how do you feel?' to the candidate who has just been voted off the island to the US marines posing in the Abu Ghraib polaroids pointing to prisoners reduced to a pile of suffering bodies. In each case the subject of enunciation indicates the occurrence of affect, usually registered on someone else's body. This ranges from the innocuous comment and link to a great music video to the 'money shot' of reality television: the look on the candidate's face as they are voted out of the house. Is not this minimalist form of indication not the worst apology for whatever happens, an indiscriminate affirmation of the existence of political events, the absolute zero degree of commentary?

This kind of radical empiricism is a false exit and not only for ideological but also for epistemological reasons. Any keyword search presupposes a decision as to the number of cognate terms allowed. Any signalling of particular events presupposes a choice of some events rather than others. Any collation of events into a practice presupposes a concept of practice. One cannot do philosophy without at least one idea.

But does philosophy's commitment to ideas – ideas of justice, of social practice, of forms of authority – irrevocably engage it in angelism or apology? Does even the driest and most detailed description of a particular kind of constitution bear little relation to the actual goings-on in the hallways and back rooms of the institutions it promulgates? Does the philosopher always end up alongside Plato in the *Seventh Letter*, head in hands, weeping at the destruction of his ideas amidst the unthinkable turmoil of public life? Does it all end in failure between philosophy and politics?

We need to begin again. And perhaps we should begin in dysfunction. Before we even get to the theory of the success and failure of political actions, we need to address the failure of the philosophical idea faced with the particular political event. We need an anatomy of this failure.

## The duck and the seagulls

Last autumn I knelt by the side of Canal St Martin and threw crusts of bread at a reluctant duck. I was hoping to entertain my daughter. At that time she liked bedtime stories about her feeding ducks, but in the stories the ducks swam towards the bread and ate it. Much to our surprise the duck was soon engulfed by a swarm of seagulls, barking and honking over the brown water, beaks tugging at sodden morsels of baguette. I was astonished by how many seagulls could fit into the same cubic metre of air without knocking into each other and as each swooped and dove into the bread zone, angling for the swiftest capture and smoothest exit, I suddenly understood that this was an event. The latest seagull slid diagonally into the squawking cubic metre of air above the hapless duck and was forced to stall and hover a foot above an quivering mass of flapping wings, and I thought, is this seagull not one factor, one single causal chain entering into a multiple interaction, an utterly contingent and short-lived synthesis? Finally the paternal instinct kicked in and I started to worry about this violent avian ontology traumatising my daughter for whom birdies and ducks had been the gentle creatures of picture books. This display of intense inter-species conflict over scarce resources was a little too much, I felt, for a 1-year-old – 'nature, darling', I said, 'is red in tooth and claw, but it's O.K., we're bigger than the seagulls'.

What if every political event were such an implosion of seagulls and ducks? Every event a contingent temporary implosion of multiple forces and causal chains? What if some of the causal chains that interact in a political event involve ideas? Sure, philosophy is a practice that works with ideas but it has no exclusive rights over them: other practices, like politics, also work with ideas. And more importantly, when philosophy works with ideas, not all of them are its own. If, during the entire history of philosophy, some philosophers had been capable of thinking while unpredictable political events occurred in front of their noses – if they paid attention to seagulls imploding over bread – then perhaps some of the ideas philosophy has taken for its own actually originated in political events. In Alain Badiou's terms, some of philosophy has actually been conditioned by politics: was not *polis* a word in Solon's mouth as he completely redistributed the voting population, long before Socrates came to think his own allegiance to the *polis*? So not only is it impossible to parse the philosophy–politics relationship as the idea–reality relationship, but also philosophy originally shares in politics; they are certainly different but they are not entirely separate practices. It is a little like the ship of Theseus whose planks are continually replaced over time: is it the same ship? At least the decking, if not the mast, in philosophy is all politics, from Socrates' heroic protest to Locke's secret coffee house reading groups that germed the *Essay*.

How can a philosopher think a political event if every philosophical attempt to think the reality of political action ends in failure?

One must begin in failure.

## How to do things when institutions fall apart

In *How to Do Things with Words*, John Austin embarks upon an anatomy of speech acts by identifying the different ways in which such actions can be said to fail: they can misfire, be defective, incomplete, subject to flaws and hitches. His famous examples are the utterance of the phrase 'I do' in a church in front of a priest with a ring in a nearby pocket, and the phrase 'I baptize this ship the Queen Elizabeth' with a magnum of champagne attached to a rope in one's hand, a temporary platform under one's feet and a long line of German monarchs in one's family tree. This analysis of the possible failures of such speech acts gives rise to a set of rules or conditions for their success, or 'felicity'. For instance, rule A2 states that all the people and circumstances must be appropriate to the procedure. Rule B1 stipulates that the procedure must be executed by all participants and correctly. Rule C1 states that the persons involved must possess appropriate intentions, sentiments or thoughts when performing the act and they must have the intention to behave accordingly afterwards. Austin's oeuvre has not yet been subject to a careful and complete reading in terms of its political valency: he starts out as a classicist with one of his foremost concerns the nature of the good in Aristotle. He visits the Soviet Union in the early 1930s. Many of his examples involve caricatural political situations: the Queen's baptism of the boat misfires because an activist clambers up the platform, grabs the magnum and hurls it at the liner shouting 'I name this ship "Mr Stalin"!'[18] Such an analysis is not the task of this book. Rather I have one simple question. If what decides the success of a speech act are institutional conventions – such as those of a marriage ceremony – and the stable elements of its context that decide its success or failure, what happens when institutions have broken down and the context of the speech act is unstable? What happens when new institutions are coming into being, whose very construction presupposes the successful performance of many speech acts? What kind of theory of overlapping contexts and institutional evolution would one need to accommodate periods of historical instability in Austin's theory? Given a period of intense political turmoil, what is it that guarantees the success or failure of political actions?

This book does not employ Austin's method, analysing the ordinary language of action. In a situation of institutional failure and political disaster, it appears unlikely that linguistic analysis alone will yield the reality of action. But at least in name the approach of this book is inspired by Austin: it will be a matter of carrying out an anatomy of failure. The task is now one of choosing the right material for such an anatomy.

## The English revolution: Ideas in practice

To not miss the practice exit from the angelism–apology dilemma, one must recognize that practice is a fundamentally historical category, and so there are practices, in the plural. Moreover, practices are not pure multiplicities of empirical events with no consistency. Historical practices vehicle ideas. Philosophers in tune with their times sometimes pick up on those ideas. Other ideas, they pass over. The focus of this book is one moment in history when philosophy and politics began to share ideas, one moment of intense political instability, when institutions fell apart, were broken and remade, but badly. One moment when philosophers stopped their endless technical debates over universals and particulars and paid attention to the actual unfolding of a political event under their noses: the English Revolution.

In the space of a few years political practices emerged that put radically new ideas into circulation, ideas that would go on to shape our very understanding of parliamentary democracy, common and private property, the value of labour and the commoner's right to a share in the nation's wealth and finally the authenticity of grassroots religion. The philosophers whose lives were shaped by the English Revolution and its long aftermath, Thomas Hobbes and John Locke, went on to invent modern political philosophy in their attempts to come to terms with the implications of these events. No longer could a political system found its legitimacy solely in inherited institutions such as the monarchy – its ground must now be sought in the practical reasoning of the people at large. In Alain Badiou's terms, the English Revolution was an event that gave rise to a new form of political practice and the creation of new kinds of political body: the New Model Army, popular counterweight to a recalcitrant parliament.[19]

The Leveller-agitators in the regiments of the New Model Army invented new forms of political action. Hobbes and Locke construct new systems of political legitimation in reaction to the English Revolution. But in doing so the philosophers do not embrace the new forms of action; rather they dismiss them under the catch-all categories of enthusiasm and the hysterical passion of the crowd. Hobbes and Locke open up the grand questions of politics – Who acts? On what grounds? To what end? – and in answering these questions the contested domain of politics is sown back together. Henceforth it is the sovereign who acts in your name to secure public safety, or it is the people who act as party to a contract, delegating their power to a sovereign body to secure public safety. But what happens when one has two different political bodies that both claim to represent the people and with widely different understandings of what is at stake in such representation, such as the New Model Army versus Westminster in the Putney Debates? This is the Leveller's question. This is not to say that Hobbes and Locke would not be able to conceptualize and judge such actions: indeed for Hobbes there is no right to rebellion and the Leveller-agitators are public enemies. Rather the point is to anatomize the agitators' own writings and actions to see if they develop a coherent account of political action.

And so in this book I shall be playing history against philosophy, but in a game in which ideas are found on both sides, a game in which any hard and fast distinction between the two sides is dissolved. Politics becomes part philosophical, philosophy becoming part political.

An anatomy of failure identifies models of political action. It isolates points of conflict and dysfunction in practices and uses them to map the model. These models are the ideas embodied in political practices. Models can be found in activists' practices, in governmental practice and philosophical practices. There is more than one model at work in the English Revolution and its aftermath. This book identifies three: Hobbes' model of sovereign action, Locke's model of contractual action and the Leveller-agitator model of joint action. Contra angelism, they have been used in practice. Contra apology, they are plural, and none of them are necessary or the best. These models are not cemented to one locality alone, however complicated, but are alive and travel from one historical context to another. Much has been written about the legacies of Hobbes' and Locke's understandings of politics, but the Leveller-agitator model has been neglected. Its legacy deserves to be brought out into the light. The point is not to critique the Lockean and Hobbesian models – they do that well enough of each other. Nor is the point, in the end, to lament their inadequacy in relation to the English Revolution. The project is not to demonstrate their conceptual incoherence, nor even to criticize their preparation of industrial capitalism. If practices are plural, then there is more than one model of political action, and no one model has all the answers to the problems of politics. The project is to construct these models, to indicate their use, to show their limits and so open up spaces for other models, and finally, in a sequel to this book, to draw out their descendance.

The Leveller-agitator experience has been kept alive by a few Marxist and not-so-Marxist historians – Lawrence Stone, Christopher Hill, Ian Gentles, John Morrill, Austin Woolrych – but it has not yet been examined for the light it could shed on the current predicament of political philosophy. This is not to engage in one more exercise in Whig history, monumentalizing the Levellers as the illustrious forebears of today's social movements. Rather it is to undertake a genealogy in reverse, finding a moment of novelty in the past to create something old in the present, something rooted, something solid.

The historicism of such an approach does not counter the expansive ambition hinted at in the very name of the project: a 'philosophy of political action'. This is not a book of history or of the history of ideas or even of the history of philosophy – it is a theoretical book on the present, it pulls each model into the present. I am trying to understand today but from a long distance away. I have been too close, my eyeglasses are scratched and smeared. And so I have stepped back and borrowed a telescope from some of the greatest political experimenters England has ever seen.

# CHAPTER TWO

# 1647 – The history of the Leveller-agitators and the New Model Army

To the freeborn people of England:

> We profess our bowels are and have been troubled and our hearts pained within us, in seeing and considering that you have been so long deprived of the fruits of all our labours and hazards, we cannot but sympathize with you in your miseries and oppressions.[1]

So declare the agitators of each horse and foot regiment of the New Model Army in an appendix to their October 1647 manifesto *An Agreement of the People*. Two years after their victory over the royalist forces, the New Model Army's fate was uncertain and the settlement of the war still undecided. For the agitators the momentous business of the war was being turned away from its proper end by a corrupt and non-representative parliament that refused to pay arrears or grant indemnities and now threatened to disband the very army that had fought for its rights. To call for the purge and reform of the parliament according to popular sovereignty was none other but an extension of the soldier's commitment in the field. The only problem was that the idea of full and exclusive popular sovereignty was new in English politics, and there was little consensus over what form it might take.

From the point of view of the state the English Revolution is a period of institutional failure and political disaster. Together the monarchy and parliament fail to assure the people's safety inasmuch as the country is led to civil war. In such a context action is naked – agents act outside or on the margins of established political procedures. The grounds for action are not habitual, nor taken for granted, but are fiercely debated and recast. As John Wildman argues in the Whitehall debates over religious toleration:

> Through the judgment of God upon the nation all authority hath been broken to pieces, or at least it hath been our misery that it hath been uncertain whether the supreme authority hath been [here or there], [so] that none have known where the authority of the magistrate is, or [how far] his office [extends].[2]

When all authority breaks into pieces people start to raise questions about who can act, on what grounds and how. Political action becomes a question and it does so not in isolation, but between people from different constituencies and within a political process. That is to say what counts as political action, what is called 'political action', is no longer certain – indeed the very question of who can act politically is subject to radical revision. In the summer of 1647, five years after the outbreak of war, the New Model Army emerges as a political agent in its own right. When the action it undertook met its end, the monarchy and the House of Lords had been abolished, the House of Commons purged, King Charles I executed and yet all hopes of a radical social revolution quashed. The political process that decided the outcome of the English revolution involved the army, the parliament, the vanquished king and a group of activists called the 'Levellers' by their enemies. Each assumed the masks of ally, rival, negotiating party and enemy; each responded to the question of political action. The object of this chapter is to analyse this political process in three moments, punctuated by key texts:

- The original constitution of the army as a political body rivalling parliament in the summer of 1647, marked by the capture of the king, and the publication of *A Solemn Engagement* of 5 June.
- The Autumn split between the rank and file agitators and the officers of central command (the 'Grandees') publicized

in the 15 October agitator manifesto *The Case of the Army Truly Stated*.

- The public confrontation between the agitators and the grandees over the constitutional settlement of the war, recorded in the famous *Putney Debates*, whose outcome was sealed, in infringement of all debating rules, by the King's escape to the Isle of Wight and the suppression of the Leveller-agitators.

The aim of this analysis is to explore how the very nature of political action – and not just particular policies or programs of reform – became an urgent question within this political process, a question that expanded and complicated itself into five fundamental queries, each to be found in lived events and distinct phases in the life and death of the New Model Army alliance. The five queries unfold in the following sequence:

- Who can act?
- Who can act on what grounds?
- Who is right about what is to be done?
- Why do we succeed or fail?
- If you and I split, were we ever united, and to what end?

If these queries can be situated in the concrete conjunctures in which the grandees, the agitators, parliament and king found themselves between the summer and winter of 1647, and if partial responses to these queries can be identified and their consequences traced, then some light may be shed on the overall shape of this political process. Historians divide over its interpretation: did it form a second revolution, after that of 1640–2? Was it merely the lead-up to a military coup d'état? Does it mark the victory of adversarial politics over consensus politics?[3] Did it form the final phase of one long revolution?[4] Does it exhibit the classic splits between a Leftist deviation (the Levellers) and a Rightist deviation (the Presbyterian members of parliament) of a revolutionary dialectic, with Cromwell taking the high road, having found the sense of history? Each of these interpretations is risky since it presumes the question of political action answered. Either the latter takes the form of negotiation between parties that recognize each other's legitimacy; or it takes the shape of gradual reform advanced through legislation passed by a parliamentary majority; or finally its true form emerges outside and inspite of institutions as a revolutionary transformation that catapults a nation from one stage of history to the next. This enquiry must remain agnostic with regard to such ready-made answers to the question of political action.

The English contribution to the modern thinking of political action is usually held by historians of philosophy to be summed up in the seventeenth century in the work of three authors: Thomas Hobbes, James Harrington and John Locke. Each provides a response as to the nature of political activity and the shape it should assume if religious and civil wars are to be avoided. Hobbes constructs the figure of sovereign action, Locke that of contractual action. Harrington is not known for an explicit model of political action – hence his absence from this book – but innovated by drawing up a republican constitution and then linking it to economic and agrarian reform. Each of these philosophers went on to enjoy a legacy well beyond the confines of the seventeenth century. The position I take here is that we are missing something in this picture: during the English revolution elements of a *third* model of political action were put together, a model of potentially similar stature, a model that was shunted offstage and forgotten, much like Thrasymachus, and to our loss. This model is to be found in the alliance between the Levellers and the New Model Army.

## Summer 1647: *A Solemn Engagement* and the creation of a political body

We were declared enemies by parliament for petitioning.[5] (*SE*, 10)

In June 1646, the New Model Army completed its defeat of royalist forces. On 18 February 1647, faced with the financial burden of maintaining the army and bolstered by reports of its rampant religious sectarianism, the Presbyterian majority in the House of Commons decided to disband most of the army before settling arrears of pay. The foot could either be dissolved or go to Ireland to quell the Irish insurrection. Recruitment for service in Ireland began but met with resistance on the part of soldiers, unhappy as their demands for arrears were not being met, and with the replacement of familiar commanders by Presbyterian appointments. Various petitions written by the rank and file were passed through the regiments. The officers attempted to channel this discontent by creating a more moderate petition *The Petition of the Officers and Soldiers . . . of Sir Thomas Fairfax* that focused on professional issues of pay and indemnity, extirpating any overly political demands.[6] At this point the historians divide over whether or not the army was already politicized. Ian Gentles, to whom we owe the most detailed recent study of the army, prevaricates: on the one hand, he claims the questions of arrears, conscription, pay and war pensions formed the 'ground bass' of all army statements that year; on the other hand, he admits that in their awareness of the country being divided between their friends and foes, the army was already politicized.[7] Note that to emphasize the professional issues at the expense of the rank and file's political concerns is to repeat exactly the same gesture as the officers when they drafted their moderate petition.[8] Mature with experience in their autumn manifesto *The Case of the Army Truly Stated* the agitators themselves refused such a gesture, interpreting it as an attempt to cut the ground from beneath their feet (CA, 4–5). In any case, as events show, there was to be no simple channelling and controlling of the soldiers discontent, and no simple division between the professional and the political.

News of *The Petition of the Officers and Soldiers . . . of Sir Thomas Fairfax* being circulated and signed by soldiers, despite orders that it be banned, threw Presbyterian members of parliament into a high rage: Holles passed a motion on the 29 March condemning the authors of the petition for spreading sedition and denouncing them as 'enemies of the state and disturbers of the public peace'.[9] This motion came to be known as the 'Declaration of Dislike', a crystal of parliament's hostility to the very army that had fought for the former's rights against the king. Throughout April and May, the parliament pressured army officers to speed up the business of conscription for the Irish service. This policy met with increasing resistance and dismal results. In response, army officers presented *A Vindication of the Officers of the Army* to parliament on 27 April, a tract that defended the banned March petition, asserted the army's right to petition its representatives, declared the officers' solidarity with the rank and file in the expression of the army's grievances, and finally demanded a vindication of the army's honour in the shape of parliament officially retracting the Declaration of Dislike.[10] Parliament postponed consideration of this document until 30 April when it was upstaged by the presentation of a manifesto *The Apology of the Common Soldiers of Sir Thomas Fairfax's Army*, drafted by 16 troopers from eight cavalry regiments stationed in East Anglia, near army headquarters. This was the first appearance in print of the famous 'agitators' or 'adjutants' or 'agents', chosen by the rank and file of each troop or company to publish and pursue their concerns. Their manifesto claimed that conscription for Ireland was 'a Design to ruin and break this army in pieces' and 'this plot is a mere cloak for some who . . . seek to become Masters, and degenerate into Tyrants'.[11] The House reacted in anger and summoned the authors to the bar – three were waiting outside. When demanded to explain just exactly who was degenerating into a tyrant, the agitators replied that 'the Apology' was the joint act of the eight regiments of horse, and that only the regiments could interpret it'.[12] One of the agitators, Shepherd, further suggested that any queries should be addressed in writing to the regiments. This formalism embodies a principle of solidarity and collective responsibility, used as a defense against parliament's attempts to intimidate, isolate and scapegoat individuals.

Other regiments swiftly emulated the eight cavalry regiments and elected two agitators for each troop or company. These agitators then formed an inter-regimental system of communication. Conservative opponents of the army – and even the Grandees at times, such as Henry Ireton – charged the agitators with being outsiders who had infiltrated the regiments to manipulate the common soldiery with demagogic propaganda. These outsiders were identified as 'Levellers' and seen to belong exclusively to a group of London-based activists. From this standpoint the New Model Army was in no way a political agent capable of concerted action. The real agents were the agitators, not the army as a whole; the soldiers were being instrumentalized, their legitimate concerns over pay and indemnity captured and absorbed within a foreign ideology. If the soldiers were ever active en masse, it was not a case of rational action, but of what Locke would later call 'enthusiasm' and Hobbes theorized as 'hysterical passion'.

There was communication between army agitators and the London-based Levellers; however the historians Austin Woolrych, Ian Gentles, Mark Kishlansky and John Morrill agree that the agitators were not outsiders but homegrown.[13] Some of the agitators were well-known Levellers and yet they had also served as soldiers and officers in the army. Other agitators were not Levellers. In any case the agitators as a group could not be identical with the Levellers for the simple reason that their political interests diverged at times. The Levellers positioned themselves as champions of the people, and the army – the agitators' cause – was often quite unpopular with the people. Soldiers, having not been given their salaries, could not pay for their housing and food, and so often demanded free quarter of the local population. Moreover, as both Woolrych and Morrill argue, the very existence of a large professional standing army was not consistent, in the long term, with the Levellers aim of democratizing and decentralizing government.[14] Morrill goes so far as to argue that any ideological alliance between the Levellers and the rank and file of the army was short-lived and fragile. There are thus two warring hypotheses on the relationship between the army agitators and the Levellers, that of hostile conservative contemporaries, and that of 1980s revisionist historians: the former hold that the agitators were all imported Levellers, the latter argue that the two groups intersect, but that any alliance was flimsy, opportunistic and involved a fundamental mismatch of political identities.

My contention is that neither of these hypotheses hold; rather, the two groups intersect and the alliance was strong – their interests did coincide and they coincided on the burning questions of the day: the settlement of the war and the future constitution of the country. Countering Woolrych's and Morrill's point, although the existence of a large professional standing army may be contrary to the Levellers ideal of a decentralized and radically democratic state, the very exercise of electing agitators from the rank and file in each regiment is an eminently democratic and decentralizing experiment – these are Leveller ideas at work. The agitators were soldiers who entered into an alliance with the Levellers precisely because they found themselves putting Leveller principles into practice in the pursuit of their own grievances and desires.

The agitators' first occasion for a full-scale campaign was offered to them when the army officers decided to canvass each regiment, troop and company as to their alleged discontent. This in response to a demand made by parliamentary commissioners on 7 May. After presenting measures for dealing with arrears and indemnities these commissioners asked the officers to embark for Ireland under Major Skippon and hoped that the officers in attendance could assure that their regiments were free of 'distempers'. Again embodying a principle of collective responsibility the officers did not immediately proffer guarantees of calm and discipline but said they would sound out their men as to their 'grievances' rather than their 'distemper'. This exercise of sounding out produced documents from each of the regiments, and the lists of grievances display extensive similarities in the numbered items.[15] This similarity signals the agitators' involvement and the emergence of collective organization.[16] However, the differences between the documents – some adding items concerning religious toleration, or reimbursement for the purchase of horses – mark their independent and authentic origin in each regiment's specific experience.

The writing of petitions is the first concrete example of non-institutional political action carried out by the New Model Army. Its means are collective: not just the addition of signatures – which generates a quantitative and serialized figure of the collective – but also the very drafting of the petition – generating a qualitative and differentiated figure of the collective. General meetings were held in which the rank and file were consulted over the formulation of their grievances. In regiments divided by their loyalties disputes broke out between officers over whether such consultation had been properly carried out, signalling how seriously they took this procedure.[17] The synthesis of the soldiers' demands continued when a group of officers produced a single consolidated petition – in moderate language – based on all of the returns from the regiments. The resultant document – *A Perfect and True Copy of the Several Grievances of the Army* – was presented to the parliamentary commissioners, headed by Major Skippon, and in turn presented to parliament on 20 May. This petition was the first step in the creation of a new political agent, it begins to develop a practical response to the first query of political action: *who can act*?

Parliament reacted to the petition on 23 May by ordering the immediate and complete disbandment of the New Model Army, calling each regiment to separate and distant rendezvous thus physically dispersing them. It promised a limited amount of arrears to the individual soldiers, thus seeking to divide them from their officers who had gone to bat for them. No compromise, no negotiation; the lines had been drawn. In response to parliament's order for separate and partial rendevous the army called a general rendezvous at Newmarket on 4–5 June. It was at Newmarket that the officers created the General Council of the Army, formalizing the inter-regimental system of communication between the agitators. The Council appears to be a radical experiment in army democracy, a united council of army soviets *avant la lettre*, but when one looks at the detail of its composition it becomes clear that the officers ensured that there was a preponderance of officers over agitators. For every regiment there were four representatives: two agitators and two officers. And then there were 15 officers from the general staff.[18] The general council was dissolved in January 1648, marking the bitter end of the first alliance between the agitators, the Levellers, the grandees and the parliamentary independents. But in Newmarket we are at its heady beginning.

On 5 June, the pamphlet *A Solemn Engagement* was accepted by the army and the existence of the general council ratified. From the standpoint of Oliver Cromwell, his son-in-law Henry Ireton and Thomas Fairfax, the commander-in-chief, the composition of the general council secured the army's fragile unity. From the standpoint of the agitators the council was overstuffed with generals and officers. Nevertheless in the lead up to the publication of *An Agreement of the People* and the subsequent Putney debates, it was the whole army's acceptance of *A Solemn Engagement* that marked the high point of public unity. This pamphlet, presented to General Fairfax to be sent to the House of Commons, begins by noting parliament's censure of the March petition and the identification of its authors as enemies of the state – in Holles' Declaration of Dislike. It explains that this disqualification of the army's voice from the political field, this blocking of 'due and regular' channels, led the soldiers to take the 'unusual (but in that case necessary)' step of choosing two or more men from each regiment to 'act in the name and behalf of the whole soldiery of the respective regiments' (*SE*, 6). These were the 'agitators' appointed to 'prosecute [the soldiery's] rights and desires' and vindicate the justice of the March petition against its criminalization by parliament. Further, the pamphlet claims that these agitators 'have accordingly acted and done many things to those ends, all which the soldiers did then approve as their own acts' (*SE*, 6).

What is at stake in this document is nothing less than the public presentation of the army as a *new political body*, complete with voice, representative structure, mission and enemies. It raises and answers the first aspect, the first query of the manifold question of political action: who can act? From parliament's standpoint, it alone can act. The army belongs solely in the field and must be disqualified from the political domain: it has no legitimate voice. But from the soldier's viewpoint there is no separation between their action in the field and politics: 'they thought we would have stood only as mercenary Soldiers, hired to serve their arbitrary power' (*SE*, 10). The soldiers' engagement in the war was political, not mercenary: in a civil war one has to choose sides, parliament or the king, and such a choice is evidently a political act.

What signs were there of the genesis of a new political body? *A Solemn Engagement* not only presents an innovative collective structure, but it is also itself the product of plural authorship, of a communal process of consultation, deliberation and debate that draws upon shared memories of past acts, events and omissions. Officers agreed, we are told, upon 'a narrative account of the grounds, rise and growth of discontent in the Army, and their proceedings in relation thereunto' (*SE*, 6). General Thomas Fairfax, the commander-in-chief, is thus not presented as the single author of the pamphlet but rather as its messenger, as an intermediary delegated to present it to parliament. But given parliament's hostile reaction to the last address, it is doubtful to what extent it forms the primary audience of the document. In so far as it does what it says, *A Solemn Engagement* is a performative in John Austin's sense – it engages each soldier in the collective fate of the army, it announces their pledge to not disband until their common demands are met:

> We the officers and soldiers of the army, subscribing here unto, do hereby declare, agree and promise to and with each other, and to, and with the parliament and kingdom as follows:
>
> 1) That we shall cheerfully and readily disband when thereunto required by the parliament, or else shall many of be willing (if desired) to engage in further services either

in England or Ireland, having first such satisfaction to the Army in relation to our grievances and desires heretofore presented, and such security; That we of our selves (when disbanded, and in the condition of private men) or other the freeborn people of England (to whom the consequence of our case does extend) shall not remain subject to like oppression, injury or abuse, as in the premisses has been attempted or put upon us while an Army, by the same men's continuance, in the same credit and power (especially if as our judges) who have in these past proceedings against the Army so far prevailed to abuse the Parliament and us, and to endanger the Kingdom. (SE, 8–9)

The primary audience for the pamphlet is evidently the rank and file, the very soldiers that the parliament is attempting to bleed away with the promise of limited arrears. As set out in *A Humble Representation of the Dissatisfactions of the Army* of 14 June, the grievances that the army holds include the following:[19]

- non-payment of arrears in the soldiers' pay, and the evident failure of parliament to secure sufficient finance for paying such arrears;
- the absence of a full act of oblivion ensuring indemnity for all soldiers for all actions performed in the war whether or not it can be shown that they resulted from direct ordinances of parliament;
- compensations for maimed soldiers and war widows;
- the insufficient law against press-ganging;
- excessive demands of accounts for all expenses incurred during the war, insufficient compensation for paid quarter when compensation is awarded;
- the requirement, against custom and tradition, that cavalry give up their horses before receiving any arrears; and,
- insufficient reparation for parliament's Declaration of Dislike, thus failing to clear the Army's name and vindicate its original March petition.

The agitators are well aware that the parliament, in its consideration of the army's concerns, is seeking every possible way to minimize them and give limited satisfaction, whether it be by the installation of onerous bureaucratic procedures, by quibbling over figures, by simple delay or partial concessions, by adding further requirements or by dividing the soldiers' claims into categories of legitimate and illegitimate. In the agitators' eyes such tactics amount to nothing more than disrespect for the principles at stake.

As a pledge to stay together until the desires and grievances are met, *A Solemn Engagement* presents a plural 'we' and projects it into the future, conditioning its existence on the performance of actions by an institution that does not even yet recognize the army as a negotiating partner. But between presenting a political body and actually creating one there is a gap: how can the publication of a mere pamphlet bridge that gap?

First hypothesis: *A Solemn Engagement* is a foundational speech act that transforms a loose set of regiments united solely by orders and supply chains into a democratically governed self-identical political agent. It is an instance of what Lacan called 'full speech', changing the subject's situation with regard to the symbolic order, manifesting the signifier's power of *creatio ex nihilo*.[20] Once the tract has been published, the rank and file come to identify with the position and historical mission attributed to them and so line up and act in line with the agitators' demands. If this were the case, the tract would join classical republicanism's family of famous political performatives, such as the original constitutions of Solon, founder of Athens, and Lycurgus, founder of Sparta. At a more banal level successful performatives in politics are quite common: a parliament could pass legislation and create, for example, a new municipal council for an expanding market town, thus creating a political body through law. However this does not hold in the case of the New Model Army. Austin states that the success of a speech act presupposes a stable and rule-bound institutional context – this is precisely what is missing during the revolution. Moreover the army emerges as a rival alongside and in spite of the parliament, not as an internal effect of the parliament's own benevolent sovereignty. And the rules, if any, that regulate the army's own internal procedures of consultation are being made up on the fly. But the hypothesis might still have some legs. Aristotle argues that in the absence of formal rules, in unstable and contingent contexts, we must presuppose mastery, and in particular, a master, a *phronimos*, like Pericles.[21] In the absence of stable encompassing institutions the tract *A Solemn Engagement* thus transforms the army through mastery of its context, mastery here being a superlative excess of skill, of savoir faire in the timing, composition, distribution and presentation of the pamphlet, a document that perfectly crystallized, heightened and expressed the soldiers' nascent political subjectivity.

But does not such a hypothesis presuppose precisely what is the supposed result of this process: unity? There is no one masterful agent behind the publication of the pamphlet but a plural process. In any case, one cannot explain the constitution of political agency through pre-existing political agency: such would be another twist on the great man theory of history. The army possesses neither mastery, nor legitimacy, nor even one identifiable and stable context: its dispossession of these elements is flagrant. So the hypothesis of this political body being generated by a foundational speech act is implausible. And yet *A Solemn Engagement* is effective in that it forms a point of reference, an anchor for many of the agitators' declarations and actions to come. So how else to explain its success?

Another hypothesis is that the engagement signs an explicit, regional and conditional social contract. Regional in that it enacts the collective agreement of the army in the absence of any agreement on the part of either the kingdom or the parliament, the other two parties named in the pledge. A contract without full agreement on the part of one of the parties amounts to a kind of prescription or requirement laid upon that party, a declaration of intent; not a threat but a warning, an announcement of the stakes of a political process to come that the other party will be involved in whether they like it or not. This contract is explicit in that it is written and presented with all of its stipulations in a pamphlet and does not have to be assumed as implicit or hypothetical: in fact it resembles an everyday legal contract far more than Hobbes and Locke's analogical concoctions. And it is conditional in that it names the term of its own dissolution, conditional upon the parliament's satisfaction of its desires. For Hobbes and Locke, our philosophers of the English revolution, a political body is most definitely generated by a social contract. For Hobbes, the contract has always already taken place: it is implicit in any dealing in civil society. For Locke, it attains moments of explicitness when a man comes of age and, for instance, inherits property thus accepting the law of the land. But for both philosophers, the social contract must involve the agreement of every individual in a state: it cannot be regional or limited in either number or temporal duration. The engagement claims that 'the soldiers did then approve as their own acts' the actions of the agitators: this closely resembles the structure of delegation and transmitted ownership embodied in Hobbes' sovereign, but with one crucial difference – the sovereign is one, and the agitators many (SE, 6). The last divergence, which renders this hypothesis even less plausible, is one noted by Hegel in *The Philosophy of Right*: a contract takes place on the basis of the 'arbitrary will of individuals', of 'self-sufficient persons' and generates nothing more than a 'common will' rather than 'a will which is universal in and for itself'.[22] As such for Hegel, a contract cannot model the genesis of the state or any other political body. Likewise for the signatories and addressees of the engagement, it is only at the term of the army's dissolution that they will be returned to 'the condition of private men'. During their 'solemn engagement' they do not act as private individuals – as the model of the contract supposes – but become part of a collective subject, entering what I shall later term a *condition of co-implication*. The engagement does not arithmetically sum up a common will that unites their private interests but rather creates a collective project that enables the naming of not just the army's but the kingdom's common good: 'the freeborn people of England . . . to whom the consequence of our case does extend' (SE, 9). And so this second hypothesis of a regional contract must also be abandoned.

The hypotheses of foundational speech act or regional social contract share the same basic problem: they take this pamphlet as the be-all and end-all of the genesis of army as political body. But the pamphlet is not alone. Its publication is but one of the actions that constitutes the new political body. Its value lies in its recording and publicizing of some of the other actions, as does the value of all of the other pamphlets issued in the army's name in 1647. But it is these actions assembled together with the sequence of pamphlets that form a political body. So what other actions, events and phenomena mark the constitution of this new political body?

The first action is so simple in its sheer physicality: the army decides to meet as a whole at a general rendezvous rather than each regiment attending the partial rendezvous called by parliament. The general rendezvous at Newmarket on the 4–5 June allows the army to present itself to itself as a coherent and massive collective of men with common concerns manifested, if by nothing else, by the simple effort of travelling to Newmarket and setting up camp. From Westminster's standpoint there is no good reason why the entire army should assemble in one place – save to conspire against the parliament, a charge that the army rejects. Cromwell was well aware of the subversive significance of a general rendezvous: in November 1647, he attempted to dampen the army's revolutionary fervour by cancelling a general rendezvous at Spitalfields, replacing it with partial rendezvous. The value of a general rendezvous is that it enables a physicalization, a simple incarnation or presentation of the whole of the political body's might without division or obscurity. Indeed, the agents could be surer of the rank and file's support – and thus of the universal address of their claims – in their negotiations with the generals and the officers if the former were ready to hand. Moreover, the very decision to assemble against parliament's orders – direct disobedience – exemplified the army's shift from being the latter's unhappy instrument to becoming an independent force and voice. The authors claim of the parliament: 'They thought we would have stood only as mercenary Soldiers, hired to serve their arbitrary power' (*SE*, 10). The action of general assembly gives the lie to a narrow understanding of the army's function.

But the rendezvous at Newmarket was only the first in a series of manoeuvres that physicalized the army's existence as a political body: the army discovered it had power over the actions and behaviour of parliament by means of its mere proximity to London. On 24 June the army marched from St Albans to Uxbridge and threatened to cut off the city's supply. In response, the 11 hostile Presbyterian members of parliament withdrew, albeit temporarily, from the House of Commons. The army, satisfied by this reaction, withdrew to Reading, but too soon: in July the Presbyterians engaged in a campaign to weed out the army sympathizers and Independents from the London militia. The agitators immediately called for a further march upon London and a great debate was held but Cromwell opposed this move, arguing that the time was not yet ripe. In August, however, ripeness was all as the London mob forced the Independent members of parliament to leave

Westminster – 9 peers and 57 members of parliament fled to the army for protection and in reaction the army occupied London for the first time.

One could object that these chessboard manoeuvres indicate nothing but a balance of force and that to embrace such as a sign of political action is to simply play Thrasymachus' game. But we do not yet know how to play Thrasymachus' game, and there is nothing simple about force, especially when it is articulate force orientated towards political ends. Not only through its physical unification but also by means of its tactical positioning the army came to understand that it possessed some power over the behaviour of a hostile parliament, power that waxed and waned according to its distance from Westminster. It had become a de facto player if not an equal to parliament through force and manoeuvre.

To physical assembly and tactical position, the marks of an increasingly complex political discourse must be added. The army began to not just judge parliament's acts with regard to the March petition but its entire performance with regard to the absence of a settlement to the civil war. In diagnosis of this failure, it charged the corruption of parliament's substance 'by the indirect practice of some malicious and mischievous persons, as we suppose surprizing or otherwise abusing the Parliament' (*SE*, 6). A further passage suggests that such persons were not external influences but formed part of the parliament and wielded some power:

> We of ourselves (when disbanded in the condition of private men) shall not remain subject to the like oppression, injury and abuse, as in the premisses has been attempted and put upon us while an army *by the same men's continuance, in the same credit and power.* (*SE*, 9; my italics)

The agents argue that if such abuse of the parliament continues the kingdom will be endangered and plunge back into civil war. This is not only to judge but also to name and circumscribe the very event horizon of the political situation, the threshold of disaster and dissolution. Given that is is on the behalf of an actor who would not simply observe but join in that war and precipitate its occurrence, the naming is more than constative: it is performative, a threat. That is to say, it is not the case that further civil war is an objective necessity independent of the army's decisions: it would result, from the army's perspective, from the conflictual twin trajectories of itself and the parliament. In the diagnosis of *A Solemn Engagement*, if this suspected abuse continues, the institution will have failed in its duty of protecting the kingdom and securing the safety of the people. It is here that the army begins to question the very legitimacy of the parliament to prosecute the business of the kingdom.

But for a political body to exist not only must it present itself to itself, sense its own weight in manoeuvre and pronounce judgement upon other political bodies; it must become aware of its existence in the eyes of the others. In other words, to take its place in the political field it must account for the quality and efficacy of its relationship with the other political bodies. One of the elemental constituents of political relationality is responsibility: to whom does one answer for one's acts, to whom does one give an account? Before it will pay arrears to any soldier of the New Model Army parliament demands that a condition be satisfied: accounts be provided for all sequestered provisions during their campaigns. In the 14 June pamphlet *A Humble Representation of the Dissatisfactions of the Army*, the agitators refuse this order as impractical and contrary to custom and insist in return that the parliament must be held accountable for the actions the army performed on its behalf during the war against the royalist forces.[23] Their challenge to Westminster takes the form of a hypothetical: if the latter did recognize and own those actions that were committed on its behalf during the war, then it would properly pay arrears, create war pensions and pass an act of indemnity for all soldiers.

And so in the summer of 1647, the dispute between the army and the parliament boils down to the latter's failure to own up to the former's actions – we fought for you, the agitators argue, and now you repudiate us, you disqualify us, you would dissolve us. Did we mistake your intentions in going to war against the royalist forces? If all that was intended was a reshuffle of pieces already on the board, ending up with a constitutional monarchy, then why so much bloodshed? The agitators argue from betrayal, an implicit contract has been dishonourably broken; the great business they had undertaken together has been abandoned by the parliament. But the army does not remain in a position of discontent and resentment for long. As it becomes aware of its own political existence and of the legitimate grounds to act, prosecute and pursue that great unfinished business one can sense the authors' pleasure in noticing and dismissing its adversaries' perception of its own existence and intentions:

> We find many strange things suggested or suspected to our great prejudice concerning dangerous principles, interests and designs in this Army (as to the overthrow of magistracy, the suppression or hindering of Presbytery, the establishment of independent government, or upholding of a general licentiousness in Religion in the name of the liberty of conscience). (*SE*, 10)

However mistaken parliamentary paranoia might be, its assignation of hidden and dangerous intentions to the army is one more proof of the latter's occupation of a place on the political field. For the army to be able to say 'this is what we are for you, but you have it wrong' is to both identify and circumvent the parliament's relationship with itself. If the agitators were to believe and identify with parliament's perception and hostile judgement of the army, then their position would falter and their project dissolve. But the agitators are amused in their dismissal of Westminster's fears.

To the army's self-presence, sense of tactical weight, judgement of other political bodies and encompassing of its relationships to those bodies, we must add one punctual Machiavellian act. On 4 June, Cornet Joyce, a lowly infantryman seized the king from his imprisonment at Holdenbury under the parliament's authority and removed him to army headquarters. In response to Charles I's demand to see his commission, Joyce famously indicated the 500 troopers standing behind him and claimed to act on behalf of the common soldiery.[24] The chief responsibility for this action is highly ambiguous: Joyce claimed he was acting under Cromwell's instructions while the latter denied this. Ian Gentles analyses the disclaimer written by the grandees as stating that they did authorize the changing of the guard at Holdenbury to secure the person of the king, but not his forcible removal to headquarters, the latter being the fruit of Joyce's own negotiations with the king.[25] If the responsibility for this action is thus joint then it becomes all the more difficult to interpret the meaning of this action – whose intentions should be analysed? Those of the grandees, or Joyce, or the agitators? On the one hand, taking the king into army custody prevented the Presbyterians in the parliament from negotiating a settlement too favourable to the army's former enemies. On the other hand, given widespread rumour of royalist sympathies among the rank and file, and Cromwell's leanings towards constitutional monarchy, many saw Cornet Joyce's act as the first step in a possible restoration of the king.[26] In any case, the army now had in its possession the key piece on the chessboard, the piece that would determine the shape of settlement. And so between the Grandees and Joyce, in Joyce's overzealous extension of the grandees instructions, the army acted in line with its demands, using the element of surprise and showing Westminster that it would not let the fruits of its labours be despoiled.

With the publication of *A Solemn Engagement* and the capture of the king, the New Model Army sealed its appearance in the political arena and began to answer the first query concerning political action: who can act? The New Model Army can act. It exists within the political arena, it has the capacity to make a difference. But this response is insufficient on its own; a second more complicated problem has emerged: on what grounds can the army act? In other words, the agitators need to explain why the army has a mandate to engage in politics and not just military matters. They need to justify its existence in the political arena and legitimate its actions.

It is in the engagement again that we find the beginning of a response. In the part entitled the Declaration the army denies having solely a particular interest to vehicle. Rather it lays claim to the common good as its interest:

> We shall much rather study to promote such an establishment of common and equal right and freedom to the whole, as all might equally partake of but those that do by denying the same to others. (*SE*, 10)

It is in the first article of the Declaration that the grounds are identified for such a claim. The authors name the 'freeborn people of England' as those 'to whom the consequence of our case doth equally extend' inasmuch as their case involves 'oppression, injury or abuse' (*SE*, 9). This, of course, is the most dangerous claim made in the entire pamphlet since it immediately sets the army in a position of being a rival to the parliament. The authors claimed that the army represented the whole of the people, and that it pursued the common good. In the drafting of the *Humble Petition* in May the officers had tried to channel the rank and file's discontent into professional concerns alone, such as arrears and indemnities, and away from constitutional questions.[27] John Wildman, a chief agitator, writes his own account of the Putney Debates.[28] In that account he claims that Cromwell, though publically joined to the cause of the army since June, was in private against the publication of *A Solemn Engagement*, fearing that it would lead to ruin and disaster in the kingdom. These signs of internal dissension – which would later blossom into the rift between agitators and grandees – indicate the radicality of the army addressing the situation of the freeborn English people as a whole. And there is a curious passage in the Declaration that signals the authors' awareness of the controversy they have invited: they write, 'neither would we (if we might and could) set up any particular party or interest in the Kingdom' (*SE*, 10). This denial is disingenuous if not downright paradoxical. On the one hand, both the army officers and the parliament would prefer the army to pursue their private interests as particulars, that is, as individuals. On the other hand, what is denied in *A Solemn Engagement* is the intention to set up a particular faction. But in the same breath the authors claim to 'study and promote such an establishment of common and equal right and freedom to the whole' (*SE*, 10). Evidently such a study is the proper work of the parliament. If the parliament is sovereign then its proper task cannot be shared with other bodies; it has exclusive rights over the deliberation and execution of the business of government. If, de facto, the army claims to participate in this great task, then it does not recognize the parliament as sovereign; rather, it is placing itself as another body alongside the latter. And if this is the case the original accusation holds: the army is in fact setting up a particular party or interest. And thus it is no surprise that the authors 'find many strange things suggested or suspected to our great prejudice concerning dangerous principles, interests and designs in this Army' (*SE*, 10).

On what grounds does the army really act? It is only in the subsequent manifesto, the *Case of the Army Truly Stated*, that the position becomes clear.

## Autumn 1647: *The Case of the Army Truly Stated* and the split between agitators and grandees

In mid July, Henry Ireton, Cromwell's son-in-law and Commissary General of the horse, had written and circulated his proposal for settlement in favour of a constitutional monarchy, *The Heads of the Proposals*. It was used as a basis for negotiations between the army generals and the King. In the meantime the agitators had drawn up a rival document *An Agreement of the People*, which had gained wide support among the rank and file. Throughout the summer the Army had engaged in a game of push and shove with the Presbyterian members of parliament, forcing their withdrawal from Westminster by marching on London, and then as soon as they withdrew seeing the Presbyterians purge and mobilize the London militia and frighten the independent members of parliament out of Westminster and into the army's care. Neither the question of arrears, nor indemnities, nor compensation for war widows had been resolved: none of the grievances of May's *A Perfect and True Copy of the Several Grievances of the Army* nor June's *Humble Representation* had been properly addressed. It was in this atmosphere that the general council of the Army met on 16 September and Ireton forced through a vote on *The Heads of the Proposals* despite opposition from Colonel Rainborough, one of the Leveller-agitators.

In reaction to Ireton's precipitation of the question of settlement additional agitators were elected to certain regiments: their new manifesto was *The Case of the Army Truly Stated*, circulating through the regiments during September and printed on 15 October.[29] Morrill and Woolrych concur in arguing that there is a change in the authorship of this tract compared to that of *A Solemn Engagement*. It is signed by agents from the five horse regiments alone, precisely those that had recently held elections for additional agitators.[30] This explains the significant shift in the rhetoric and the arguments of this document with regard to *A Solemn Engagement*. Where the June pamphlet suggested that the parliament had been misled, abused and manipulated by certain persons with malicious intent towards the army, the 15 October pamphlet charges that parliamentary authority per se remains subject to infamy as long as the record remains of its shameful criminalization of the army's March petition. Moreover, given that;

> None of the public burdens, or oppressions, by arbitrary committees, injustice in the Law, Tythes and Monopolies, and restraint of free trade, burdensome Oaths, quality of assessments, Excise and otherwise are removed or lightened . . . [It is thus the case that] . . . the rights of the people in their parliaments concerning the extent and nature of that power are not cleared and declared. (CA, 2)

In *A Solemn Engagement* the agitators claim that the consequences of the army's case extend to the freeborn people of England. The authors of *The Case of the Army* simply assume that extension and flatly state that they have not yet seen 'the rights and freedoms of the nation cleared and secured' (CA, 1). Furthermore they claim not only the commonality but the identity of the army's case with that of the people as a whole by arguing that they fought for the parliament not as mercenaries who served the state but *as commoners*:

> We, by their invitation, took up arms in judgement and conscience, to preserve the nation from tyranny and oppression, and therefore were obliged to insist upon our rights and freedoms as commoners. (CA, 10)

This is the argument that clarifies the problematic claim of *A Solemn Engagement*: the army is not a particular faction and yet it works towards the good of the whole; the army sees itself as *more representative* of the commoners of England than the parliament. Indeed, the army sees itself as *more than* representative: it is identical with the commoners of England. The soldiers of the New Model Army took up arms and fought for the parliamentary cause as commoners. If the parliament is deserting its own cause, then evidently the army can and will step in to pursue that cause. And so, by October 1647, the army had stepped from public protest, from declaring its grievances to the recognized legislative authority of the land, to a position of rivalry if not potential usurpation. That it was able to do this is a sign that it found the grounds for its action: the soldiers fought for the parliamentary cause as commoners. They will abandon neither the cause nor the nation's commoners.

But then the unthinkable happens in terms of the army's gathering of strength: as soon as it consolidates and grounds its own unity it is subject to a split that will eventually lead to its political death. Army headquarters and the general council are frequently targeted in the pamphlet and accused of failing to act in line with the principles and desires declared in *A Solemn Engagement*. Headquarters is named as participating in same procrastination as parliament when it comes to redressing the army's grievances (CA, 1). The Council has affirmed 'that the Army is not to insist upon or demand any security for their own or other the freeborn peoples' freedoms or rights, though they might propound any thing to the Parliament's considerations'. In response the agitators claim that this would be to 'pervert' the 'whole intent of the *Engagement*' (CA, 3). The pamphlet's authors go so far as to claim that the army's enemies will gain hope from the words of the general council that 'will not oppose [these enemies] or disturb them in their proceedings' (CA, 9). This public split will widen into a divide during the Putney Debates in which Cromwell and Ireton voice their opposition to the Levellers constitutional program, a divide that amplifies into a gulf when Cromwell moves to violently suppress a Leveller-inspired mutiny in January 1648. But in the autumn of 1647 agitators are still members, though a minority, of the general council, and the army, though subject to a split, is still the site of concerted political action such as the very holding of the Putney Debates. The army is thus involved in struggle on two fronts: external and internal, split from the parliament, split between grandees and agitators. If the external struggle is primary, army unity predominates – as Cromwell always wishes – but if the internal struggle is primary, then dissolution threatens.

The first two queries of political action are: *Who can act*? And *who can act on what grounds*? At this stage in the New Model Army experience they have met with responses. It is in the situation of internal and external struggle that the third query opens up: *who is right about what is to be done*? Should the army seek settlement according to Ireton's *Heads of the Proposals* or along the lines of *The Case of the Army Truly Stated* – soon to be elaborated in the alternative Leveller constitutional program *An Agreement of the People*? In the Autumn of 1647 the split is already so deep that it is not merely a question of negotiating between alternative programs and arguing their merits and weaknesses: the agitators accuse the grandees of having already betrayed *A Solemn Engagement*. When negotiations do not take place and parties pursue their program without any modification – as Ireton does, pushing *The Heads of the Proposals* through the general council on 16 September – then the disagreement goes beyond content to form and motivation.

In targeting those members of the general council who would conciliate or negotiate with parliament, the agitators reinforce and affirm the independent and legitimate political vocation of the army. That vocation is neither to be bargained away nor suppressed, nor misdirected: it has given rise to a transparent and principled course of action that cannot but continue. This is the most striking aspect of the agents' thinking of political action. Again and again they return to the declarations of *A Solemn Engagement* and declare that they have not been satisfied, and that certain members of the Army headquarters would abandon them: for the agents, action flows from principle, and the principles cannot be negotiated. What are these principles? They go under the name of 'the common rights and liberties' or 'our native Rights' (*AG*, 1, 5). The first is the principle of popular sovereignty. The government rules by consent of the people alone, as Rainborough puts it in the Putney Debates:

> The poorest he that is in England hath a life to live, as the greatest he; and therefore truly sir I think that every man that is to live under a government ought first by his own consent to put himself under that government. (*PL*, 53).

The second agitator principle is to insist on the people's rights by limiting the government's powers, namely by granting full religious toleration, putting an end to press-ganging and guaranteeing equality before the law. For the agitators the action of the war will remain incomplete until a satisfactory settlement is reached, a settlement that clears the rights and freedoms of the freeborn people of England. That is to say, military hostilities may have officially ceased, yet the action of the war remains incomplete inasmuch as it flows from the principle of defending the parliament as a political authority founded on popular sovereignty. If the action of the war was based on principle, only actions that further realize those principles can complete that action and secure a true settlement. This is what I call a *logic of entailment*.

In the eyes of the agitators, the grandees do not act on principle but negotiate with various forces, royalist and parliamentarian; and the intentions behind their negotiations are unclear. On the first day of the Putney Debates, Cromwell and Ireton are condemned by Edward Sexby for engaging in independent negotiations with the parliament over the settlement of the kingdom: 'your credit and reputation have been much blasted . . . for seeking to settle the kingdom in a way wherein we thought to see satisfied all men, and we have dissatified them – I mean in relation to the King' (*PL*, 2). In his account of the Putney Debates, John Wildman goes further and claims that Cromwell and Ireton were simply traitors to the cause who had never shared the principles enshrined in *A Solemn Engagement*. Rather they had espoused those principles during a certain period because it suited their long-term game – purging the parliament of the enemy Presbyterian faction of Hollis, Stapleton and Waller. Moreover the grandees' enmity with this faction cannot be based on principle since otherwise they would not do exactly the same thing they accuse the Presbyterians of: negotiating with the king behind closed doors. Wildman concludes that the grandees are engaged purely in revenge and their intentions are to realize their private interests alone. Without taking Wildman's extreme diagnosis as gospel it must be admitted that Cromwell did have a reputation for prevarication, insincerity, affectations of piety and the instrumentalization of his temporary allies. Indeed S. R. Gardiner, in the fourth volume of his monumental history of the civil war, mentions his own struggle with the question of whether Cromwell was an honest man in his dealings.[31] John Morrill and Philip Baker recall 'the charges of hypocrisy, double-dealing and a craving for power levelled against him by almost all of his contemporaries' and signal the consensus among historians that clears him of these charges.[32] The fact that Cromwell was continually subject to such accusations indicates the force of the query posed by his former allies – *why do you act as you do*? The shape Cromwell's actions take in the agitators' accusations is that of private negotiations with the king. For the agitators at least, the split between themselves and the grandees can be understood as a divorce between two models of political action: action based on principle, and action as negotiation.

From the standpoint of the agitators, it is impossible to negotiate principles.

But would the grandees have ever accepted such an account? Do they merely negotiate without any basis in principle? Cromwell argues that he negotiates on the basis of principles, indeed he claims during the Putney Debates that the grandees and the agitators have much in common:

> I cannot see but that we all speak to the same end and the mistakes are only in the way. The end is to deliver this nation from oppression and slavery, to accomplish that work that God has carried on in us, to establish our hopes of an end of justice and righteousness in it. We agree thus far. Further too: that we all apprehend danger from the person of the King and from the Lords. (PL, 104)

Ireton argues against the Leveller constitutional program on the basis of both principle and consequence. Moreover he has his own positive political program: *The Heads of the Proposals*, whose publication as the army's program was precisely where all the trouble started. So it is far from being the case that the divide between grandees and agitators can be simply parsed as a difference between principled action and negotiation. Negotiations, such as the Putney Debates, can be driven by conflict between different standpoints, not just between different private interests. In any case, the difference between negotiating interests and actualizing principles does form an open problem for the actors in this political process. Before pursuing the concrete differences between the agitator and grandee political programs a brief exploration of this problem may shed some light on the difficulties each side faced.

In a broad perspective on the evolution of the parliament during the Interregnum Christopher Hill argues:

> As parliament became an effective sovereign body, majority decision was a necessary means of settling disagreements. Divisions on party lines in the sixteen-forties foreshadowed the rise of a party system a generation later. Majority government, like religious toleration and Hobbes's political theory, recognizes that society is a group of atoms: it abandons the fiction of a one-minded community.[33]

If Hill is right then the dominant model of political action that emerges in the seventeenth century is contractual. If the passage of policy through the parliament requires a majority then it must involve calculated negotiation between voting parties and their interests. Note that once the party system arises in the 1680s the 'fiction of a one-minded community' is abandoned at a global level only to re-emerge at a regional level: the level of the party. In any case, the situation of the Levellers, agitators and grandees is not one adjudicated by majority government. For the agitators, negotiation itself seems to have a bad name: all the negotiations they have attempted have broken down. They address the parliament with a series of reasonable demands. Parliament's response – limited satisfaction of economic demands, ordering the army to disband – forecloses any possibility of dialogue on larger political questions. In the general council, the agitators are outvoted by the grandees and they suspect they have been outmanoeuvred. In their political landscape the only significant instance of prolonged negotiations is that between the grandees and the king, and for the agitators these negotiations are opaque. Nevertheless, these negotiations on the part of the grandees do have a public face: the document at their basis is *The Heads of the Proposals*, which contains a detailed program for a constitutional monarchy. This document thus enables a confrontation of principles, and so in *The Case of the Army* the agitators object to such a program:

> In the declaration of June 14th, page 10, as in all other Remonstrances and Declarations it was desired, that the rights and liberties of the people might be secured, before the Kings business should be considered. But now the grievances of the people are propounded to be considered after the restoring him to the regal power, and that in such a way according to the proposals *viz.* with a negative voice, that the people that have purchased by blood what was their right, of which the King endeavoured to deprive them, should yet solely depend on his will, for their relief in their grievances and oppressions. (CA, 6)

Indeed during the Putney Debates the most intransigent obstacle, involving long disquisitions on technical and historical constitutional matters between Ireton and Rainborough, concerned the *Proposals* awarding of a royal veto over parliamentary legislation.

Morrill and Baker argue that it was the vexed question of what to do with the king in a future settlement that ultimately caused these talks to break down.[34] The agitators' position was clear: no further negotiations with the king should be entered into. In the *Case of the Army* the authors require that:

> Before [the king's] business be further considered, because the people are under much oppression and misery, it be forthwith the whole work of Parliament, to here consider or, and study effectually redress for all common grievances and oppressions, and for the securing all other the peoples rights and freedoms. (CA, 17)

At Putney on 5 November, they voted for the general council to send a letter to parliament stating that it was the army's position that no further propositions of settlement should be addressed to the king (PL, 453).[35] In reaction Ireton walked out of the talks. To an unrelenting catalogue of accusations John Wildman in his *Putney Projects* adds the charge that Cromwell and Ireton 'maintained the most constant possible correspondence with the King, though they declared it treason in Mr Hollis to make private addresses to the King's part, yet they have multipled private addresses to the Capital enemy, the King himself' (PP, 12). But Wildman is not content with condemnation alone, he must diagnose the grandees' duplicity, he must sound out the heart of their actions. In the light of their public declarations, Wildman argues, 'common right and freedom was visibly the choicest object of all their actions and intentions . . . seemingly the golden ball of their contention, the ultimate end of their hazardous race' (PP, 5). Wildman subjects these appearances to a test: 'It's a known maxim that the end of an action is where the heart rests' (PP, 10). The test is then refined to focus on a specific moment: Wildman argues that once Cromwell, occupying London with the army; 'having subjected even *ad nutum* to his beck both King and Parliament, his first public actions could be then no other than the express character of his intentions' (PP, 9). And Cromwell's first public actions, in Wildman's interpretation, add up to no commitment to the common rights and freedoms of the people of England, rather to little more than a demand that the situation of the army be regularized. For Wildman, Cromwell and Ireton demand but 'partial justice' restricting their projected purge of the parliament to 11 Presbyterian members whereas 'they could have produced as high a charge against ten times 11' (*PP*, 8). Wildman states his methodological rule for the interpretation of action and then concludes his diagnosis:

> It's a known maxim that the end of an action is where the heart rests. I wish the application be not true, that their private interest was their highest end, and therefore in the enjoyment of that they acquiesced (PP, 10).

Here the charge is complete: Ireton and Cromwell negotiate with the enemy, thus de facto ensuring that he has a place in any future settlement, thus engaging in a restoration, and they do so on the basis of their private interest. At least for Wildman, if not for the other Levellers and agitators, there is a clear opposition between action as negotiation based on private interest and action as the actualization of principles; indeed Wildman gives us a dire and dramatic portrait of the latter as ascesis:

> Had single simple justice been the object of their desires then they could have known no bounds or limits, no respects or relations. But injustice, oppression, and corruption in whatsoever subject would have been the object of their hatred, and the execution of the law upon them their desire and intention. They would have known no difference between the meanest Scavenger and the highest Lord, yea (that original of injustice) the King himself ... Had the cries and groans of the Oppressed took such deep impressions on their hearts as they professed, had their hearts been fired (as they appeared) with the sacred flames of love of their native country, they would have travailled in the birth of its perfect peace and freedom and been pained until they were delivered. They would have said like Pompey, taking ship in a dangerous storm, *Necesse est ut eam non ut vivam*, it's more necessary that we relieve the oppressed, than preserve our lives.[36] (*PP*, 9–10)

For Wildman to actualize principles is to stop at nothing until they are completely realized. As such there is no room for negotiation. To negotiate is to admit another necessity than that of principle, namely the necessity of recognizing and accommodating the existence of other political parties as both legitimate and as embodying different interests and standpoints. Wildman goes so far in his opposition to private interest as to deny even the principled agent's own interest in survival faced with the exigencies of the mission. Wildman, of course, does not represent all of the agitators in this document. The agitators are clearly against private negotiations with the king, but it is not clear that they are against negotiation per se. And nor is it the case that they are in exclusive possession of principles for their action; Ireton is quite at home arguing from principle in defending the *Proposals*.

It is at Putney, during four days of recorded discussion, that the differences between agitators and grandees come to a head. Putney is the last moment in which the agitators and grandees are able to talk through fundamental political issues face to face. By December the general council is dissolved, and by January the agitators suppressed. In this long summer of agitation and manoeuvre the question of political action unfolds in all of its complexity:

- Who can act?
- Who can act on what grounds?
- Who is right about what is to be done?'
- Why do we succeed or fail?
- If you and I split, were we ever united, and to what end?

It is at Putney that the Leveller-agitators and grandees have their last chance to agree on the answers.

## The *Putney Debates* and the end of the alliance

On 28 October 1647, the general council held its weekly meeting at Putney. Ten days previously it had received *The Case of the Army*. From an initially hostile and punitive reaction on the part of the senior officers the council had moved towards a policy of conciliation and accommodation, appointing a committee to study the document.[37]

The central question of the Putney Debates is what is to be done for settlement. It is the highpoint, in this political process, of the third query concerning political action: who is right about what is to be done? The notes taken by the army secretary Clarke record deep disagreement over the content of the constitutional programs outlined in the rival documents – Ireton's *The Heads of the Proposals* and the agitators' *An Agreement of the People*. Should a settlement be reached by negotiating with the king towards a form of constitutional monarchy, or should a new constitution be imposed that extends the franchise, abolishes monarchy and the House of Lords and decentralizes government? However the disagreement went even deeper to touch the very form of political action. Hence in the first of the four major quarrels animating the debate, Cromwell and Ireton charge that the very publication of *An Agreement of the People* is illegitimate. The second quarrel concerns the grounds and consequences of the *Agreement*'s proposal to extend the franchise. Cromwell opens the third battle by charging the agitators with willfully and divisively instrumentalizing the army, which is in no position to decide constitutional matters. The fourth round is rung in with the agitators' counter-attack: the *Heads of the Proposals* amounts to nothing more than a restoration of the king and the lords' interests.

Each speaker is forced to reveal and clarify his ideas in the heat of exchange: nowhere else in the seventeenth century do we have a record of lowly common soldiers arguing with no hesitation for their view on the most pressing constitutional issues of the kingdom. And yet speakers continually question the very possibility of discussion given the heights of disagreement – accusations of bad faith and professions of good faith abound, God is continually called upon for guidance, the whole proceedings are interrupted by a prayer meeting, compromises are seen as impossible, and wildly different grounds for action are called upon: historical precedent, God's providence, right reason and the people's safety. And as the arguments intensify some become more and more uneasy at the threat of division given rumours of hostile forces being raised by the royalists and parliament. Audley voices the anxiety: 'This dispute is long. If we are stuck here we are lost' (*PL*, 76).

The danger of the interlocutors getting stuck in this dispute is palpable: indeed, with hindsight it is worth asking whether or not the dispute was not what Jean-François Lyotard calls a 'differend' rather than a disagreement.[38] In a differend, antagonists employ conceptual frameworks so dissimilar that no agreement can be reached, even concerning the basic terms of the debate. Such a hypothesis would explain the interlocutors' frequent expressions of frustration with the form of the debate and with the absence of agreement over common rules for the discussion. Individuals propose various conditions for the debate. Audley attempts to get all antagonists to recognize the common danger threatening the army. Cromwell valorizes unity over division: 'Consider that we may be one in one Christ though we think diversely, and we may be friends though not brethren, and let us attain to union though not to unity' (PL, 182). In a less idealistic tone he urges that military authority must be recognized otherwise ordinary military operations cannot be carried out. But all calls for unity and common ground were frustrated by disagreement. To understand the shape of the political process after Putney it is vital to comprehend how such a deep dispute could ever come to any conclusion.

## *The publication of* An Agreement of the People

On the first day of debates, in which much is made of the order of business, who is to be admitted to the meeting and what exactly is to be discussed, the agitators urge that their constitutional programme *An Agreement of the People* be taken into consideration. Upon hearing it read out Cromwell exclaims: 'Truly this paper does contain in it very great alterations of the very government of the kingdom' (PL, 7). In his eyes it attempts to 'leap out of one condition into another' and he urges that it is their duty to not only consider ends, and the good of the country, but also 'ways and means to accomplish [the things proposed]', for in his consideration 'there will be very great mountains in the way of this' (PL, 8). Ireton will lay exactly the same charge against a second version of the *Agreement* at Whitehall in December 1648: to be a true 'Agreement of the People' it must actually secure the consent of the people themselves, and that is far from provided for in the document. Cromwell's second objection is to the very publication of the *Agreement*, and it takes the form of a comic hypothetical: if everyone were to start publishing manifestos such as this, confusion would result and England would be Switzerlanded into separate cantons. His target here is what he sees as the utter contingency of its emergence: nothing in its logic of radical democratization is to prevent another such constitutional project from emerging, and another, without end, creating one opaque oppositional group after another. Ireton joins in the accusation: to publish such a manifesto is to break prior engagements and obligations. These men seem to think that they are 'at a loose end' but he would remind them that they do have obligations and he proposes that these must be considered in their proper balance with freedom before the 'paper' is considered (*PL*, 9). We will meet such authoritarian contractualism again – in Hobbes.

The agitators' defense is simple: they hold that they have higher engagements, namely to God and to their conscience. Moreover they hold that if an engagement is unjust it is right to break with it. This immediately brings the retort from Ireton that such a right is equivalent to an embrace of anarchy and thus an absence of government. This exchange anticipates Hobbes and Locke's treatments of the right to resistance within their theories of the social contract. On the one hand, Hobbes argues that there is no right to resistance: to act against the sovereign is to act against oneself, which is against natural law. Locke, on the other hand, places the sovereign as subject to the contract, rather than above it. Consequently if the people judge that the government is no longer assuring their safety, they may rightfully engage in resistance. The agitators do not, of course, have Locke's argument to hand, and it is easy for Ireton to dismiss the individual judgement of injustice as not only arbitrary but also necessarily leading to the dissolution of the entire institution of engagements. But the agitators make another argument – the real engagement is the one they undertook in the field, against the royalist forces (*PL*, 33). This engagement is yet to be fully carried through; the *Agreement* is part of the fulfilment of that engagement. As such it is to be understood as an extension of *A Solemn Engagement* that was in turn an extension of the rank and file's action in the field. Ireton concedes that there is a principle of consistency in what the army has done, but prefers to identify this principle in abstract terms – God's will and providence. He then claims that this principle of consistency nevertheless does not lead to levelling, to the destruction of all social degrees (*PL*, 50, 68).

In the analysis of action from principle versus negotiation we already met the agitators' *logic of entailment*. It can be arranged into a syllogism:

- Soldiers engaged and fought in the war against the royalist forces on principle.

- The action of the war is incomplete, settlement has not yet been achieved.

- Hence the completion of that action can only take place via the same principles.

According to this logic current actions can be explained as continuations or prolongations of an as-yet-incomplete and encompassing action. This is a crucial element in the Leveller-agitator model of political action. It provides a schema for the collectivization of single actions; they share in a larger overall action through this logic of entailment. Each action partially fulfils and fleshes out an engagement taken in earlier actions. When explaining their actions the agitators repeatedly claim that they ensue from *A Solemn Engagement* of June 1647. In turn they explain the enemy's actions as the destruction of the chain of implication: 'The Armies engagement, Representations, Declarations, and Remonstrances, and promises in them contained, are declined and more and more daily broken . . . in diverse particulars of dangerous consequence to the Army and the whole Nation' (*CA*, 2). In the pamphlet *Two Letters from the Agents of the Five Regiments of Horses*, published in September 1647, the agitators express this logic of entailment in the form of a negative implication: 'let it be remembered that if you had *not* joined together at first, and chose your Agents to act for you when your officers thought it not sage for them to appear, you had been now in *no* capacity to plead for your own or the people's freedoms'.[39] In an affirmative form: to join together and to choose agents entails the capacity to plead for the people's freedoms.

In his opposition to the publication of *An Agreement of the People* Ireton has recourse to another model of political action – *the contractual model* – which is elaborated in its most sophisticated form 40 years later in the writings of Locke. It forms one of the objects of Chapter 5. The contractual model of action employs another schema for the collectivization of action whereby one action is joined, by legal obligation, to the performance of another action. Ireton argues:

> There is no other foundation of justice I know . . . but that men should keep covenant with each other. This is the foundation of right: covenants freely made and entered into . . . What right does any man have to anything – lands, goods, estate – if you lay not down that principle, that we are to keep covenant. If they hold to natural right alone, then he as much as the next man has a right to this piece of land. (*PL*, 26)

In an economic contract, the two actions involved are commensurate insofar as they involve the same universal: the exchange value of the items or services that are bought and sold. The two actions are thus collectivized or joined through each possessing a common property, exchange value. Likewise in the contractual model of politics actions are joined through an external property: they do not belong to each other, they are not part of each other. As Hegel argues in *Elements for a Philosophy of Right*, the two wills involved in a contract are but arbitrary individual wills that create a common will, they do not give rise to a universal will in and for itself.[40]

There are not only two but three competing schemas for the collectivization of action at work in the Putney Debates. The third schema emerges in the agitators' suspicions as to Cromwell's and Ireton's activity in parliament concerning negotiations with the king. The third schema is that of instrumentalization: one action serves as a means to the other action's end. For instance, as Colonel Rainborough clarifies in response to Edward Sexby's opening accusation, when the motion was carried in parliament for making a second address to the king, 'it *was* urged in the house that it was the sense of the Army that it should be so' (*PL*, 4). As Sexby feared, the opinion of the army *was* falsely represented (the means) to sway members of parliament into voting for a policy of negotiation with the king (the second encompassing action, the end). Cromwell defends himself by claiming that he never misrepresented the army's sense of the matter. Sexby makes another far more serious accusation of instrumentalism: if, as Cromwell and Ireton hold, the engagement of fighting in the war for parliament does *not* entail reforming the institution according to the principles of popular sovereignty then:

> Many of us fought for ends which we since saw were not those that caused us to go through so much hardship. It would have been good of you to have advertised it and I believe you would have had fewer under your command. (*PL*, 74)

Ireton's response, refusing the charge of instrumentalizing the soldiers, confirms his adherence to a contractual model of politics:

> I ask those men when they drew out to join the army at Newmarket, whether then they thought of any more interest or right in the kingdom than this; whether they did think that they should have as great an interest in parliament men as freeholders had? Or whether from the beginning we did not engage for the liberty of parliaments, and that we should be concluded by the laws that such did make. Unless somebody did make you believe that you should have an equal interest in the kingdom . . . there is no reason to blame men for leading you so far as they have done. (*PL*, 76–7)

Ireton holds that there was no promise to extend the franchise on the part of army recruiters. In the absence of such a promise there are no grounds to argue that such a policy is implied by the army's action in the field. This position is disingenuous, legalistic and rigid. It disallows any possibility of political ideas emerging during a collective experience, any possibility of politicization.

Sexby was not alone in his suspicions of having been instrumentalized by the grandees. It has long been part of the historical understanding of Cromwell's uneasy alliance with the Leveller-agitators that he acted on expediency alone, using their numerical and ideological support against a hostile parliament when it suited him, and breaking the alliance when the agitators made too many political demands for comfort.

Thus the contest of three schemas for the collectivization of action – the contractual, the instrumental and that of entailment – is already at stake in the opening quarrel over the legitimacy of the very action of publishing *An Agreement of the People*. But what of the latter's detail: what exactly opposes it to Ireton's *Heads of* the *Proposals*? Nothing more than who had the right to participate in the field of politics, who could be represented in parliament: at stake was the number of voting subjects.

## *What grounds for extending the franchise?*

In 1647, there was a property qualification for the right to vote: each elector had to demonstrate ownership of land worth 40 shillings or more or be freeman in a trading corporation. In his famous study *The Political Theory of Possessive Individualism* Crawford Macpherson refers to this as the 'freeholder franchise'.[41] In Macpherson's estimate there would have been around 212,000 such electors in the 1640s. *An Agreement of the People* removes this property qualification and so extends the franchise to all copyholders, leaseholders, traders, shopkeepers, artisans and tradesmen who were not freemen. Macpherson argues that this franchise would have comprised of around 417,000 men. Note that if the franchise were extended to all males save criminals, regardless of their social status, it would have implied 1,170,000 voters. These figures give some measure of just how restrictive the freeholder franchise was, and how much of a change the Levellers were arguing for. In the Putney Debates at least, the Levellers excluded those they called 'servants', wage-earners in today's terms, and those receiving alms on the grounds that they were economically dependent upon their masters and thus would fear to vote differently to the latter (*PL*, 83).

Ireton makes two arguments against any extension of the franchise: the first from principle, the second from consequence. In principle he claims that the only ground for extending the franchise is natural right (*PL*, 53, 58). According to natural right – and here he is in accordance with Hobbes – 'you take away all property since the right of nature states that you and I have equal right to the same goods' (*PL*, 58). Again Locke would have rushed to the agitators aid, at least in this argument: the *Second Treatise on Government* offers an account of how natural law does provide for the emergence of property rights. Ireton's argument from consequence, on the other hand, is a little fanciful: he claims that if men without fixed property were given the vote, and if they outnumbered those with property, then the former could vote against property per se (*PL*, 63). Sexby's retort targets Ireton's paranoia: to say giving the poor their birthright will destroy the kingdom is to distrust providence (*PL*, 70).

Ireton supports his argument from principle by advancing an interpretation of the reasons behind the current constitution:

> I think that no person has a right to an interest or share in the disposing of the affairs of the kingdom, and in determining or choosing those who shall determine what laws we shall be ruled by here – no person has a right to this who has not a permanent fixed interest in this kingdom, and those persons together are properly the represented of this kingdom. (*PL*, 53–4)

Ireton defines a 'permanent fixed interest' as one that cannot be removed from the kingdom: freemen in corporations and freeholders do possess such immovable interests (*PL*, 57). In contrast, 'he that is here today and gone tomorrow' or he that 'may carry about with him' his interest, does not. It is ironic that Locke develops a metaphysical conception of just such a mobile proprietor as the foundation of his commonwealth. In Ireton's eyes a leaseholder whose only income results from what he makes by using the land, is in as good an economic condition in this kingdom as another: according to Ireton he has no direct ties to the country (*PL*, 63). Ireton is in favour of rationalizing the electoral system – removing rotten boroughs for instance – but sees anarchy as not only the ground but the result of any widespread extension of the franchise.

His arguments meet with various responses. To the claim that any constitutional reform must seek its grounds in natural right Rainborough, Wildman and Audley respond that to be bound to the old law is to be bound by a law in which people have no voice. Such a law is tyrannical given that the source of all political obligation is the free consent of all (*PL*, 61, 66, 81). This is the Leveller doctrine of popular sovereignty – note that Locke's contractual theory of government can accommodate such a doctrine.

To the specific claim that natural law holds no grounds for private property the agitators make four objections. Rainborough begins by noting that civil law does not have a monopoly in guaranteeing property: divine law in the shape of the commandment 'thou shalt not steal' bids that we respect the division between mine and thine.

Ireton responds that this is a general principle and not enough to guarantee the specific features of the current electoral system, but this is to beg the question since it is precisely the historically specific features of that system that the agitators are targeting as unjust. Ireton's original claim was not about legitimating specifics, but grounding the entire institution of private property: general principles are thus required. The form of Rainborough's argument here resembles that of Antigone: the injustice of the present civil law is demonstrated on grounds of a higher law, that of God.

The second objection, made by Rainborough and Clarke, proceeds by redefining property: Clarke argues that the clothes on my back constitute property, and that these are guaranteed by the right of nature (*PL*, 80). Rainborough completes this thought by arguing that the end of government is the safety of the people, and that my person is more valuable to me than my estate (*PL*, 67). Based on the natural right of self-preservation, this line of argument defines property as both my own person and whatever enables my survival. The consequence is that natural right guarantees that all are property owners: as such none would vote against 'property' per se.

The third objection to Ireton is historical. In its simplicity it anticipates Marx's approach to the origin of capital and class division. How is it, Rainborough asks, that some happen to have property and others do not: is this, in itself, just? (*PL*, 63). Though no one is willing to take up the argument on grounds as wide as those of history, the Levellers do actually possess an account of the historical origin of injustice in England – it is the Norman conquest. Wildman refers to it when he claims – against Ireton's emphasis on positive civil law – 'our very laws were made by our conquerors. Much is spoken of chronicles but I would not credit them because our lords would not suffer anything else to be chronicled' (*PL*, 65–6). Wildman thus posits both a historical origin of injustice and warns that history itself, drawn from a written record, is not a neutral source of information if history is written by the victors.

The fourth objection brought against Ireton is an argument from consequence. What, asks Rainborough, of those soldiers who lost their estate through engaging in the war, shall they have no vote? (*PL*, 56). Many who engaged in the New Model Army would not have qualified for the 40 shilling property franchise, but some were in the ironic position of initially being qualified, and then having lost their estate through a combination of military and financial misfortune. Macpherson estimates that around 22,000 soldiers qualified as wage-earners and alms-takers before the war: the Levellers argued that they had earned their franchise through fighting for the parliament.[42] Ireton is quite confident in refuting this argument: he classifies it as an 'argument from consequence' and claims he can give greater ill consequences of changing the constitution than of keeping it (*PL*, 71–2). But the agitators are not engaged in some kind of cost-benefit analysis in which consequences of one course of action are weighed up against consequences of an alternative course of action. The argument for the extension of the franchise for those classes who ventured their lives in the war for the parliament is part of the larger argument for the publication of the *Agreement* as a direct consequence of the soldiers' engagement in the war. The form of the argument, as Sexby puts it, seconded by Peter and Rainborough, is the following:

> We have engaged in this war and ventured our lives: and it was all for this, to recover our birthrights and privileges as Englishmen; and by the arguments urged is there is none . . . I wonder we were so much deceived. If we had not a right in this kingdom we were mere mercenary soldiers. (*PL*, 69)[43]

This general argument does not measure the consequences of one policy against those of another inferior policy. The agitators do not claim that it is of greater utility to award 'birthrights and privileges' to soldiers. Rather they argue that their constitutional vision is entailed or implied by their actions on the field. When Ireton engages with this general argument, in contrast with the argument about the franchise, he does not dismiss it as proceeding from consequence alone; rather he understands it as a claim about a broken contract. As mentioned earlier, in return he disingenuously demands who it was that explicitly promised the vote to soldiers when they engaged. Ireton argues there was no such contract to be broken, and if there was, then its content – the very meaning of the war – was rather to fight against one man's will determining everything, against absolute monarchy (*PL*, 72). But the agitators are not arguing that they have been cheated in a contract. When Rainborough asks 'I would fain know what a soldier has fought for all this while? He has fought to enslave himself, to give power to men of riches', he is not protesting that a contract has been broken but that a great action, a project, a mission has run off the rails, has gone astray, has come to bear no fruit (*PL*, 71). Indeed, to apply the model of a contract would be to reduce the soldiers' engagement to some form of exchange – they were promised a certain compensation in return for services rendered. But this is to treat them, as Sexby puts it, as 'mere mercenary soldiers'. Rather it is on the basis of their engagement in the war that they have come to understand what it means to possess a right in their kingdom, what it means to participate in the reconstruction of the commonwealth after the war.

Cromwell and Ireton are well aware of the scope of the agitator ambition hence their attack that opens the third major quarrel of the debates.

## The willful and divisive actions of the agitators

On the third day of debate, Cromwell opens by charging the agitators of mistaking the entire position of the army, which, not being the supreme authority in the kingdom, cannot decide the settlement of the war, the latter being properly the business of parliament alone, including any decision that might be made to further negotiate with the king (*PL*, 97–8). Earlier he marks his dissatisfaction with one of Edward Sexby's interventions, claiming that 'it did savour so much of will' and claims 'some gentlemen speak more of will than . . . of satisfaction [of conscience]' (*PL*, 73, 76). Ireton echoes this critique when he claims that taking anything away from the current constitution is to take away 'for matter of wilfulness' (*PL*, 77). He goes one step further when claiming that the authors and subscribers of *The Case of the Army Truly Stated* have gone far further in dividing and disbanding the army than the grandees: indeed 'here is not one part of the Army is divided [in body] farther than the outcries of the authors of it [are in spirit]' (*PL*, 86). The kind of disbanding that concerns Ireton is not that of dispersing to separate camps, but ideological; it is a

> dividing which makes no army, and that dissolving of that order and government which is as essential to an army as life is to a man – which if it be taken away I think that such a company

are no more an army than a rotten carcass is a man . . . For my part I profess it seriously, that we shall find in the issue that the principle of that division [which they seek to raise on the question] of disbanding is no more than this: whether such [men] or such shall have the managing of the business. I say plainly, the way [they have taken] hath been the way of disunion and division, and [the dissolution] of that order. And I shall appeal to all men: [whether] the dividing from that General Council [and from the resolution] wherein we have all engaged [that] we would be concluded by [the decisions of] that [Council], and [whether likewise] the endeavouring to draw the soldiers to run this way [with them – whether this is not the real dividing of the Army]. (*PL*, 86–7)

Ireton's accusation of instrumentalism is clear: the Leveller-agitators have caused ruinous division within the army by seducing common soldiers with their foreign ideology to the point of destroying army discipline. Faced with their accusations of his own double-dealing between the army and parliament, and his own breaking of *A Solemn Engagement* of June he accuses the authors of *The Case of the Army* and *An Agreement of the People* of breaking with their engagement to abide by the decisions of the general council. Recall that the agitators were never happy with the composition of the general council – designed to both formalize and channel the inter-regimental communications between agitators – since it was 'overstuffed' with officers and grandees. Not only does Ireton insist on formal engagements – abiding by the council's decisions – but he also detects a hidden agenda behind the agitators' activism. All of their ostensive political differences over the expansion of the franchise and constitutional monarchy versus a republic come down to nothing more than a desire to rule: 'The principle of that division . . . is no more than this: whether such [men] or such shall have the managing of the business' (*PL*, 87).

Whether these accusations are made in bad faith or not and whether they are in keeping with Cromwell's and Ireton's overall attempts to negotiate with the Leveller-agitators is besides the point here. What is important is that within these charges the instrumental model of action emerges again. Previously it emerged in the quarrel over whether or not the agitators had any right to publish *An Agreement of the People*, and there it contrasted with two other models for the collectivisation of action; that of the contract, and that of entailment. Here the instrumental model gains more detail: it is not just a matter of treating people as means towards an end. It is deciding what to do sheerly on the basis of individual will. In Cromwell's charge of voluntarism, the individual will is understood as arbitrary in its separation from any public consensus over the common good. This anticipates Locke's critique of absolute monarchy as based on arbitrary will of one man. As Ireton informs the agitators: 'I [will] tell you what the soldier of the kingdom hath fought for. First, the danger that we stood in was that one man's will must be a law' (*PL*, 72). In Cromwell's vocabulary willfulness refers to what he interprets as an attempt to justify and ground a policy or a political obligation in nothing more than individual will or conscience, with no reference to previous formal engagements or to the functioning of established institutions, such as army discipline – 'how they can take the determination of commanding men, conducting men, quartering men, keeping guards, without an authority otherwise than from themselves I am ignorant' (*PL*, 97). At one point Cromwell complains that the agitators speak as if they were firmly resolved to impose the *Agreement* as if it were already law, without any interest in discussion or alternative propositions (*PL*, 31). The instrumental model of action thus imposes one man's will as law; but to what end? In Ireton's opinion, the concealed end of the agitators' divisive activity is nothing more than the acquisition and retention of political power: 'whether such men shall have the managing of the business'. The model of instrumental action thus involves a curious kind of tautology: the end of action is not the common good, nor any other determinate content, but rather the formal and abstract capacity to engage in further instrumental actions through the maintenance of a position of power.

The agitators' responses to these accusations are short and to the point: they understand that the substance of the debates does not lie in these matters and they brush aside the charge of willfulness. Wildman plays the contractual model against Ireton in a Lockean manner: the agitators are most definitely bound to the general council's decisions, but only so far as it promotes their safety (*PL*, 90). After Cromwell speaks, Rainborough dryly remarks 'I wonder how that which should be termed wilfullness in one man be called reason in another' (*PL*, 74). After Ireton speaks, however, Rainborough is astounded: 'If . . . this was the sense of the army in dividing, and it was meant that men should not divide in opinions! To me that is a mystery. It is a huge reflection, a taxing of persons' (*PL*, 87). An anonymous agitator immediately backs up Rainborough, targeting Ireton's claims:

> Whereas you say the Agents did it, [it was] the soldiers did put the Agents upon these meetings. It was the dissatisfactions that were in the Army which provoked, which occasioned, those meetings, which you suppose tends so much to dividing; and the reason[s] of such dissatisfactions are because those whom they had to trust to act for them were not true to them. (*PL*, 88)

Sexby makes a similar defense in response to Cromwell: 'Concerning my making divisions, if I were a particular I could lie down and be trodden but I am truly sent by a regiment' (*PL*, 74–5). The agitators reject the charge of having instrumentalized the soldiers. Their defense is based on the democratic decentralized organization that they have put in place within the regiments – we are the voice of the rank and file, we do not ventriloquize, we solely organize. It is here that the crucial differences emerge between the competing models of political action. The agitators' model is one of entailment. They position and legitimize their activity as a continual *expression* and *advancement* of the rank and file's shared concerns. The publication of their apparently 'divisive' pamphlets concretizes the principle of the rights of commoners to freedom and political representation. Ireton, on the other hand, says the following:

> I will not arrogate that I was the first man that put the Army upon the thought either of successive Parliaments or more equal Parliaments; yet there are some here that know who they were [that] put us upon that foundation of liberty of putting a period to this Parliament, [in order] that we might have successive Parliaments, and that there might be a more equal distribution of elections. There are many here that know who were the first movers of that business in the Army. I shall not arrogate that [to myself]. (*PL*, 77)

Here Ireton implicitly accuses the agitators of seeding ideas among the soldiers, of initiating the spread of a divisive ideology. The 'first movers' of the ideology are thus specific individuals, and not the rank and file as a whole. He continues by vaunting his good faith and ideological flexibility by claiming agreement – though limited – with such ideas:

> But I can argue this with a clear conscience: that no man hath prosecuted that with more earnestness, and will stand to that interest more than I do, of having Parliaments successive and not perpetual, and the distribution of elections [more equal]. But, notwithstanding, my opinion stands good, that it ought to be a distribution amongst the fixed and settled people of this nation. It's more prudent and safe, and more upon this ground of right for it [to be so]. Now it is the fundamental constitution of this kingdom; and that which you take away [you take away] for matter of willfulness. (PL, 77)

The agitators' proposition to extend the franchise to common soldiers who were not freeholders is thus neither prudent, nor safe, nor is it as grounded on right as Ireton's position. If the soldiers have come to believe in it then they have been duped and manipulated. Ireton has already named the end of instrumentalization: the acquisition and maintenance of power. In the passage cited above we have the beginning of instrumentalization: initiation in a single foreign unit, the introduction of ideas. The propagation of action then proceeds through a multiplicity of means that are essentially passive and do not contribute to the orientation of the action. The corresponding figure of the collective, the rank and file, is precisely what we find in Hobbes when he argues that outside the sovereign there is no such thing as collective action, only hysterical passion.

The fourth quarrel animating the Putney Debates concerns the degree to which Ireton's *Heads of the Proposals* restores the power of the king. It reopens the third query of political action: who is right about what must be done, the agitators in the *Agreement* or Ireton in his proposal? The discussion also reveals one further ontological determination of instrumentalism. Cromwell, defending *The Heads of the Proposals*, makes the following argument:

> For the actions that are [now] to be done, and those that must do them, I think it is their proper place to conform to the Parliament, that first gave them their being; and I think it is considerable whether they do contrive to suppress the power [of

the King and his party] by that power or no, if they do continue [their endeavour] to suppress them. And [indeed] how they can take the determination of commanding men, conducting men, quartering men, keeping guards, without an authority otherwise than from themselves I am ignorant. And therefore I think there is much [need] in the Army to conform to those things that are within their sphere. (*PL*, 97)

This is an ontological argument in that it uses Aristotle's concept of ontological priority: the parliament gave the army its being therefore the army depends on it. In contrast, the parliament, as ontologically prior, is independent of the army. This asymmetry is the ground of parliamentary authority: the army's actions should thus conform to its decrees. It might appear as though Cromwell is making an argument from practice when he exclaims: 'how they can take the determination of commanding men, conducting men, quartering men, keeping guards, without an authority otherwise than from themselves I am ignorant' (*PL*, 97). However the inverse is the case: he is arguing from ontology to practice: instrumental actions such as commanding men, quartering men, keeping guards can only take place in so far as there is an external authority at work. External in the sense that the officer who commands is external to the soldiers who are commanded, and also external in the sense that the authority of the officer depends in turn on that of parliament. The ontological determination of the initiation of instrumental action is thus not only that it must be a single unit, but also that single unit should be in some sense external and prior to the means employed in the execution of the action.

Cromwell does not have a problem with instrumental action per se. If it were not for instrumentalism there would be no such thing as military discipline. His problem with the Leveller-agitators is rather that they *pretend* to incarnate another democratic logic of action whereas in fact their logic is instrumental. Furthermore, being instrumental, it lacks the vital ingredient of legitimate external authority.

What external authority could the Leveller-agitators appeal to? In their eyes, their vocation and actions are given legitimacy through their appointment by the rank and file. This is an internal or 'bottom-up' form of authorization. During the debates the agitators also make claim to another apparently external form of authority: God.

The agitator whom Clarke names 'Buff-coat' in his transcription declares: 'Whatsoever hopes or obligations I should be bound unto, if afterwards God should reveal himself, I would break it speedily, if it were an hundred a day' (*PL*, 34). Ireton agrees, declaring twice that if he sees the hand of God in it, he will proceed himself to the destruction of the king and the House of Lords (*PL*, 50, 69). The New Model Army as a whole had a reputation for devoutness and piety.[44] Indeed Ireton claims 'the Army . . . has carried with it hitherto the name of God' (*PL*, 49). At the very beginning of the debates Lieutenant-Colonel Wolfe asks for guidance from God and proposes a prayer meeting the following morning (*PL*, 18). Clarke, who is also recording the proceedings, seconds Wolfe in urging all to 'lay down our reason, our goods and let the spirit of God work in us. We should be ready to submit to the will of God' (*PL*, 39). Everard goes so far as bring a direct message from God to the meeting: 'This message God hath sent me to you: there is great expectation of sudden destruction' (*PL*, 43). Yet the problem, as Cromwell points out and Locke after him, is that of knowing whether someone genuinely speaks as from the mind of God (*PL*, 101). Cromwell offers three responses to this question. In the immediate heat of counter-accusations as to the authenticity of divine inspiration he stipulates that all should judge as to whether one has spoken with the mind of God (*PL*, 101). His second response actually names a positive criterion: when the debaters actually succeed in agreeing upon something, then that agreement is of God. Finally, faced with the enthusiasm and heat of some of the agitators, he asserts 'I know no outward sign of the mind of God but meekness, mildness, gentleness, love and the desire to save those who can be saved' (*PL*, 105). These latter two criteria allow him to dismiss any policy that would engage in destruction of existing institutions. With regard to Sexby's claim that in restoring the king they are setting up a power that God will destroy, he says let us not make rules for our actions by claiming to know the mind of God. All we can attain is a negative rule in that we know we ourselves should not engage in destruction, but if God wills it, then God will carry out such destruction (*PL*, 106). This is disingenuous since elsewhere Cromwell is in no way a proponent of such quietism. As Gentles records:

> Trumpeting the crushing victory [over the King's forces] at Naseby, he told the Speaker, 'Sir, this is none other than the

hand of God; and to him alone belongs the glory.' A month later, after the equally decisive victory at Langport, he demanded of a member of parliament, 'to see this, is it not to see the face of God?'[45]

The agitators shared Cromwell's belief: the preamble to *An Agreement of the People* opens with the following claim:

> Having by our late labours and hazards made it appear to the world at how high a rate we value our just freedom, and God having so far owned our cause as to deliver the Enemies thereof to our hands. (*AP*, 1)

Thus both Cromwell and the agitators invoke an entirely different mark of the mind of God than that of meekness and mildness: victory in battle. Providence is the name of the event interpreted as a sign of the God's will. To invoke providence is to furnish a definite answer to the fourth query of political action: why do we succeed or fail? Cromwell's actions succeed or fail in so far as they are in line with God's plan for humanity. Unfortunately this answer gives rise to great ambiguities, since the agitators and the grandees are able to draw entirely different conclusions from the same events, the army's victories. If one is going to adopt a providentialist vision then one is also going to need a hermeneutics. God may decide the outcome of all action, but the problem remains of deciphering the meaning of those outcomes. What is curious about the providentialist vision is that it invokes a consistent ground of action outside and beyond any established political institutions, and unlike the laws of nature, which offer another such ground, the mind of God is inaccessible to reason. In a debate over what should be done, any invocation of the will of God without a corresponding hermeneutics is nothing but a wager in favour of the chances of the proposed action.

From the agitators' standpoint it is entirely consistent with the action of the war to disestablish the House of Lords and the king: they should have no further role in government. Here opens the final quarrel of the Putney Debates, taking place on 1 November, 1647, the last recorded day of debate.

## The Heads of the Proposals, *the King and the Lords*

The agitators argue that Ireton's constitutional document, *The Heads of the Proposals*, does not provide for settlement because it restores and reinforces the king's and the lords' interest. In particular, the king is said to retain a negative voice in the parliament in so far as he must confirm the laws that are passed and retains the power of veto. When Cromwell seeks to identify the common grounds for agreement between grandees and agitators, he recognizes that:

> We all apprehend danger in the person of the King and of the Lords ... there is not any intention in any of the army, in any of us, to set up the one or [the] other ... Neither is it our intention to preserve one or the other with a visible danger to the public and people.

He then identifies the fundamental source of disagreement: 'That part of difference that seems to be among us is whether there can be a preservation [of them with safety to the kingdom]' (*PL*, 104–5). Cromwell's position, mentioned above, is that it is neither just nor right to proceed to a complete destruction of the king's and the lords' part in government. Moreover in his eyes the creation of a constitutional monarchy does not amount to restoring the king: the threat, as Ireton makes explicit, was royal absolutism and the end of the war was to remove that threat. In opposition, Wildman holds that all the legislative power in the kingdom should be vested in the House of Commons alone (*PL*, 118).

Ireton and Wildman lock horns from the outset when it is a matter of defining their disagreement. Wildman states the disagreement concerns 'whether this power [of veto] should be given to the King and Lords or no' (*PL*, 109). Ireton immediately corrects him:

> The question is not, whether this should be given to King and Lords, or no; but the question is: whether that interest that they have in this (if they have any), whether it should be now positively insisted upon to be clearly taken away. (*PL*, 109)

For Wildman, on the one hand, to alter the existing forms of government – given the present situation of civil war – is to engage in reconstruction through a new distribution of political power. For Ireton, on the other hand, the institution of the king's oath remains intact, and to alter it is not to build but to take away one of the king's privileges. Wildman makes two arguments against the existence of the king's veto: one from history, and the other from safety (*PL*, 108–9). From historical precedent he argues that by the constitution of England the king did not previously enjoy legislative power to the point of choosing which laws to assent to and which to dismiss. From safety he argues that giving the king the power of veto does not safeguard the liberty of the people. Rainborough adds that if the lords are not bound to laws passed by the commons that they have not affirmed, then they may join together and act against the parliament (*PL*, 115).

Ireton answers the historical argument first: he insists that the king's veto does not amount to legislative power. The sense of the existing king's oath is rather that he 'ought to affirm those laws that the Commons chose' (*PL*, 111). Moreover, he claims that in line with the parliament's current practice – which is to pass laws without the king's assent – in the *Heads of the Proposals* he provides for those cases in which the king refuses to give his assent to the law; these laws remain 'in point of safety' laws despite the absence of royal confirmation. In so far as he recognizes that for the past five years the parliament has operated de facto without the royal assent, the difference between his position and that of the agitators appears quite minimal, as Audley, a participant in the debate, immediately remarks. Rainborough makes a methodological point: history cannot be cited as a ground for the legitimacy of established institutions in so far as these are exceptional times; never has a like event occurred in which a king makes war upon his people (*PL*, 121).[46]

Ireton's response to the argument from the people's safety is to insist, against any spectre of a lords' revolt, that if it came to a breach of the peace, the lords would be subject to common law. Lords can be arrested by a civil magistrate. It would then be their right to be tried by their peers (*PL*, 115). On the negative side, if their privileges were completely taken away, then so would be all recourse they might have in case of injury to their person. He again uses an extreme hypothesis: the commons could take it upon themselves to pass a law so as to take away the lords' 'honour, title, estate, liberty or life' (*PL*, 114). In such a case the lords would have no recourse. As Ian Gentles remarks, the grandees have evidently made extraordinary concessions to the agitators' position: the king and lords would only exercise their veto concerning laws that affected 'their own persons or estates' (*PL*, 115). Gentles remarks 'this very slender concession to the first two estates of the realm again generated much more heat than its significance justified'.[47] However it is clear from Wildman and Rainborough's remarks that they do not see what would justify *any* exceptional position for the lords; by what right – save hereditary! – should they not be bound by all laws passed by the commons? In their eyes they should enjoy no 'distinction from other men', as in Ireton's words (*PL*, 123). Gentles thinks their heat is unjustified, but he is thinking in a framework of negotiation, whereas the agitators are arguing from principle. Given that the lords gain their seats by inheritance rather than election, it ends up being the bicameral system per se that poses a problem. Wildman claims 'it will never satisfy the godly people in the kingdom unless that *all* government be in the Commons, and freely' (*PL*, 118; my italics). Wildman's position in this particular argument about veto is entailed by the principle of popular sovereignty, as incarnated in the soldier's prosecution of the war against the king's forces. From the perspective of negotiation, on the other hand, if holding to a principle leads to a breakdown in negotiations, then perhaps that principle was the wrong one to have chosen in the first place. However, from the agitators' standpoint, if negotiations break down it is either because the grandees hold to different principles, or because the grandees have a hidden agenda and are thus engaged in some instrumental manoeuvre. If the grandees are arguing from principle, then the discussions can continue since for the agitators arguments about principles can be concluded. If, however, the grandees are hiding some agenda, then the negotiations are lost in any case.

At this point Ireton, Wildman, Cowling and Rainborough engage in an abstruse historical debate about whether or not the king's and lords' hereditary rights were the product of an original usurpation. Gentles claims that at this point most members of the general council were no longer interested in such subtleties since 'virtually everyone in the meeting wanted [the royal veto] abolished once and for all'.[48] Both Bishop and Wildman have already announced positions that anticipate the change in attitudes towards the king the following autumn. Wildman asks whether or not it is just to punish with death those that made war upon the king's command and yet give mercy to him? Bishop is far blunter, calling Charles 'that man of blood' (PL, 107). So ends the final quarrel of the Putney Debates. The draconian judgement expressed in this phrase will find wider acceptance in late 1648 and eventually end in the king's execution.

The principles at stake in this debate concerned nothing less than the form of government and its concretization of aristocratic distinctions between king, lords and commoners. For the Leveller-agitators the king's right of veto, however ceremonial its role, is fundamentally undemocratic. Any government issuing from the experience of the war should be a fully representative body, answering to the commons alone. Any restitution of aristocratic or royal privileges amounts to restoration.

## *The end of the Putney Debates*

In the records we possess the debate ends on an uncertain guarantee given to Wildman by Ireton. Wildman fears that no law in a constitutional monarchy guarantees his safety, as a private individual, against the king if the latter decides to kill him. Ireton protests that the king is much bound by many laws and as such would not 'hazard himself to kill this, or that, or any other man' (PL, 124). Wildman's last response is not just one more display of good faith: rather it is a formula for ending a debate that has – despite agreements and compromises – revealed deep differences of principle:

> It will be thought boldness in me [not] to agree. If God will open your hearts to provide so that the King may not do me injury, I shall be glad of it. If not, I am but a single man, I shall venture myself and [my] share in the common bottom.

That is to say, if the grandees can provide for the agitators and thus for the peoples' safety, then Wildman will be glad of it and the alliance between Leveller-agitators, the New Model Army and the grandees will remain intact, complete with 'open hearts'. However, if such provision cannot be found, the alliance will dissolve and Wildman, like all others, will be but 'a single man' free to wager himself and his share in 'the common bottom'. This formula proves prophetic. There appeared to be much agreement between the agitators and other members of the general council at the end of the Putney Debates. On the following day, 2 November, the council agreed to a number of points to be put into a declaration to be addressed to parliament. By 3 November *An Agreement of the People* was available in London bookstalls, advertised as having the support of 15 regiments of the army. On Friday, 5 November, the council, at Rainborough's instigation, moved to write to parliament requesting that the latter cease all negotiations and addresses to the king. Ireton stormed out in protest. Gentles records that London was rife with rumours of possible attacks on the king and of Leveller-agitator plans to arrest the grandees and purge the parliament.[49]

At this point the grandees acted. At the general council meeting on 8 November, Cromwell reopened the debate on the franchise and argued the Leveller position led to anarchy. He then succeeded in persuading the council to vote to send the agitators back to their respective regiments. On 9 November, the general council ordered three separate rendezvous for the regiments, against the Levellers' request for a general rendezvous. Fairfax was to personally address all 18 regiments and present them with a 'Remonstrance', prepared by a committee, that would reconcile all army pamphlets. Fairfax – and this gained him credit with the general council – had also been very active in Westminster pursuing the army's material demands concerning arrears and indemnities. These measures were still not enough: tensions remained high. On 11 November, the king escaped from army custody in Hampton Court. Parliament refused to implement the measures Fairfax had suggested to meet the financial costs of paying full arrears to the soldiers. At the same time, the Levellers were holding meetings in London, arranging alliances, such as with the guild of weavers, and publishing tracts about the split in the army between grandees and soldiers. Everything came to a head at the first of the three army rendezvous at Ware on 15 November.

Seven regiments were present at Corkbush field outside Ware. When the grandees arrived on the field certain officers had already been proselytizing for the *Agreement* among the soldiers – a delegation led by Colonel Rainborough marched up to Fairfax and presented him with a petition in favour of the *Agreement*. The grandees immediately had three officers arrested and several agitators on the grounds that they had not been summoned to the rendezvous. Harrison and Lilburne's regiments had indeed turned up to the rendezvous without having been summoned, both with copies of the offending *Agreement* actually pinned to the soldiers hats. Harrison's regiment, seeing that none of the other seven regiments would join them in mutiny, bowed under Fairfax's reprimand. Lilburne's regiment, however, presented more trouble having actively disobeyed orders to march to Newcastle and having split from most of their officers. They drew up on the field in unruly fashion late in the afternoon, plonking themselves down next to another orderly regiment and so drawing the ire of one of latter's officers. Digusted by their manner he insisted they show some military discipline. He was promptly stoned in return. Once Fairfax had completed his long review of the other regiments – in which he set out to each his own moderate program of reform and blamed the new Leveller-agitators for sowing discord among the army – he came to Lilburne's regiment and ordered them to to remove the *Agreement* from their hats. Upon the soldiers' refusal Cromwell charged into them waving his sword, and officers followed, ripping the papers off. No resistance was offered. Military discipline was established. Fairfax had nine instigators arrested and condemned to death on the sport. Ever the benevolent commander he exercised the right of mercy and pardoned six, allowing the unlucky remaining three to cast lots to decide who – the unluckiest – should die. Mathew Arnold, scapegoat for an entire army's political ambitions, was shot by the other two instigators.

The grand alliance between the Levellers, the agitators, the soldiers of New Model Army and the grandees thus came to an ignominious end. At the two other rendezvous at Watford and Kingston harmony reigned and all regiments present accepted and signed Fairfax's Remonstrance. In London, five Leveller leaders were arrested upon their presentation of a petition to the House of Commons. Henceforth all were free to wager themselves and their shares in the common bottom, isolated and as individuals. By force, by betrayal, the basic condition of liberalism had been established: atomization.

The dissolution of the alliance was not by any means the end of the grandees' political career. They still had to manage a course between the exigencies of the soldiers, the failure of the parliament to finance arrears, the hostility of the population to the army's practice of free quarter, and the difficulty of any negotiations with the king faced with his escape from custody and his attempts to forge an anti-parliament alliance with the Scottish. And before the end of 1648, despite a massive and concerted reduction in the army's size aimed at most of the radical regiments, the grandees would find that they were in need of the Levellers again, but that is another story.

## Conclusion

In June of 1647 the New Model Army, complete with agitators in each regiment, publishes its grievances and concerns, addresses parliament, and engages in its own definition of the stakes of settlement. A new voice, a new actor emerges within the field of politics and embarks upon a process unimaginable for previous generations. The army becomes a political agent solely in the form of an alliance between soldiers, agitators, Levellers and grandees. The process ends and the political agent dissolves in failed mutiny and the enforcement of military discipline. During the experience five queries concerning political action emerge:

- Who can act?
- Who can act on what grounds?

For parliament, only the king – despite his disgrace – the House of Lords and the House of Commons can engage in political action, and on the historical grounds of the constitution and established law. The agitators counter that the New Model Army acts on the grounds of its prosecution of the cause of all commoners in the victory over royalist forces. Its decentralized inter-regimental organization of democratically elected agitators ensures that the voice of the common soldiers is heard. The alliance acts on behalf of a greater whole than the parliament, addressing all 'freeborn men of England', and calling for an extension of the franchise and the reform of government.

- Who is right about what is to be done?

How is the grand action of the war against royalist forces to be completed: by the creation of a constitutional monarchy or a democratic republic with an expanded franchise? Is it the *Heads of the*

*Proposals* or *An Agreement of the People* that finds the way forward? The Leveller-agitators answer if it is the people who fought for the parliament against the king, then it is the people who will agree and henceforth participate in the political constitution of the nation. What is to be done is decided by a logic of entailment, whereby the long incompleted action of settlement is continued through the concretization of its principle in diverse contexts. Each local action entails further actions, further efforts to draw the consequences of the principles of the people's common rights and liberties and that of popular sovereignty.

- Why do our actions succeed or fail?

Cromwell rolls his eyes upwards to the heavens and claims that if his actions have been successful it has been because they were God's will: providence secures victory in the field. The agitators also invoke providence – 'God having so far owned our cause so as to deliver the enemies thereof to our hands' – but flesh it out with more concrete stipulations. The agitators' actions succeed in so far as they remain their actions in all of their consequences, and they do so if they maintain the alliance. To act so as to maintain the alliance is to extend and expand the engagement that the alliance had already entered into when fighting against the royalists for the parliamentary cause.

- If you and I split, were we ever united, and to what end?

What lies behind Ireton's and Cromwell's opposition to the *Agreement*? Is theirs ultimately an argument on principle or from interest? Do the Leveller-agitators really speak, as they claim, for the whole of the common soldiers, or only for a radical London clique? For whom do these former members of the grand alliance act, if it was not for each other and for the soldiers of the New Model Army? Faced with arguments from the established constitution, civil law and consequence, the agitators argue that the principles of action emerge from the long experience of the action itself, from the soldiers having risked their lives as commoners for the parliamentary cause.

Once betrayed by the grandees, the Leveller agitators, Wildman at their head, accuse Cromwell of acting on grounds of expediency alone, to have manipulated, accommodated and instrumentalized the agitators and their demands so as to retain political control over the army. But this is not the whole truth of the matter. To be able to instrumentalize one's partners in a temporary alliance and to continue one's political career after the dissolution of said alliance is to enjoy a position and a political identity that transcends and is separate to the alliance. Both Cromwell and the Levellers possess a political identity before and after the New Model experiment, but *Cromwell as grandee* and *Levellers as agitators* only exist as long as the alliance lasts. It is as a grandee that Cromwell achieved his greatest successes and enjoyed his greatest support; he drew his strength from his active implication with the army. Before and after the alliance the Levellers were relatively impotent activists with a narrow urban base, more irritants than actors. But as united in the alliance, Cromwell and Ireton became grandees, Levellers became agitators. To be united was to share in the extension and application of those principles of action that emerged during one long incomplete action.

- What do these answers to the five queries amount to?

They add up to a model of political action, the *Leveller-agitator model of joint action*, where a model is a historically active conception of how political action takes place, found not only in documents, but in historical practice. Long forgotten and neglected, the Leveller-agitator model rivals in its ambitions the sovereign and contractual models of Thomas Hobbes and John Locke. Such is the hypothesis of this book.

To prove it two tasks must be carried out.

First it must be shown how the agitator model differs from those of Hobbes and Locke. Chapters three, four and five progressively put together this demonstration through an analysis of the philosophers' metaphysics of action, of their treatment of the question of religious dissidence and of their conception of politics. Chapter five sets out the sovereign and contractual models of political action by identifying the Hobbesian and Lockean answers to the five queries.

Second, the agitator model must be constructed. This is the task of the final chapter.

As Hegel says, *hic Rhodus, hic salta*.

# CHAPTER THREE

# Hobbes' and Locke's metaphysics: Substances no longer act, institutions act

## The desubstantialization of action

In 1640, Thomas Hobbes argues that there is no collective action:

> One must not attribute to a crowd [*multitude*] a single action of any kind. Hence a crowd cannot make a promise or an agreement, acquire or transfer a right, do, have, possess, and so on, except separately, or as individuals, so that there are as many promises, agreements, rights, and actions, as there are men. For this reason a crowd is not a natural person.[1]

When he does analyse the activity of a crowd it is in terms of hysteria – the spate of suicides in a Greek village, or the compulsive spouting of Iambic verse by a heatstruck theatre audience – these are cases of inspiration, of enthusiasm or of passion.[2] For there to be action one condition must be satisfied: there must be a single person as agent. But in Hobbes' thinking, personhood is not restricted to human individuals. The church, for instance, can be 'one person'. Indeed the entire problem is that at certain moments in its history – during doctrinal disputes and the protestant reformation – the church was not a single person but suffered dispersion and fragmentation. In the *Leviathan* he writes, 'If the church be not one person, then it hath no authority at all; it can neither command, nor do any action at all' (*L*, 268).

These claims have an important consequence for our enquiry: a 'person' is not a permanent ontological category but rather a condition that may be attained, a condition of integral self-identity, of distinctness and unity. In turn, this conception of personhood implies a different understanding of agency. The sovereign himself – sole and exclusive actor in Hobbes' model of political action – attains agency and personhood solely *as* leviathan, *as* composite of the wills of the people, an 'artificial man' created through the 'art' of the social contract (*L*, 9).

A scholastic adage states *actiones sunt suppositorum*. In Thomas Aquinas' thirteenth-century formulation:

> Actions belong to supposits and wholes and, properly speaking, not to parts and forms or powers, for we do not say properly that the hand strikes, but a man with his hand, nor that heat makes a thing hot, but fire by heat.[3]

A 'supposit' is a substance, an entity that exists independently of any other entities. A supposit is also said to 'underlie accidents', where accidents are qualities and properties that are united in this entity, such as the whiteness and raggedness of the same T-shirt. Aquinas stipulates that what gives unity to accidents – 'this whiteness', 'this raggedness' – is the one T-shirt, the supposit or substance they belong to. Substances include a subcategory of 'persons'. Hence whenever an action occurs one must suppose the existence of a substantial person underlying that action. If an action of striking occurs, then there is always a person responsible for that action. The action belongs to a person. The massive difference between Hobbes' and Aquinas' concepts of action lies not in the attribution of actions to persons but in the very nature of personhood. For Aquinas, on the one hand, a person is a substance, a simple given entity, a natural individual. For Hobbes, on the other hand, a person can be an artificial composite, the product of an art, an institution – such is the church or the state.

This is but one sign of the change in the metaphysics of action manifest in Hobbes' philosophy. Other traces of this transformation can be found in Descartes and Locke. Despite the immense complexity of its roots and its consequences, the change that takes place can be summed up in one simple formula: *it is no longer substances that act, but institutions.* In other words, action is desubstantialized.

The object of this chapter is to explore this shift in the metaphysics of action as it emerges in Hobbes' and Locke's philosophy. This will lay the groundwork for the investigation of political action. There are two evident connections between the new metaphysics of action and the shape of political action. The first, which we have already met, concerns the articulation of action, substance and personhood, and it forms the object of the present chapter. The second concerns the question and practice of religious toleration, specifically the split between the internal actions of conscience, and the external actions of institutional rites. This connection will form the object of Chapter four. Chapter five will be devoted to a full analysis of Locke's and Hobbes' models of political action.

Concerning action and substance, the following caricatures can be advanced:

- For the scholastics wherever there is action there is a real substance behind it.

- For Hobbes there is no action – all is passion – save when an artificial composite substance is constructed and then it alone acts.

- For Locke we have no knowledge of substance, and actions can only be assigned to persons qua agents as a function of the judgements of juridical institutions.

This was not the only path open in the seventeenth-century metaphysics of action. For both Spinoza and Leibniz:

- There is substance or there are substances.
- There is adequate knowledge of substance(s).
- Not only do substances act, but also the very being of substance, conceived as all-encompassing, *is* action.

In this chapter, by way of contrast with Hobbes, we shall briefly explore Spinoza's mechanism and concept of action. Leibniz, however, will remain out of reach.

In Locke and Hobbes, the impact of this basic metaphysical position on political action is clear: individual persons no longer act, institutions act. The commonwealth takes centre stage and the prince and the citizen shuffle off towards the wings. Locke does allow a right to resistance and imagines situations in which people rise up against an oppressive government, legitimating their action through a 'call to heaven'.[4] But it remains the case that within any stable political body – including that recomposed after a rebellion – political action is reserved for government alone.

As I say, a full investigation of Spinoza's and Leibniz's metaphysics lies outside the scope of this enquiry. Nevertheless, a curious affinity emerges in the final chapter between the Leveller-agitator model of joint action and their holistic models of substance. For the New Model Army thinkers a political action is part of a larger political action, and the place within which actions occur is composed of parts that are actions. Institutions and judgements are secondary phenomena that may be derived from an accumulation of actions, but they do not provide the fundamental determinations of any action.

But such recondite references lie far ahead, after we have made our way through many tangles in the enquiry. To begin, what is the nature of action in Hobbes' mechanist anthropology?

## Mechanism: There is no action, only passion

### Sequencing internal and external motion in the Leviathan

In the *Leviathan*, Hobbes replaces the notion of free will with a mechanistic explanation of the causes of action. He takes a compatibilist position by reducing the concept of freedom to the absence of physical obstacles:

> Liberty and necessity are consistent; as in the water, that hath not only liberty, but a necessity of descending by the Channel; so likewise in the actions which men voluntarily do: which, because they proceed from their will, proceed from liberty;

and yet, because every act of man's will, and every desire, and inclination proceedeth from some cause, and that from another cause, in a continual chain . . . they proceed from necessity. (L, 146)

He adds that if one could see all of these causes – as God does – one would see the necessity of men's actions (L, 147). What is called an action is thus but one link in a long causal chain: it is not the case that individual persons initiate new and separate causal sequences in the world. To use Aristotle's terminology, individuals are not self-movers for Hobbes. The first step in the mechanist reduction of action is thus the *sequencing* of action: an action is removed from its throne of being a unique and autonomous causal event and inserted into the ubiquitous threads of efficient causality. The second step is the ontological qualification of all parts of these causal sequences: all is motion. In the anthropological treatise constituting Part I of the *Leviathan*, Hobbes classifies action under the term 'voluntary motion'. For Aristotle, a voluntary action is one in which the moving principle is inside the actor, and an involuntary action one that has 'an external principle, the sort of principle in which the agent, or [rather] the victim, contributes nothing'.[5] Aristotle's example of involuntary action is that of a person being kidnapped: he is carried somewhere by men who have him in their power. In this situation it is the kidnappers who are acting; they are said to be 'agents'. In turn Aristotle's abducted protagonist suffers their action, and is termed a 'patient'. Agents act voluntarily and retain the principle of their action inside themselves. Patients act involuntarily, or suffer, and the principle of the action is external to them. In contrast, for Hobbes involuntary motions do not necessarily have external sources: his key examples are breathing and the circulation of the blood, 'concoction, nutrition, excretion, etc'. The difference between involuntary and voluntary motions is that the former are not accompanied by mental images (L, 38). All voluntary motions are preceded by the imagination or fancies in the mind.

It is not clear whether such a criterion will restitute Aristotle's ontological distinction between agents and patients. A mental image would seem to occur inside a person. Indeed Hobbes does identify qualify imagination as the *'internal* beginning of all voluntary Motion' (L, 38). Yet Hobbes has already defined imagination, otherwise known as 'Fancy', as nothing but the relics, the decayed remainder or after-effect of 'Sense' where sense 'is Motion in the organs and interior parts of man's body caused by the action of things we See, Hear, etc.' (L, 38). Behind imagination there lie sense-perceptions and behind sense-perceptions the causal actions of external things that press upon the sense organs – all in long linear sequences. Voluntary actions may well begin internally in the imagination, but the imagination has its own external beginnings – the agent–patient distinction will not find its grounds here.

When external objects stimulate sense organs and cause sense-perceptions that affect the imagination, the imagination in turn stirs 'small beginnings of Motion, within the body of Man' which take the general name 'Endeavour'. Endeavour comes in two forms: appetite or aversion (L, 38). As Quentin Skinner notes it is already controversial to claim that action has its beginnings not in the faculty of reason, as the schools have it, following Aristotle, but within the passions.[6] If a person experiences a simple appetite or aversion there is an immediate passage to action. If, however, conflicting appetites and aversions succeed one another 'concerning one and the same thing', that is to say if 'diverse evil and good consequences of the doing . . . come into our thoughts' then we engage in 'deliberation'. In Aristotle's treatment of action, deliberation occurs within the realm of prudence or practical wisdom. Deliberation identifies the appropriate means to achieve a desired end given the singular complexity of a practical situation. It is required in situations that depart from the norm, in matters that cannot be resolved by routine. Yet for Hobbes deliberation is nothing but a simple summation of alternating aversions and appetites, a mechanical cost-benefit analysis. The result of this addition is the balance, a final appetite or aversion, and this is called the 'will' (C, 38; L, 44). The will is not a separate faculty with the capacity of controlling the passions by means of reason, as it was for the schools – and as Bishop Bramhall will remind Hobbes in his attack *In Defense of True Liberty*.[7] Nor is the will a faculty capable of overshooting the faculty of the understanding in its affirmations as in Descartes' theory of error.[8] 'The will', the presumed centre of autonomous action, is a mere epiphenomenon, a result of a chain of counteracting appetites and aversions.

The reduction of the will to a sum of appetites is Hobbes' second controversial doctrine on action. Its results for morality were considerable. In *On the Citizen*, Hobbes writes; 'It is self-evident that men's actions proceed from their wills and their wills from their hopes and fears; hence they willingly break the law, whenever it seems that *greater good* or *lesser evil* will come to themselves from breaking it' (C, 69). What determines an individual to act is thus neither a sense of duty, an estimation of virtue, nor practical reason but a summation of 'hopes and fears' that, if resulting in the perception of a 'greater good' to be attained through action, will lead to that action.

Sense-perception, imagination, deliberation, desire, the will: Hobbes reduces all components of action to types of mechanical motion.

Hobbes' attack on the notion of free will, and on the underlying assumption that actions begin from an internal principle in their agents, would not be complete without a redefinition of freedom. In line with his mechanism he defines freedom as the absence of external physical impediment to motion (L, 145). As such bodies alone can be described as 'free': the terms 'free speech', 'free way' or even 'free will' are all metaphorical, and refer ultimately to a free man who is: 'he, that in those things, which by his strength and wit he is able to do, is not hindered to do what he has a will to' (L, 146). Freedom thus does not consist in the equal and indeterminate possibility of two or more courses of action open to an agent. An individual will always undertake just that action which is already determined by the chains of causality in which she is caught up. Just after the famous passage cited earlier on the liberty of the water flowing down a channel Hobbes maps out this intrication:

> Every act of man's will, and every desire, and inclination proceeds from some cause, and that from another cause, in a continual chain ... they proceed from necessity. So that to him that could see the connexion of those causes, the *necessity* of all mens' voluntary actions, would appear manifest. (L, 146–7)

As noted above, this causal intrication or 'sequencing' of action forms the first step in the mechanist reduction. The second step is the ontological qualification of all components of action as types of motion, as has been shown with reference to imagination, deliberation and the will. This reduction allows Hobbes to speak of human action under the heading of 'voluntary motions, commonly called the passions' (L, 37). Though voluntary motions may well have 'internal beginnings' in the imagination, the imagination in turn has 'external beginnings' in objects pressing upon our sense organs, and each of these causal links could not have been otherwise.

The consequence is simple: what seems to be an *agent*, a principle of action, is, in fact, a *patient*, traversed by causal chains. There are no autonomous actors initiating change in the world. Changes do occur, but they flow through every single body, bodies being but waypoints, links among links in causal chains. At an ontological level, all talk of agents is meaningless. Under Hobbes' mechanism, there is no action, all is passion.

## *The dissolution of cosmos, polis and psyche*

Not only does mechanism dissolve the classic Aristotelian conception of action, it also dissolves its context, the *polis* or city-state. At an ontological level, Aristotle's city-state belongs to sublunar world of contingency and its substances are populated by infinite accidents beyond the grasp of rational discourse. Nevertheless, the city-state is a finite whole that also belongs to the natural world and like any organism its changes take the form of growth, of the development of a form, regulated by a final cause. Under mechanism every phenomenon can be reduced to matter in motion. All causality takes the form of efficient causality: the encounter of bodies and the subsequent transmission of movement, which halts, accelerates or redirects the motion of the second body. All changes that occur, whether they be qualitative, intensive, generative or corruptive, can be reduced to local movement. Bodies are differentiated by geometrical and dynamic properties alone: size, shape and motion. The encounters of bodies conform to universal laws of motion, such as inertia. In his analysis of sense-perception and imagination Hobbes defines inertia as follows: 'When a body is once in motion, it moves (unless something else hinder it) eternally; and whatsoever hinders it, cannot in an instant but in time, and by degrees quite extinguish it' (L, 15). The universality of such a law, applicable at any scale of reality, immediately erases the hierarchical order of the Aristotelian *cosmos*. There are no longer any privileged regions of being such as the reign of mathematical necessity in the heavens versus the imperfection and contingency of the sublunar world. Both the moral and ontological priority of the whole over the parts, and of unity over multiplicity is also lost. Given the uniform regularity of the laws of motion, scientific knowledge of a phenomenon can be attained without placing it within a higher unified whole; a phenomenon can be studied locally.

Under mechanism a phenomenon is no longer understood by referring to its place in a global order of things or a region of being. Rather a phenomenon may be measured and given spatial and temporal coordinates. The universe is rendered dynamic – all is matter in motion – any apparently finite static being becomes a temporary effect of motion occurring at another level. The twenty-third proposition in part two of Descartes' *Principles of Philosophy* states: 'All the variety in matter, all the diversity of its forms, depends on motion'.[9] Stasis is the exception rather than the rule, appearance rather than reality. Paradoxically, under mechanism's dynamization of being, time loses its chaotic powers. No longer does it dissolve identities and threaten the ontological grounds of knowledge as in Plato and Aristotle. Time now provides the measure of order and predictability, the frame for the comparison of speeds and the mapping of phenomena.

It appears that under mechanism action should become irrelevant, anachronistic, a leftover from an obsolete ontology.

The mechanization of the universe also leads to the derealization of perception and a withdrawal of the *psyche* from the world. The individual no longer has immediate access to the basic units of reality. Ordinary language is disqualified as leading to persistent illusions. In Descartes' analysis of the inconstant wax, it is language that makes us think we perceive the wax rather than a bunch of properties. The errors of ordinary language will be rectified by philosophy, teaching us that we do not see wax but *judge* these properties to be wax.[10] In Hobbes' analysis of perception, it is the simple movement of external bodies 'pressing' against our sense organs that give rise to the rich and complicated world of perception. There is a split between sensuous appearances and the minute motions of real bodies that lie at their base: 'The said image or colour [of the object] is but an apparition unto us of that motion, agitation or alteration, which the object worketh in the brain or spirits, or some internal substance of the head' states Hobbes in his third proposition on 'the cause of sense' (*EL*, 23). Locke sealed this split between *psyche* and *cosmos* with his distinction between 'primary properties', figure, size, motion; and 'secondary properties' such as smell, colour, taste, texture and sonority. Primary qualities inhere in the bodies themselves whereas secondary properties are relative, emerging solely from interactions between such bodies and an individual's sense organs. The Lockean individual senses a world of her own making. Not only that but to achieve scientific knowledge of reality she must forget the sensuous world of secondary qualities.

The far consequence of this split between matter in motion and the individually perceived world is that any talk of action is like talk of secondary qualities. What is called an action is a function of perception, not of social reality, which ultimately proceeds, underneath the passions, at the level of the shock of bodies. Philosophical discourse can become a cure for our illusions, a therapy correcting the errors of ordinary language. As Locke writes in the *Essay*'s 'Epistle to the Reader', the philosopher is 'an Under-Labourer in clearing Ground a little, and removing some of the Rubbish, that lies in the way to Knowledge'. Part of that rubbish may be the very notion of action, and of politics as an art made up of actions.

Under mechanism, action is not only demoted to an illusion of perception but also reduced through its proliferation. In the semi-heroic Aristotelian concept of voluntary action the unique individual, the citizen, rationally intervenes within the whole of the city-state to contribute to the collective good. Under mechanism action is no longer a single cause but one effect, one passion among others. With regard to the cause of sense perception, Hobbes explains:

> Originally all conceptions proceed from the *action* of the thing itself, whereof it is the conception. Now when the *action* is present, the conception it produces is called sense, and the thing by whose *action* the same is produced is called the object of sense. (*EL*, 22–3; my italics)

Heroic action only vanishes to become ubiquitous, the name of any shock between two bodies, the name of brute efficient causality. Do Hobbes and Locke dare go the full length of this idea in their political philosophy? Certainly they reinstate action in the form of institutional operations; but what lies under the institution?

Mechanism dedifferentiates the realm of action; action no longer occurs solely between rational citizens in the city-state, it occurs in every natural change. Mechanism *levels* action.

## *Spinoza's countermodel: Imperial action*

Spinoza's mechanist metaphysics provides immediate confirmation of this thesis. Nevertheless he manages to rescue a concept of individual human action, and his understanding of political action is remarkably different to that of Hobbes. How can he start on the same path and then fork off and travel so far? At the outset of his treatment of the affects Spinoza declares 'Man is not an empire within an empire'.[11] 'It is believed', he explains;

> that man disturbs the order of Nature rather than he follows it, that he has an absolute power over his actions, and that he is determined by himself alone. Further they ascribe the cause of human impotence and inconstancy not to the common power of nature but to some defect or other in human nature, which they accordingly lament.[12]

Spinoza's nameless opponents belong to a scholastic tradition that, in following Aquinas, amalgamated Aristotle's model of voluntary action with the Christian conception of original sin. Spinoza's own analysis of the affects, of morality, of how men live and of action thus begins with a critique of what can be called the *imperial model of action as command*. The same critique, the same warning, is repeated at the outset of his *Treatise on Politics*:

> Yet most people believe that the ignorant violate the order of Nature rather than conform to it; they think of men within Nature as a state within a state. They hold that the human mind is not produced by natural causes, but is directly created by God and is so independent of other things that it has an absolute power to determine itself and use reason in a correct way.[13]

In chapter six of the *Theologico-Political Treatise*, Spinoza develops a similar argument with regard to the existence of miracles. He shows that in the biblical presentation of miracles the circumstances and proximate causes of the phenomena are omitted to generate the appearance of a punctual, dramatic and transformative action. To persuade people to believe in God a short circuit is operated in the presentation of 'God's action', that is, a short circuit between command and the result. However, if we pay close attention to the scriptures we will notice that 'the details of such miracles plainly show that they involve natural causes' hence 'all things that are truly reported to have happened in Scripture necessarily happened according to the laws of nature, as all things do'.[14] The upshot is that 'the edicts and commands of God, and hence of providence, are nothing other than the order of nature'.[15] Precisely the same critique of action as command is at stake in Spinoza's disagreement with Descartes over the existence of free will and latter's power to control the passions (E, V, Pref). Finally one of the major tasks of the first book of the *Ethics* is to dismantle the anthropomorphic notion of God as a separate individual creator, master of the universe. The critique of imperial action is the grand polemic of the *Ethics*.

In Spinoza's diagnosis what is at stake in imperial action is not only a short circuit between command and result, omitting proximate causes, but also the illusion of independent agency, of autonomy in the initiation of action. As in Hobbes so for Spinoza; humans are but one part of the natural order. In particular, they are embedded in a web of affects that ties each of them into a dynamic set of relationships with other individuals and objects. Any individual being is not understood as a static and closed entity but as *conatus*, that is, as a continual endeavour or striving to persevere in being. In humans this endeavour is called 'appetite' at the level of the body and 'desire' at the level of the mind. Endeavour can also be understood in corporeal terms as a 'power to act' and in mental terms as a 'power to think' (E, III, P7). The body is constituted such that it is able to enter into multiple connections with other bodies and humans. This multiplicity also exists on a temporal plane in that these connections can leave traces and impressions in the body. Any such connection is termed an 'emotion' that is an 'affection of the body by which the body's power of acting is increased or diminished, helped or hindered, and at the same time the idea of these affections' (E, III, D3). Thus to have an emotion is to connect with another body and have one's power of acting and thinking increased or decreased. This power, *conatus*, is thus a kind of registering scale of intensities; an increase in power is what we call 'pleasure', and a decrease 'pain'. With this minimal apparatus Spinoza can thus already define three primary affects: desire, pleasure and pain. To define other emotions, beginning with love and hate, all that is required is the addition of the idea of an external cause. Love is pleasure, that is, an increase in the powers of acting and thinking, combined with the idea of an external cause responsible for such pleasure (*E*, III, P12Sch). The emotion of love thus involves an idea of agency, an attribution of responsibility to a unique external cause. However, in imagining the presence of the external body Spinoza stipulates that the mind is in fact simply indicating its own state. It is also possible for the imagination to assume that it is being affected by one body when it is actually being simultaneously 'affected by two bodies' (*E*, III, P15). Hence error may creep into the composition of the web of affects.

For this composition to become a network a few additional elements are required. First there is the dimension of time: to the image of the external object affecting the body in a positive or negative manner is added an image of past of future time, thus generating definitions of 'hope, fear, confidence, despair, delight and remorse' (*E*, III, P18Sch2). Hope, for instance, 'is simply an inconstant pleasure, which has arisen from the image of a thing that is future or past, about whose outcome we are in doubt' (*E*, III, P18Sch2). Second there is the existence of other individuals who may affect, in turn, the objects that affect us. That is to say, the object of my love may be destroyed by another person: this causes me both pain and hatred towards this person. Or the object of my love may also become the object of another person's love, causing rivalry between us. Through such triangulations we come to love and hate other objects and people.

## *Spinoza's expressive and participative model of action*

It is from within this dense tangle of affects that a human being acts for Spinoza; not by means of a separate faculty working against the emotions, but rather along with them. In short, to act is not to command but to understand. Spinoza generates this counter-intuitive concept of action by beginning with the following definition:

> I say that we act when something occurs either in us or outside us of which we are the adequate cause; that is . . . when there follows from our nature, either in us or outside us, something that can be understood clearly and distinctly through that nature alone. Conversely, I say that we are passive when something occurs in us, or when something follows from our nature, of which we are only a partial cause. (*E*, III, D2)

Proposition one of Book III states: 'Our mind sometimes acts, but sometimes is passive; namely, in so far as it has adequate ideas, so far it necessarily acts, and in so far as it has inadequate ideas, so far it is necessarily passive.' Hence to be an adequate cause of an event is to have an adequate idea. But what is the object of these adequate ideas? According to their definition in Book II they concern universals or properties of bodies. These common properties are those involved in interactions between external bodies and our bodies (*E*, II, P39Dem). The basis of action – an adequate idea – thus involves knowledge of the precise interactions in which our body is engaged. To act is thus to know how one is implicated within a situation – where a situation is nothing other than a sticky web of affected and affecting bodies.

At this point in his construction Spinoza has come a long way from the mechanist ground he shared with Hobbes. The similarities, however, persist: Spinoza, like Hobbes, is a compatibilist. Freedom and necessity are not mutually exclusive determinations of human action. At the very beginning of *Ethics* freedom is defined in the following manner:

> That thing is called free which exists solely by the necessity of its own nature, and is determined to action by itself alone. However that thing is called necessary, or rather compelled, which is determined by another to exist and to operate in a certain and determinate way. (*E*, I, D7)

In the treatment of freedom in the realm of human action within the *Political Treatise* Spinoza dismisses what he calls the notion of freedom as contingency; the freedom to not do something:

The more free we consider man to be, the less we can say that he is able not to use his reason, to choose evil rather than the good; and so God, who exists, acts, and understands with absolute freedom, also exists, acts and understands necessarily, that is, from the necessity of his own nature.[16]

To exist solely by necessity of one's nature is thus to exist according to the laws of one's own nature. And to exist according to law, for Spinoza, is simply to understand those laws. He writes:

And so I call a man altogether 'free' in so far as he is guided by reason, because it is to that extent that he is determined to action by causes that can be adequately understood solely through his own nature, even though he is necessarily determined to action by these causes.[17]

So to act freely is not to command but to *understand* the laws of one's own nature. Here it becomes evident that Spinoza has paid a price for his mechanism: he certainly has an original concept of individual action, but he has turned it into a species of contemplation.

To understand the laws of one's own nature is to understand one's location in a web of affects. Spinoza then makes one last connection that clarifies his alternative model of action. In his metaphysics, each particular thing, including each person, is a mode of the infinite substance, God. As such each thing expresses one of the attributes of God in a determinate way (*E*, I, P25Cor). In the *Political Treatise* Spinoza states: 'The power of natural things by which they exist and act is the very power of God'.[18] To act is thus to express the power of God. Furthermore, in Book V of *Ethics* Spinoza explains 'The more perfection each thing has, the more it acts, and the less it is acted on; conversely, the more it acts, the more perfect it is' (*E*, V, P40). To act is thus not only to express the power of God but to approach the perfection of God. 'The essence of God', Spinoza proclaims in his *Short Treatise*, 'contains an infinite action': his project is to show how humans can participate in such infinite action.[19]

Departing from the same mechanist ground as Hobbes in the critique of autonomous 'free' action, Spinoza diverges in his development of a model of political action. Hobbes, on the basis of an ontological desubstantialization of action, constructs the sovereign model of action. Spinoza carries out a similar mechanist reduction of action to Hobbes – through the critique of the imperial model of action – yet he develops an entirely different conception of political action: neither sovereign nor contractual, it can be termed the *expressive* and *participative* model of action. The ground for this development (and this is the Aristotelian thread) is his holism: the concept of one all-enveloping substance, avatar of the original city-state. In the sixth chapter of this book the enquiry into the Leveller-agitator model of action leads into the question of whether action can be expressive and participative in the absence of a whole, in the absence of a global unified political body.

Locke lies at a fair distance from Spinoza. He dismisses ontology in favour of epistemology, sources all ideas in experience rather than reason, and argues that our ideas of substance are obscure. Yet he joins Spinoza and Hobbes in embracing mechanism, and at the same time attempting to develop a concept of action.

## *Locke and the difficult derivation of the very idea of action*

Locke defines action as voluntary motion on the part of a free agent. This definition emerges within his investigation into our idea of active power in chapter 21 of the second book of the *Essay Concerning Human Understanding*. Locke states:

> The forbearance or performance of that action, consequent to such an order or command of the mind, is called voluntary. And whatsoever action is performed without such thought of the mind is called Involuntary.[20]

For a voluntary action to be performed by a free agent, the following specification is required:

> The Idea of liberty is the *Idea* of a Power in any agent to do or forebear any particular Action, according to the determination or thought of the mind, whereby either of them is preferred to the other; where either of them is not in the power of the agent

to be produced by him according to his *Volition*, there he is not at liberty, that agent is under *Necessity*. (*EHU*, II, 21, §8)

Locke then examines under what conditions a human may be said to be a *free agent*; it is not enough that his action be voluntary. The demonstration passes by way of the example of a person who while asleep is brought into a room in which he will find a friend he wanted to see. At least he has not been kidnapped, as in Aristotle, but has been forced to immediately socialize upon awakening: the door to the room is locked from the outside. Upon waking our sleepy protagonist willingly remains in the room, so as to converse with his friend. Yet we cannot say that he freely remains in the room since he has no power to leave if he should wish so (*EHU*, II, 21, §10). Our will determines which action we should prefer to perform whereas our liberty concerns our capacity or power to either perform or forebear that action. Our dozy conversationalist is not a free agent because he does not have the power to leave the room.

Locke states above that the idea of liberty is derived from our idea of power. Consequently, so is the idea of free agent, which in particular is derived from the idea of 'active power'. When Locke begins his investigation of the idea of power he explains the novelty of his approach. He is not concerned with the existence and type of powers to be found in different kinds of being but rather with 'how we come by the idea of [Power]' (*EHU*, II, 21, §2). His approach is thus epistemological; he wants to identify the origin of our ideas. In the introduction to the *Essay* he explains that it is 'my *Purpose* to research into the Original, Certainty, and Extent of humane knowledge' (*EHU*, I, 1, §2). The immediate corollary of this approach, for Locke, is the dismissal of any investigation into the physics of the mind: 'I shall not at present meddle with the Physical Consideration of the Mind; or trouble my self to examine, wherein its essence consists' (*EHU*, I, 1, §2). Such 'speculations' may be 'singular and interesting' but Locke dismisses them as outside his purview. This prefatory gesture, though not fully followed through in Locke alone, opens a new epoch. Epistemology is separated from ontology, which is requalified as physics. Ontology is then removed from the position of first philosophy and epistemology takes its place. Nothing will ever be the same again in philosophy's division of labour.

This gesture also allows Locke to bypass mechanism's ontological leveling of action, its effacement of action's singularity and the annulment of the 'agent' and 'patient' categories. Through Locke's identification and privileging of epistemology, he can attempt an entirely different construction and justification of the category of action: the question is no longer one of the being of action, but of the origin of the idea 'action'.

The purpose of an anatomy of failure is, of course, thoroughly ontological. At this point one can play a rationalist, or dare I say, continental game against the British empiricist and show how Locke's epistemology presupposes certain ontological theses. There is one place in which Locke's neat separation and inversion of philosophical disciplines breaks down: his distinction between active and passive power. This is an ontological, indeed, Aristotelian distinction if there ever was one. An active power is defined as the power to make changes. A passive power is the power to receive changes (*EHU*, II, 21, §2). Locke claims we have distinct ideas of passive and active power as a result of experience. Our observation of the constant changes in the qualities of sensible things leads to the idea of passive power in so far as those things are supposedly 'liable still to the same change' (*EHU*, II, 21, §4). However, the observation of sensible things is not sufficient to generate an idea of active power. He remarks:

> A body at rest affords us no *Idea* of any *active Power* to move; and when it is set in motion itself, that motion is rather a Passion, than an Action in it. For when the Ball obeys the stroke of the Billiard-stick, it is not any action of the ball but bare passion: Also when by impulse it sets another Ball in motion, that lay in its way, it only communicates the motion it had received from another, and loses in itself so much, as the other received; which gives us a very obscure idea of an *active Power* of moving in a Body, whilst we observe it only to transfer, but not produce any motion. (*EHU*, II, 21, § 4)

Locke does not say that balls in motion give us *no* idea of an active power, only that they give us a 'very obscure idea'. And indeed we need to have some kind of idea of an active power to frame for ourselves the very idea of a passive power, which is supposed to emerge spontaneously from observation of the physical world.

As Locke stipulates, wherever change is observed, 'the mind must collect a power somewhere, able to make that change, as well as a possibility in the thing itself to receive it' (*EHU*, II, 21, §4). To assume that something has a *passive* power to receive change is also to assume that something else has actually initiated that change. In other words, no passive powers without corresponding active powers, otherwise one has an infinite regress on one's hands – another Aristotelian and ontological argument. If the idea of an active power among tangible bodies is 'very obscure', then, by implication, so is the idea of a passive power: the only clear idea is that of physical differentiation. This obscurity suggests a Kantian line of argument: the active–passive distinction is a kind of logical schema that is imposed upon experience to make sense of it.

Fortunately for Locke there is another source for our idea of active power, and hence, by implication, of passive power: the operations of the mind, namely the will. He claims that we develop an accurate idea of active power by reflection upon our ability to call ideas to mind or to simply move our limbs. The exercise of this power 'directing any particular action' is called volition. When Locke argues for this derivation he makes a similar claim to Descartes in the thirty-ninth proposition of part one of the *Principles of Philosophy*. Descartes writes: 'That there is freedom in our will, and that we have power in many cases to give or withhold our assent at will, is so evident that it must be counted as among the first and most common notions that are innate in us'.[21] Locke writes: 'Everyone, I think, finds in himself a Power to do or forebear, continue or put an end to several actions in himself' *EHU*, II, 21, §7). Unfortunately for Locke, at this pass, a simple appeal to innate ideas will not do. For the empiricist there are no innate notions, only ideas generated on the basis of observations from experience. And yet what feature of our mental experience gives rise to the idea of an absolute beginning of change? Surely we are simply ignorant of the causal chains bringing ideas into our mind. In the case of moving our limbs many factors – heat, cold, hunger – can be identified that lead to that movement, factors that themselves are entangled in causal chains as Hobbes and Spinoza point out.

From whence, then, the idea of active power? It is in the postscript to chapter 21 – a postscript that could stand as a mini-treatise on action – that Locke reveals a further inextricable determination of this idea.

> Sometimes the Substance, or Agent, puts itself into *Action* by its own power, and this is properly active power. Whatsoever modification a substance has, whereby it produces any effect, that is called action; v.g. a solid substance by motion operates on, or alters the sensible *Ideas* of another substance, and therefore this modification of motion we call action. But yet this motion in that solid substance is, when rightly considered, but a passion, if it received it only from some external Agent. So that the active power of motion is in no substance which cannot begin motion in itself, or in another substance when at rest. So likewise in thinking, a power to receive *Ideas* or Thoughts, from the operation of any external substance, is called a *Power* of thinking: but this is but a *Passive Power* or capacity. But to be able to bring into view *Ideas* out of sight, at one's choice, and to compare which of them one thinks fit, this is an *Active Power*. (*EHU*, II, 21, §72)

Behind the idea of a free agent, one thus finds the idea of active power. A free agent is a substance that exercises active power; that is to say, without any external assistance or impulse, it moves itself and initiates modifications in another substance. This derivation of the idea 'free agent' reveals a further idea behind the idea of active power, and that is the Aristotelian idea of substance as a self-mover. Despite his apparent modernity, Locke appears to adhere to the scholastic doctrine *actiones sunt suppositorum* whereby any action supposes a substance. And in this case he cannot join Hobbes and Spinoza in the mechanist desubstantialization of action. But Locke's investigation is not over yet.

From whence, in turn, the idea of substance? If Locke can anchor the idea of substance in the observation of experience then he can interrupt this apparent circularity whereby:

- The definition of action presupposes a free agent.
- The idea of a free agent is derived from our idea of active power.

- The idea of active power is based on our experience of acting by means of the will.
- Our idea of an acting will is based on the idea – or experience? – of a self-moving substance.

The problem is that two chapters later in the *Essay* Locke engages in a thoroughgoing critique of the very idea of substance. According to Locke, the idea of substance is extremely indeterminate; it refers to a kind of support for qualities, a substrate to which qualities belong, or within which they are said to subsist. The nature of the support remains entirely unknown; it is merely supposed inasmuch as it is assumed that qualities cannot exist without existing in something primary. When we examine 'the ideas that we have of particular distinct sorts of substances' we find they are 'nothing but several combinations of simple Ideas' (*EHU*, II, 23, §6). Those simple ideas belong to three categories: primary qualities, secondary qualities and active or passive powers. A substance thus has primary qualities 'discovered by the senses' consisting of the 'Bulk, figure, number, situation and motion of the parts of Bodies which are really in them' (*EHU*, II, 23, §9). Secondary qualities, on the other hand, such as sound, taste, colour and smell are brought about by the interaction between human sense organs and substances. In chapter 8 Locke says secondary qualities 'are in truth Nothing in the objects themselves, but Powers to produce various sensations in us, and depend upon those primary qualities' (*EHU*, II, 8, §14). The other simple ideas included in our ideas of particular substances are those of active and passive powers. These ideas refer to the capacity we attribute to substances to change their primary qualities; and thus change our perceptions of them. For instance, part of the complex idea 'wood' is the simple idea of its capacity to produce heat when burnt.

Locke admits that the idea of a free agent is primary in our conception of spiritual or immaterial substances. He says that we have two distinct and clear ideas of the substance of spirit, namely, thinking and the power of acting. Nevertheless, we have no understanding of how exactly it is that we can freely move our limbs, that we can act with our minds (*EHU*, II, 23, §28, §30). For this reason, it is the case that – contra Descartes – the idea of spiritual substance is just as obscure as the idea of physical substance (*EHU*, II, 23, §22–3). If the idea of active power is based on the experience of willing ideas into our mind, or willing our limbs to move, and yet that experience is interpreted through the idea of substance as self-mover, and if, in turn, the idea of substance depends on the idea of active power, and is obscure, then it does appear as though Locke has ended up in a circle. That there are possible exits from this circle is obvious: on the basis of a phenomenological analysis of mental experience one could defend Locke by arguing that the experience of willing does not presuppose the idea of substance but does generate the idea of a self-moving 'I'. Such an argument could analyse, say, the parsing of mental experience through grammatical structures, asking whether it is accurate to make a distinction between sentences such as 'I'm moving my arm' and 'I will to move my arm'. But we will leave such adventures for the twentieth century.

What confirms Locke's own circularity is the way he shifts ground when he meets with this obscurity in the idea of substance. At the beginning of the *Essay* he takes up the banner of epistemology and rejects that of ontology. Yet at this point under the guise of warding off scepticism he reassures us that although their ideas are obscure this is no reason to doubt the existence of both physical and spiritual substance (*EHU*, II, 21, §31). He does not make an outright ontological claim; rather he disallows his epistemological enquiry from having ontological results. In other words, substances could well exist, it is just that we have a very obscure idea of them. It is quite possible to avoid scepticism and defend the existence of external reality without holding to the notion of substance. Moreover, the ontology Locke ends up adopting is that of mechanism, and mechanism does not leave much place for self-moving substances. So there is a possibility that Locke will join Hobbes and Spinoza after all in the desubstantialization camp. But back to the circularity.

Locke embraces a mechanist ontology in his doctrine of primary versus secondary qualities. At the level of primary qualities all bodies are composed of imperceptible particles encountering other particles. The level of secondary qualities arises as the aggregate results of the motion of these particles and their interaction with someone's sense organ. If this is the case then there are no grounds for distinguishing a 'free agent' and its motion from other kinds of movers. Any appearance of a body beginning to move will be the result of imperceptible micro-motions at the level of its particles that are necessarily in continual contact with the body's environment, composed of minute particles itself. Indeed our very experience of seeing an external body, for instance, is the result of the impact of a stream of imperceptible particles upon our sense organs. As Hobbes and Spinoza argue, under mechanism there is neither substance nor action but passion alone. If Locke adopts a mechanist ontology, he cannot simply claim that there are physical and spiritual substances despite our foggy ideas about them.

But Locke also manages to dance around this trap. He adopts a Cartesian dualism: there are two fundamental kinds of substance, physical substance and spiritual substance. Inasmuch as spiritual substance is immaterial, it is not subject to a mechanist explanation of its workings. He even adopts Descartes' terminology, calling the mind a 'thinking thing'. So at the last moment Locke retains the possibility of there being spiritual substances that are free agents, though we have a very obscure idea of them. And if the workings of spiritual substance do not allow a mechanistic explanation, then a 'free agent' is a term that does not pick out any particular item in his ontology. Indeed at the outset of the *Essay* Locke warns us that he will not present any detailed theory as to the physical working of minds.

The consequence for Locke's philosophy of action is simple. It is not the case that idea of a free agent, and subsequently that of action, remain undemonstrated and constitute a dead end. Rather the idea of a free agent is primary. It is axiomatic. It is used in the construction of other important ideas, yet it admits of no further explanation. The implications of Locke's construction of a model of political action become very clear when Locke turns to the epistemological question of the judgement of particular actions. Judgement as exercised by individuals, and judgement as exercised by judicial institutions lead Locke far further into the embraces of nominalism than we have suspected so far. The idea of a 'free agent' will turn out to be a kind of framing device that not only allows actions to be assigned to persons, but also personal identity to be assigned to individuals.

## *Rule-following action*

Locke and Hobbes declare the possibility of a science of morality that would proceed by demonstration. 'Moral philosophy is nothing else but the science of good and evil, in the conversation, and society of mankind' claims Hobbes, and in turn Locke announces 'Morality is capable of demonstration, as well as mathematics' (*L*, 110; *EHU*, III, 11, §16).[22] The basis of this science would be the laws of nature, which provide universal rules for action. The device used to expose the working of these laws is the hypothesis of the state of nature. This hypothesis removes all social determinations of action: neither custom, nor habit, nor obligation, nor duty, nor institutional practice nor even morality shape action in the state of nature. Hobbes writes, 'nothing one does in a purely natural state is a wrong' since 'injustice against men presupposes human Laws and there are none in the natural state' (*C*, 28). Action is stripped of its clothes and exhibited in the raw.

The foundational thesis of social contract theory is that action minus all social determinations does not lead to absolute chaos, it does not produce an undifferentiated state. There may well be a 'war of all against all' but this already requires a certain level of organization, and presupposes that individuals act according to the laws of nature. For Hobbes a law of nature is a 'precept, or general rule' for action, 'found out by reason' that forbids a human from doing anything which would destroy her, or from omitting any action that would lead to her preservation (*L*, 91). This obligation is joined to the primary Right of Nature according to which every individual has the liberty to use their power by any means to preserve themselves. Everyone thus has a right to anything including any other person's life and property in the name of self-preservation (*L*, 91). Locke does not grant a right to harm other human beings, but he does concur on some points with Hobbes: 'Man being born . . . with a title to perfect freedom, and an uncontrolled enjoyment of all the rights and privileges of the law of nature . . . hath by nature a power . . . to preserve his property, that is, his life, liberty and estate, against the injuries and attempts of other men' (*ST*, §87). If individuals act in line with the laws of nature, it is possible to predict the collective result of such actions: a general state of dysfunction in which no individual is able to enjoy the fruits of his action; a 'war of every man against every man' (*L*, 90). At a collective level, without government, rule-following action fails. Individuals cannot secure their own safety since they are under the constant threat of being robbed by others. In his analysis of the state of nature Hobbes carries out an anatomy of failure, and it gives rise to his new model of political action.

However, and this is one of the fundamental difficulties of Hobbes' theory, rule-following actions also lead to a diametrically opposed result: the peace of the social contract.[23] Hobbes thinks to manage this inversion by stipulating that the second law of nature, derived from the first, runs as follows:

> That a man be willing, when others are so too, as farre-forth, as for Peace, and defence of himselfe he shall think it necessary, to lay down this right to all things; and be contented with so much liberty against other men, as he would allow other men against himselfe. (*L*, 92)

The goal is still survival but here rational deliberation – understood as 'reasoning about actions that might conduce to an [individual's] advantage or other men's loss' – has identified a global condition for survival: peace. The first law of nature gives rise to total war. The second law, though derived from the first, contains the seed of the social contract.[24] At the level of the collective the laws of nature bring about both the state of nature and its antinomy, law-governed civil society.

Locke and Hobbes ambitiously declare the advent of a science of morality (*EHU*, IV, 3, §18–20; *EHU*, IV, 12, §8). Hobbes speaks of a 'civil science', 'the science of virtue and vice' and the 'science of natural justice' (*C*, 7; *L*, 111, 234). This project alone signals just how far seventeenth-century philosophy of action has travelled from its Aristotelian origins. Aristotle repeatedly warns in the *Nicomachean Ethics* that the matter of morality, action, does not admit of geometrical method and is not a subject of precision. For Aristotle action follows upon deliberation, and deliberation only ever occurs in unusual situations. Where routine, habit and standard practices prevail there is no need for deliberation, but when something anomalous occurs one must ask what should be done, and how. This is where prudence comes into play. Yet for Aristotle the definition of prudence posed a problem: how can one know what the true course of virtuous action is – where virtue is a mean between two extremes – in a singular, infinitely complex and contingent situation? What rule is there that explains how to apply the rule? In the absence of a definite concept of prudence, Aristotle is reduced to supposing its possession in the hands of reputedly prudent individuals, such as Pericles – a supposed subject of knowledge.[25] Prudence is what we suppose some prudent people happen to have: the circularity is evident.

This entire problem disappears under the mechanist reduction of action. When action falls from its throne, when its singular and heroic status is erased and it is banalized to the point of ubiquity, then it becomes predictable in a universe reigned by universal laws. Deliberation is no longer a rational process that must reconcile the universal with the singular, the rule of virtue with a practical situation. Now deliberation is simply an alternation of appetite and aversion, a cost-benefit calculation, with the stronger winning out. In short, there are two bases for a science of morality. The first is mechanical. Under mechanism all is matter in motion, and motion obeys universal laws that can be mathematically formulated. Even if a particular sphere of material interactions is walled off and classified as 'human action' it must still obey these quantitative laws. Hobbes identifies such quantitative forces at work in action in the summing up of appetite and aversion in the 'will', an arithmetical result of deliberation. The second basis for the science of morality, as explained above, is natural law, which is qualitative. There might appear to be a gulf between these two different foundations, one quantitative, one qualitative; one referring to fact, one to value. But the first natural law is that of self-preservation, and Hobbes' concept of deliberation as calculation refers exclusively to the individual's estimation of how an action might enhance or diminish his chances of self-preservation. Locke finds another way of unifying these quantitative and qualitative foundations for a science of morality in his mechanist justification of majority rule in parliament: 'it is necessary the Body should move that way thither the greater force carries it, which is the *consent of the majority*' (*ST*, §96).

All actions have their measure and all actions may be subject to judgement. The practical promise of this moral science is as immense as its outlines remain vague. Hobbes exclaims:

> For if the patterns of human action were known with the same certainty as the relation of magnitude in figures, ambition and greed, whose power rests on the false opinions of the common people about right and wrong, would be disarmed, and the human race would enjoy such secure peace that (apart from

conflicts over space as the population grew) it seems unlikely that it would ever have to fight again. (C, 5)

Unfortunately the science of morality has not yet been drawn up, nor established in the curricula of all schools and universities.

> But as things are, the war of the sword and the war of the pens is perpetual; there is no greater knowledge of natural right and natural laws today than in the past; both parties to a dispute defend their right with the opinions of Philosophers; one and the same action is praised by some and criticized by others. (C, 5)

This is precisely the situation that both Hobbes and Locke would remedy. As we shall see, it is quarrels over the nature and names of actions that are the very root of political conflict. The science of morality, in the hands of government and promulgated by state schools for the people, will prevent all such quarrels.[26] In this ambition our authors show themselves descendents of Socrates: the correct philosophy, taught correctly to the right people, will give rise to a just city. Thrasymachus will never tire of laughing at this absurd enterprise.

## Nominalism and the framing of action

If Hobbes and Locke carry out the desubstantialization of action under mechanism, and so it is no longer substance that acts, what then acts? And what bestows unity on action?

Both Hobbes and Locke embrace a nominalist solution to this problem. It is the judgement of action that not only interprets actions, assigning them a moral value, but actually frames and constitutes them as unities. And behind the work of judgement lies the agency and solidity of judicial and political institutions.

### *The sovereign's decision and political conflict in Hobbes*

Hobbes' nominalism concerning actions is found in his doctrine of legal positivism.[27] Despite the existence of natural right in the state of nature, Hobbes holds that there is no justice nor injustice prior to the social contract. Actions become just or unjust solely under the law of the sovereign:

> And the Makers of the Civil Laws, are not only Declarers, but also Makers of the justice and injustice of Actions; there being nothing in mens manners that makes them righteous, or unrighteous, but their conformity with the law of the sovereign. (L, 386)[28]

In themselves, actions possess no moral quality – if they can be said to be just or unjust it is solely as a function of their outward conformity to the law of the land. In *On the Citizen* Hobbes is even more explicit:

> *Just* and *unjust* did not exist until commands were given; hence their nature is relative to a command; and every action of its own nature is indifferent. What is *just* or *unjust* derives from the right of the ruler. Legitimate kings therefore make what they order just by ordering it, and make what they forbid unjust by forbidding it. (C, 133)

It seems Hobbes is resuscitating Thrasymachus! Justice is what the ruling authority decides it to be. Yet unlike Thrasymachus' ruling authority, Hobbes' sovereign is under a constraint: that of forever maintaining the people's safety.

Nominalism is central to Hobbes' theory of political conflict; it plays an important role in his diagnosis of the causes of the English civil war. If actions in themselves are neither just nor unjust but become so by the commands of authorities, then if there is more than one authority claiming to determine the nature of justice, confusion will result. One and the same action will appear to be just or unjust according to different authorities. This is precisely the situation with regard to the influence of Greek and Roman moral philosophy in situations of sedition and civil unrest. 'The ambivalent dogmas of the moral philosophers' warns Hobbes in the Preface to *On the Citizen*, are 'the causes of all quarrels and killings' (C, 9). In the *Leviathan* Hobbes claims:

> As to rebellion in particular against Monarchy; one of the most frequent causes of it, is the reading of the books of policy,

and histories of the ancient Greeks, and Romans . . . From the reading, I say, of such books, men have undertaken to kill their kings, because the Greek and Latin writers, in their books, and discourses of policy, make it lawful and laudable, for any man to do so; provided before he do it, he call him tyrant. (L, 225–6)

In the *Behemoth* Hobbes repeats this diagnosis and applies it specifically to the causes of the English civil war (B, 43). In the Preface to *On the Citizen*, Hobbes identifies two problems behind ancient philosophy's insidious influence. The first problem, doctrinal, is that ancient philosophers hold that justice can be 'measure[d] . . . by the comments of private men' rather than 'by the laws of the commonwealth' (C, 9). In the chapter on 'Causes dissolving a commonwealth' Hobbes specifies this charge by sourcing the 'third seditious doctrine . . . that tyrannicide is licit' in 'certain theologians in our own day and all the sophists of the past – *Plato, Aristotle, Cicero, Seneca, Plutarch* and the rest of the champions of anarchy in Greece and Rome' (C, 133). He then identifies the only possible basis for such doctrine, in his eyes, and he does so drawing on and adopting the mode of address of Gen. 3.11 which he sees as 'the first reproach God made to men' (C, 132). First God, then Hobbes:

And he said, Who told thee that thou [wast] naked? Hast thou eaten of the tree, whereof I commanded thee that thou shouldest not eat? (*King James Bible*, Gen. 3.11)

If [the tyrant] holds power rightly, the divine question applies: *Who told you he was a tyrant unless you have eaten of the tree of which I told you not to eat?* For why do you call him a *Tyrant* whom God made a king, unless you, a private person, are claiming for yourself a knowledge of good and evil? (C, 133)

Encouraging the pretense to private knowledge of good and evil – this is the first fault to be charged to ancient moral philosophy. Not only its doctrines but also its very practice by individuals encourages the belief that 'private men' can question and investigate and come to a decision on the nature of justice and right. On the contrary, it is the sovereign alone who will judge and assign the nature of actions.

The second major problem with moral philosophy is institutional, and it is a direct consequence of the doctrinal problem. It is the case, at the time of Hobbes' writing, that not only 'great philosophical intellects' but 'philosophers of all nations' and then 'gentlemen also in their leisure hours' have occupied themselves with the business of 'civil science' (C, 8). In doing so 'almost everyone is delighted to have even a false semblance of it' (C, 8). Earlier in the Preface to *On the Citizen*, just after he claims that moral philosophy could become a science – as cited above – Hobbes laments its current state:

> But as things are, the war of the sword and the war of the pens is perpetual; there is no greater knowledge of natural right and natural laws today than in the past; both parties to a dispute defend their right with the opinions of Philosophers; one and the same action is praised by some and criticized by others. (C, 5)

Not only do a multitude of people engage in the practice of philosophy, despite the most part lacking qualifications and discernment, but also the field of philosophy is characterized by permanent controversy between many different doctrines. If moral philosophy were pursued as a science, such controversies, Hobbes supposes, would cease. The combination of the doctrinal and the institutional problems contributes to civil conflict. Multiple doctrines imply multiple authorities. Multiple authorities determine the moral nature of the same actions in different ways. Conflict thus arises over the interpretation of 'one and the same action'. In other words, parties disagree about not only what is to be done – the third query of political action – but also about what has been done. In 1647, the Presbyterian dominated parliament holds that its action is the just settlement of the civil war. The agitators hold that the very same action amounts to prevarication at best and at worse a restoration of the monarchy. The naming of actions constitutes a primary ground of political conflict. Better to have one single authority – the sovereign in politics, scientific method in philosophy – than many: only then will actions mean one and the same thing to all, since in themselves they mean nothing.

Hobbes, on the one hand, reveals the institutional basis of the *nature* of actions, of their moral quality. At an ontological level, however, actions precede and remain independent of institutions.

How actions might have unity under mechanism is highly problematic, as argued in the previous section. Nevertheless Hobbes presumes such unity with no explanation of its origins.

Locke, on the other hand, takes institutional nominalism far further. Not only do institutions determine the name and nature of actions, but they also frame the unity of both actions and their agents. They do not construct actions and agents out of thin air, but they endow certain elements of experience with a particular unity.

## *Locke on personhood: Attribution and individuation of actions*

Chapter 27 of Book II of the *Essay* is consecrated to the genesis of our ideas of identity and diversity, and in particular the idea of personal identity. The term 'Person' signifies:

> A thinking intelligent being, that has reason and reflection, and can consider it self as it self, the same thinking thing in different times and places; which it does only by that consciousness, which is inseparable from thinking, and as it seems essential to me: It being impossible for anyone to perceive, without perceiving, that he does perceive. (*EHU*, II, 27, §9)

Hence a person is 'the same thinking thing' but not as an independent substrate; rather inasmuch as this thing is considered to be the same *by* consciousness. A person is thus an entity whose existence depends on the activity of consciousness. Locke anchors personhood in self-consciousness, it being a function of the self regarding 'it self as it self'. But within such a regard, what content is contained in this self? Locke explains that a person's identity extends as far as the past actions of which she has consciousness and which she attributes to herself. The attribution of personhood creates an identity between the self that reflects upon the past action and the self that performed the past action. This nominalist doctrine both excludes any substantial identity of persons, and places a primacy on action in the constitution of personal identity.

Half of Locke's work in examining personal identity consists in dismissing the traditional criteria of the identity of substance. On his account it is quite possible for the same self to inhabit two different substances – the hypothesis of mind swaps or memory implants (*EHU*, II, 27, §13). It is also possible for two selves to inhabit one and the same substance – the case of absolute amnesia (*EHU*, II, 27, §14). To highlight the difference between substantial identity and personal identity Locke mentions situations in which consciousness is interrupted: people forget past actions, they are not always conscious of their entire past lives, they are absorbed by present thoughts and indeed they sometimes sleep. Given these phenomena, in which we '[lose] sight of past selves', Locke says:

> Doubts are raised whether we are the same thinking thing; i.e. the same substance or no. Which however reasonable or unreasonable, concerns not personal identity at all. The question being, what makes the same person, and not whether it be the same identical substance, which always thinks in the same person, which matters not at all. (*EHU*, II, 27, §10)

That is to say, if one presumes that an identity is maintained across the interruption of consciousness, if one holds that it is the same entity who performed actions ten years ago and who has now forgotten them, then one is thinking identity in terms of substance. One is thinking according to the scholastic adage cited earlier: *actiones sunt suppositum*. As such, the ground of identity would be an independent substrate that remains the same throughout change. But Locke simply dismisses such an idea; it 'matters not at all'. Personal identity is rather a function, at any moment, of the contents of reflective consciousness, that is, of the consciousness of present and past actions as performed by the same self (*EHU*, II, 27, §16). The substantial agent could be unitary or multiple: this is not important, what is important is *unity of attribution of actions*. It does not matter whether it is the same substantial person who committed a crime one year ago and yet has forgotten it now: what matters is the sentence handed down by the judge that treats an individual *as* the same person (*EHU*, II, 27, §22). For justice to be had, the judge's attribution of agency must match up with the accused's own attribution of agency, with his own consciousness of having performed the crime in question. Otherwise Locke could never account for miscarriages of justice, where the innocent are condemned and identity mistaken.

This leads us to the second aspect of Locke's thesis. Personal identity is a function of consciousness, specifically consciousness of actions. Chronologically it seems that first there is a series of actions, and then there is a reflective perception of those actions that attributes them to the self as its own actions (*EHU*, II, 27, §17). Consciousness of action involves an operation of possession and identification: 'I am doing this', 'I did that'. In owning actions consciousness is treating itself *as* a thinking thing, that is, *as* a substance even though the entire question of the substantial identity has been bracketed. But more importantly the reflexive constitution of personal identity primarily concerns action: the person is not a personality, a set of static properties, but an agent who has left traces in the world. Self-consciousness of personhood is thus not simply consciousness of my inner mental contents, nor even of the veil of perception, but consciousness of my agency, of having caused changes in the environment. Although in the chronological register these actions appear to occur first, strictly speaking, agency does not pre-exist the operation of reflexive consciousness. Consciousness coexists with the performance of actions: at the very moment of action there is a 'reflex Act of perception accompanying it' (*EHU*, II, 27, §13). Yet at the same time consciousness is not the same thing as individual actions; it is separate. It is this separation that allows consciousness to be not just the presentation of contemporary actions, 'but a present representation of past actions' (*EHU*, II, 27, §13). Agency is thus attributed through the operation of reflexive consciousness, and it cannot be said to pre-exist this operation.

This nominalist operationalization of agency is crucial in Locke's treatment of what we may call, after James Tully, 'the juridical apparatus'.[29] For Locke there are three institutions of judgement, in accordance with the threefold nature of the law: divine law, civil law and the law of opinion and reputation (*EHU*, II, 28, §7). Civil law enters immediately into Locke's definition of personhood: 'person', he stipulates, 'is a *forensic* term appropriating actions and their merit' (*EHU*, II, 27, §26). It is the term that anchors juridical responsibility – to be the same person is to be accountable for past actions (*EHU*, II, 27, §17). Once one disposes of a concept of responsibility, one can develop an account of the legitimate use of punishment. Indeed in the same chapter Locke stipulates that an individual deserves punishment solely for actions that she owns up to and was conscious of (*EHU*, II, 27, §26). This is the ground, as mentioned earlier, for anyone who has been falsely accused and charged with a crime to contest the judge's attribution of agency. The juridical apparatus and its mechanisms of judgement and punishment finds its seat in individual's personhood, in her self-consciousness as an operation attributing actions to herself (*EHU*, II, 27, §18).

In the section above, 'Locke and the difficult derivation of the very idea of action', it was shown how the idea of a 'free agent' cannot be derived from experience. Rather it plays a kind of axiomatic role. It is here in the operations of the juridical institution that the importance of that axiomatic role comes to light. The idea of a free agent is a crucial element in the juridical framing of persons and actions.

Locke does not develop what is now called a social constructivist account of action. Certainly he takes a nominalist position on the existence of agents, but he does not go so far as to say that the attribution and constitution of agency is purely carried out by juridical institutions. It is consciousness that owns actions, and it is consciousness that may own up to actions once faced with the juridical apparatus. This individual operation is not the product of the institutional mechanisms of judgement, rather it is the latter's anchor.

But individual consciousness does not operate in isolation; it always has a social context. In society, the discourses that most often connect personhood, responsibility and actions are the juridical discourses: the providential apparatus of divine law and judgement, the state apparatus of the civil laws and penal system, and finally the social apparatus of the court of opinion and reputation (*EHU*, II, 28, §7). Men 'refer their actions', Locke writes, to these three kinds of laws, thus framing and understanding their own behaviour in the terms of the law. Individual consciousness is thus inhabited by juridical discourse.

What is it for a juridical discourse to frame individual behaviour? At the very beginning of the chapter on identity Locke reveals that not only is 'personhood' a forensic term, but also action. He does this by laying out general conditions of identity: any entity is said to be identical if it is compared with itself at two different moments in time and it remains the same. This holds for the three kinds of substance – God, finite intelligences and bodies – and for all modes and relations that 'ultimately terminate in substance' (*EHU*, II, 27, §2). There is an exception, however, to this reign of identity and that is the case of:

> ... the Actions of finite beings, *e.g.* Motion and Thought, both which consist in a continued train of Succession, concerning their diversity there can be no question: Because each perishing the moment it begins, they cannot exist in different times, or in different places; and therefore no motion or thought considered as at different times can be the same, each part thereof having a different beginning of Existence. (*EHU*, II, 27, §2)

Locke channels Heraclitus. An action, from an ontological perspective, does not possess a stable identity. As a change that takes place through time action is composed of parts that have disjunct identities, robbing the whole of any integrated identity. However, in juridical discourses actions do have identities. For instance, according to providentialist discourse, each of a man's sins will be known, named and judged at the last judgement. The consequence is simple: not only is *agency* a framing device that bestows unity and responsibility on persons but so is *action* itself. Neither term corresponds to a distinct ontological kind. Locke's desubstantialization of action is complete.

Unity is not bestowed on action through it belonging to a single substance. It is the juridical institution that individuates actions. But if actions do not exist at the level of supposed substances, they certainly exist at the level of our ideas – as vehiculed by juridical discourses. As in Hobbes, so with Locke: the nominalist position on action forms part of a theory of political conflict based on the names of action. If there are multiple names for action, or multiple institutions, there will be trouble.

## *Locke and the plurality of ideas of action*

In Locke's epistemology our ideas of particular actions fall under the general category of *complex ideas* and the subcategory of *modes*, where a mode is the idea of an affection of substance.

Within the subcategory of modes, action is a *mixed mode*. Mixed modes are:

> Combinations of simple ideas, as are not looked upon to be the characteristical Marks of any real Beings that have a steady existence, but scattered and independent ideas, put together by the mind, are thereby distinguished from the complex Ideas of substances. (*EHU*, II, 22, §1)

Thus the 'original' of a mixed mode lies 'more in the Thoughts of men, than in the reality of things' (*EHU*, II, 22, §2). That is to say, the mind 'exercises an Active Power in the making of [these] several combinations', wherein it joins together various simple ideas. For instance, the mixed mode 'lie', Locke explains, is made up of the simple ideas of 'articulate sounds', 'ideas in the mind of the Speaker', 'words as signs of those ideas', 'those words assembled otherwise than they are as ideas' and so on. The same kind of analysis could be carried out on mixed modes such as 'murder', 'sacrilege' and 'parricide'. In none of these cases is there one 'real being' with a 'steady existence' that serves as model for the idea.

If there is no original discrete object to which a mixed mode corresponds, from whence its unity? The response is that the unity of a mixed mode – itself a multiplicity of ideas – results from the single act of the mind that forms it (*EHU*, II, 22, §4). This unity is marked by a single name assigned to that combination of ideas, for instance 'parricide'. Two other questions then arise: First, how do individuals learn mixed modes? This is the question of transmission. Secondly, the question of origin: In the creation of mixed modes why are certain 'scattered and independent ideas' put together and not others? Locke answers the question of transmission by explaining that an individual can learn a mixed mode if he already possesses the simple ideas from which it is composed. If someone possesses the idea of murder and that of a father, he can be taught the term 'parricide' (*EHU*, II, 22, §3). Later in the chapter, Locke identifies two other manners in which people learn mixed modes: through the observation of experience, and by invention. If we observe two men wrestle, Locke claims, we can acquire the idea of wrestling.[30] The second way people learn mixed modes is by invention; the 'voluntary putting together of several simple Ideas in our own minds', 'without having any pattern to fashion it by' (*EHU*, II, 22, §9, §2). For instance, the man who invented the technology of printing developed an idea of it before it was constructed as a mechanical apparatus.

The second question of origin concerns why some mixed modes exist rather than others. Locke's answer refers to practice. The goal of language is to enable individuals to communicate their thoughts to one another. As such, certain ideas are combined into those mixed modes that happen to enable greater facility in people's 'way of living and Conversation' (*EHU*, II, 27, §5). In the following paragraph he explains further:

> For the several fashions, Customs and Manners of one Nation, making several Combinations of Ideas familiar and necessary in one, which another people have never had any occasion to make, or, perhaps, so much as take notice of, Names come of course to be annexed to them, to avoid long Periphrases in conversation; and so they become so many distinct complex Ideas in their Minds. (*EHU*, II, 22, §6)

It is repetition and convenience that lie behind the emergence of mixed modes. The convenience of a mixed mode is determined by the frequency of certain events and situations, which in turn are determined by custom.[31] Custom enjoys a foundational role in this account. The immediate consequence is a problem with translation, or to be more exact, a problem in international understanding. This problem directly indicates the modality of mixed modes; they are contingent, they could be otherwise. Locke writes, 'it comes to pass that there are in every language many particular words, which cannot be rendered by any single word of another' (*EHU*, II, 22, §6). Hence translators must have recourse to paraphrase and circumlocutions to convey these singular mixed modes. But the problem is not simply one between nations: even inside a nation, incommensurability and translation difficulties may arise inasmuch as customs change from one epoch to another, and even between different social strata, as does language use (*EHU*, II, 22, §7). If the question of the origin of mixed modes – why some rather than others? – is simply 'custom', then our ideas of action have been entirely historicized and culturally relativized. Any stability in the knowledge of action becomes a pure function of statistical frequency in the shape of custom.

## *Truth and the names of action*

Locke returns to the cultural origin of mixed modes in his treatment of truth as adequation. The peculiar advantage of mixed modes is that they 'cannot but be adequate Ideas' given that they are not 'copies of things really existing', but 'Archetypes made by the mind to rank and denominate things by' (*EHU*, II, 31, §3). As such, given that it is 'the Mind' that combines simple ideas into a mixed mode, it cannot but be satisfied with its perfection. For this reason our ideas of mixed modes – of actions – are always more adequate than our ideas of substances, which are only ever an approximation of the complexity of the really existing thing. Here the chances of a science of morality seem really quite good.

However, and here is the rub, when it comes to the communication of our ideas of mixed modes it is quite possible for our own idea of a mixed mode to be inadequate.[32] When someone is learning these terms, such as 'courage', it is quite possible for her to assign the term to a slightly different combination of simple ideas than that of her teacher. If the student then assumes that her idea of 'courage' is exactly the same as that of the teacher, then her idea is 'defective and inadequate'. But who says the teacher has access to the original archetype? Locke entertains such a hypothesis at length with regard to ideas of substance: based on his experience, a watchmaker is said to have a different idea of a clock than that of your average man on the street (*EHU*, III, 6, §31). However, with substances it is easy to decide whose idea is adequate: the watchmaker's idea is superior and closer to reality than that of the layman. But who can say who has the original and most adequate idea of courage? Socrates? He is long dead, and even when he was alive he caused havoc by quibbling over the meaning of actions, hence the hemlock.

Locke's nominalist and then pragmatist account of the genesis our ideas of action leads to the problem with transmission and communication. Locke is well aware of this trap and he is ready for it with a strikingly modern solution, but before we get there another problem raises its head. In the chapter on the truth and falsity of our ideas, Locke admits that although our ideas of action, as archetypes, are always adequate, it is difficult to know which archetype should be applied to a given action: 'it being not so easy to determine of several actions; whether they are to be called *Justice* or *Cruelty*; *Liberality* or *Prodigality*' (*EHU*, II, 32, §10). If one attempts to resolve this difficulty by referring to someone else's ideas, 'called by the same names', our idea as noted above might turn out to be inadequate. Locke juxtaposes these two epistemological problems in consecutive sentences. Their relation can be explained as follows. I resolve my difficulty in judging whether an action was liberal or prodigal by referring to someone else's judgement. That authority says that the action in question was liberal. But this is not the end of my problems because I might have a different idea of liberality than she does. Let us call this *the problem of application*. The upshot is that Locke's proto-pragmatist concept of an archetype cannot avoid the problem of adequation: inadequacies open up between different people in the understanding of mixed modes, and between people and particular actions in the naming of action. Indeed Locke is led to admit that 'our Ideas of mixed modes are the most liable to be faulty of any other' though he then restricts this problem to being one of proper speaking rather than one of knowledge (*EHU*, II, 31, §5).

To return to the contingent origins of archetypes, in a chapter entitled 'The Reality of our Knowledge' Locke raises the objection that if human beings make their own archetypes of action, 'What strange Notions will there be of Justice and Temperance? What confusion of Virtues and Vices if every one may make of them what ideas he pleases' (*EHU*, IV, 4, §9). This is the problem of arbitrariness. His response is that changes in the names of moral ideas do not affect their properties nor reasonings about them. On the basis of an extended analogy with mathematical knowledge, whereby a triangle retains its properties however it is named, he claims that the same actions will fall under the idea of injustice whatever its name; that idea involving things being taken from a man without his consent. It is in the same book that Locke advances the idea of a science of morality (*EHU*, IV, 3, §18–20; *EHU*, IV, 12, §8). Such a solution presumes the problem of application solved: evidently this science applies to cases in which there is no doubt about the nature of the action at stake.

The other solution that Locke proposes to the problem of arbitrariness is that the name of a kind of action is not fixed by one individual but rather by a community of users. Specific mixed modes arise on the basis of a context of custom and use. The normal application of mixed modes is shaped by our continual exposure to them in everyday social situations. In an earlier chapter on the 'Imperfection of Words' Locke palliates the 'variability' and 'doubtfulness' of the names of mixed modes by stating that '*common Use*, that is the rule of Propriety, may be supposed here to afford some aid, to settle the signification of Language; and it cannot be denied, but that in some measure it does' (*EHU*, III, 9, §8).

But then another obstacle crops up. In Lacanian terms, one could say there is no meta-language of use. In plain English, how do we know who, among a community of users, is using a term correctly? Locke continues:

> Common use *regulates the meaning of words* pretty well for common conversation; but no body having an Authority to establish the precise signification of Words, nor determine to what *Ideas* any one shall annex them, common use is not sufficient to adjust them to philosophical discourse; there being scarce any Name, of any very complex *Idea* . . . which, in common Use, has not a great latitude, and which keeping within the bounds of propriety, may not be made the sign of far different *Ideas*. Besides, the rule and measure of propriety it self being nowhere established, it is often matter of dispute, whether this or that way of using a Word, be propriety of Speech, or no. (*EHU*, III, 9, §8; emphasis in original)

Not only is it a matter of dispute, but also the great political and religious disputes that tore England and Europe apart during the seventeenth century can be traced back to fundamental disagreements about mixed modes, that is, about the moral or immoral, the substantial or fanciful nature of particular actions, such as having a wafer placed in one's mouth. An epistemological problem, which has turned out to be a semantic problem, is also a political problem in Locke's diagnosis:

> Where shall one find any *controversial debate*, or *familiar discourse*, about honour, faith, grace, religion, Church, etc. wherein it is not easy to observe the different notions men have of them; which is nothing but this, that they are not agreed in

the signification of those Words; nor have in their minds the same complex *Ideas* which they make them stand for: and so all the contests that follow thereupon are only about the meaning of a sound. (*EHU*, III, 9, §9; emphasis in original)

The stakes of this problem are high. And it appears that Locke is not quite so confident in his first solution – a proto-science of morality – in these contexts. He does, however, dispose of a practical solution to the absence of secure definitions of normal usage. One can resolve the problem of 'the rule of propriety being nowhere established' by reference to authority. Locke says there is no sensible standard to compare real actions to save the proper use that we suppose certain men to make of them (*EHU*, II, 32, §12). In another passage on remedying the defects of speech he says, 'The proper signification and use of terms is to be learned from those, who in their writing and discourses, appear to have had the clearest notions, and applied them to their terms with the exactest choice and fitness' (*EHU*, III, 11, §11). In other words, in ambiguous cases, the correct name for actions may be decided through reference to authority. This is an analogous solution to that of Aristotle when faced with the difficulty of defining prudence: let us suppose there is knowledge (of the correct name, of the prudent thing to do) and let us attribute such knowledge to an authority, to a master.

There are two solutions to the problem of the semantic indetermination of action in the *Essay*: first, a science of morality according to which there is an invariable moral idea that can be applied to certain actions, whatever word might be used to name that idea. The second solution is that the applicability of terms such as 'justice' and 'courage' is more or less fixed by the context of common usage, and when that context allows too much latitude one can always refer to some authority's use of the word, presuming the latter to be in the right. There happens to be two further solutions to the same problem that Locke briefly mentions then passes over. In one passage he says that any confusion about the idea of a mixed mode can be cleared up by simply explaining what one understands by, for instance, *justice* or *courage* given the action in question (*EHU*, II, 22, §9). And then at the end of the chapter 'Of the Imperfection of Words' he proposes a principle of charity in interpretation, specifically in reference to our interpretation of ancient authors:

> It would become us to be charitable one to another in our Interpretations or Misunderstandings of those Ancient writings, which though of great concernment to us to be understood, are liable to the unavoidable difficulties of speech . . . And in Discourses of Religion, Law, and Morality, as they are matters of the highest concernment, so there will be the greatest difficulty. (*EHU*, III, 9, §22)[33]

It is evident that Locke has the bible in view when giving such counsel. The interpretation of the bible fuels many religious conflicts in the seventeenth century. Other ancient texts, which speak of action, justice, ethics and the city-state, also play a part in determining the use of the very notions we use to understand social and political conflict. This appeal to charity in interpretation, and the counsel to use explanation to resolve disputes over the meaning of mixed modes, reveals Locke's astonishing modernity. It is as though he briefly glimpses the possibility of a pragmatist philosophy of dialogue for the resolution of social conflict.

Yet this is not the path Locke chooses to follow in his political philosophy, preferring to ground government in atomized individual judgements.

## From mechanism to nominalism to the indeterminacy of usage

On the basis of a mechanist reduction of action, Locke and Hobbes develop a nominalist metaphysics of action. Henceforth substances no longer act but institutions act. The argument is complex, passing through various detours, but its sequence runs as follows.

Under mechanism, action is reduced to passion and becomes ubiquitous, referring to every physical shock of bodies. On the basis of a mechanist ontology Spinoza explicitly critiques an imperial model of action whereby a separate and autonomous agent transforms its environment in line with its commands. In contrast he develops an expressive and participative conception of action where to act is no longer to command but to understand one's own intrication in the world, a conception that will hold some affinity with the Leveller-agitator model of action.

When Locke attempts to derive the idea of action from experience he ends up in a circle: the idea of action depends on the idea of a free agent that depends on the idea of active power which in turn depends on our idea of the exercise of our will which turns out to depend on the idea of a free agent. What Locke admits to be an obscure idea – 'a free agent' – must therefore enjoy the status of an axiom, an undemonstrated starting point for a construction.

Under mechanism's promulgation of universal laws of motion action, like any phenomenon, can be reduced to the level of primary properties and the shock of bodies. As such it may be measured. At the level of reason and social interaction action follows another set of universal laws: the laws of nature, unwritten precepts of reason accessible to any individual. These laws of nature lead to the social contract, which in turn institutionalizes action under the sovereign. They also render possible a science of morality.

Hobbes develops a nominalist position on action. Actions in themselves, as revealed in the state of nature, have no moral status; they are neither just nor unjust. It is the sovereign in the form of civil law that makes actions just or unjust. This doctrine has two direct consequences, the first being the indivisibility of the sovereign. On pain of perpetual social conflict over the nature of actions, there must be one authority alone that legally determines the nature of actions. The second consequence is that no freedom for private men to judge good and evil can be admitted into public affairs. Such a notion becomes a seditious doctrine to be stamped out, and one of the chief sources of this doctrine is ancient moral philosophy.

Locke extends the nominalist desubstantialization of action far further than Hobbes. He first dissolves any substantial personal identity, rendering personhood a function of reflexive consciousness. A person is an agent that has been attributed, by consciousness, to an action. It is the juridical institution that grounds its operations in such attributions. 'Person' is a forensic term used by courts in their attributions of agency, allowing them to assign responsibility for crimes. It is not the philosopher, but the juridical institution that uses the idea of a free agent as an axiom in such attributions.

If the juridical attribution of agency matches with an individual's own attribution, then the latter is guilty. In turn individuals frame their own behaviour in reference to juridical norms. In a Foucauldian turn, individual consciousness is inhabited by institutional judgement. Locke then puts one more turn on the screw: not only is 'personhood' a reflexively and institutionally generated unity, so is action. An action is not a distinct natural entity but is framed as such by consciousness and institutions.

Perhaps actions possess stability not at the level of being but at the level of ideas. Locke's investigation of our ideas and names for action takes a pragmatist turn by identifying their origin in custom and use – we invent and use those names for action that are convenient in practice. This thesis leads to two problems: transmission and application. When a person learns an idea for action, they may understand it as a slightly different combination of simple ideas than their teacher. But who is to say who has the correct combination? And how can it be determined which is the correct name to apply to a particular action in the case of conflict over its nature? In society there is no universal definition of the correct use of names for action. The realm of practice, custom and usage is fundamentally indeterminate. Locke brings two main solutions to bear on these problems: conflict over the names of action can be decided by reference to norms, or by reference to an authority's use of those names, much like Hobbes' sovereign.

Substances no longer act, the institution acts, and within the realm of usage. But what is an institution?

# CHAPTER FOUR

# Hobbes and Locke on religious conflict: When institutions act, subjects act

Hobbes' and Locke's most controversial and sensitive writing about institutions occurs not in their social contract theory but in their treatment of the established church. Both Locke and Hobbes called for the subordination of ecclesiastical power to civil power and for an end to religious conflict. Their solutions occupy opposite ends of the spectrum: Hobbes advocates the imposition of religious conformity through the offices of a single state church; Locke advocates religious toleration and embraces the subsequent emergence of a plurality of free and tolerant churches. Despite the massive contrast between the authoritarian and the liberal solution, both approaches suppose a thorough rethinking of the very nature of the church, the institution par excellence.

In proposing an alternative articulation of civil and ecclesiastical power, Hobbes and Locke sought to quench one of the fires that began and fueled the civil war. Each of the major factions during the civil war held different religious allegiances: Charles I, a High Anglican was married to a Catholic, Marie-Bourbon of France, and thenceforth was forever suspected of papist leanings; the Long parliament was dominated by Presbyterians, and the New Model Army was suspected of every form of radical Protestantism and heresy under the sun. Distinct political parties did not emerge until the time of the glorious revolution of 1688; and so during the civil war each faction understood the other factions to be united by religious ideology. One of the war cries or rallying slogans of the soldiers of the New Model Army was 'freedom of conscience' which meant nothing less than freedom to openly and publically practice alternative forms of worship: this is a little stronger than 'toleration'. Lay-preaching and iconoclasm – the destruction of graven images, of stone altars and stained glass images – were two of the most well-known religious practices of the New Model Army soldiers.[1] The nature of a genuinely christian church was an open question and an active investigation for the New Model Army.

It is precisely when Hobbes and Locke examine the nature of a Christian church that a new figure of action emerges: that of a subject split between internal and external action, the inner action of conscience and the outward performance of ecclesiastical rites; this was none other than the philosophical concept of the religious subject who remains a citizen. For Hobbes, a citizen-dissenter inwardly worships according to his heretical beliefs while outwardly conforming to the civil authority's edicts concerning religious worship. A citizen-dissenter keeps public order, does not cause public trouble, and does not engage in lay-preaching or iconoclasm. For Locke all members of the church are split between their individual calculations of their chances of salvation and their outward belonging to that particular church that, for the moment, appears to maximize those chances.

Behind Hobbes' and Locke's figure of the religious subject, whose action is split between inner conscience and outward practice, lies Luther's original problematic: if all ritual action, if all established and thus habitual religious ceremonies, if all religious works of charity can be perfectly performed with absolutely no inner faith, nor pious intention behind them, then what activity genuinely makes a person a member of the church? Seventeenth-century philosophy of action must not only come to terms with the advent of mechanism, it must also come to the end of the consequences unleashed by Luther's *Ninety-Five Theses*.

## Luther's problem

In the *Theological-Political Treatise*, Spinoza engages in a long and elaborate critique of what he depicts as the institutional conception of religious action. 'It is certain, therefore', he argues, 'that ceremonies do not belong to the divine law and hence contribute nothing to happiness and virtue. They are relevant only to the election of the Hebrews, that is, to the temporal and material prosperity and peace of their state'.[2] In opposition to ceremonies, which find their guarantee and their end in the state, it is the moral teaching found in divine and universal law that has virtue as its end. Spinoza's argument, though not Lutheran to the letter, develops and expands consequences found in Luther's original argument: no institutionalized action will guarantee your relationship to God.

Luther's original problem – as he himself recounts in his autobiographical Preface to the 1545 edition of his *Complete Latin Writings* – was not with the Roman Catholic Church per se nor with corrupt practices on the part of certain bishops and priests. The sticking point that led to his reformulation of theology lay in one phrase in Paul's Epistle to the Romans: 'In it the righteousness of God is revealed' (Rom. 1.17). But what is the 'righteousness of God'? As a young monk Luther had been taught it was God's punishment of unrighteous sinners. The righteousness of God was thus a principle of division, dividing the righteous from the unrighteous. Luther's problem was that he felt this to be harsh and excessive: as if it were not enough for the sinner to suffer and be eternally lost due to original sin, but 'God add[ed] pain to pain' with his punishment! But not only was there excess on the side of God, there was also deficiency on the side of humans: 'Though I lived as a monk without reproach, I felt that I was a sinner before God with an extremely disturbed conscience. I could not believe that he was placated by my satisfaction'.[3] Luther was reputed in his monastery for both the frequency of his confessions and the triviality of the sins he confessed: the urgency underlying his actions was caused by his desire to render himself worthy of God's grace and by his complete dissatisfaction with the means available for such a task. Luther wanted to justify himself before God, and 'God's righteousness' was the name for his objective failure to do so. In short, what is at stake in Luther's problem is nothing less than the establishment of a measure, of a relation, between human and God. Luther's breakthrough was to realize that it was possible to understand the term 'God's righteousness' in a different way, not as referring to an action or property possessed by God, such as his punishment of sinners, but rather to his action within humans, that is, as a gift to humans. God's gift to humans, which allows humans to attain righteousness, is faith. Hence Luther's concept of justification by faith.

## *The empty work: Hypocrisy, pride and the law*

Luther presents the concept of justification by faith by contrasting it with the doctrine of justification by works which holds that we can 'prepare ourselves for grace through works' (*ML*, 21). This is a doctrine originally critiqued by Paul. Luther sees it as a permanent temptation in both theology and ecclesiastical practice. He condemns the 'sophisticators wrangling in our schools' who teach such a doctrine. The kinds of works that could mistakenly be held to justify man before God include all the sacraments of the church – baptism, circumcision, confession, the eucharist and the mass – and even virtuous actions such as Christ washing his disciples' feet (*ML*, 25).

Luther charges the doctrine of justification by works with three grave faults: the faults of hypocrisy, pride and the law. The simplest fault, which also bears the greatest significance for the conception of action under religious toleration, is that of hypocrisy and its figure is that of the empty work. It is all very well to 'perform the works required by the law', but such works remain 'vain and useless' in the eyes of God as long as they are performed with a reluctant and hostile heart that 'dislikes the law' (*ML*, 21). The problem is that despite their inauthenticity, the performance of works does serve a useful function among men, that of maintaining the 'outward appearance of . . . living an honourable life' (*ML*, 20). Thus Luther accuses the performer of empty works not only of having no pious intentions, but also of harbouring intentions to enjoy an earthly reputation and goods. The empty work, conforming to the law but with no heart behind it, is not so empty after all: it is animated by a sinful desire for earthly gain. Hence, Luther's simple equation: 'such works produce nothing but hypocrites'. The hypocrisy lies not only in the division between intention and act, reality and appearance, but also in the exercise of judgement. As Luther says, 'as is the way with all hypocrites, they habitually judge others' (*ML*, 26). Such judgement seeks to assess people's piety according to whether or not they correctly perform works. But to use such a criterion is to fall into the position of what Luther calls a 'mere ceremonialist' (*ML*, 28). Unfortunately hypocrisy is not an evil that solely affects those who would elevate themselves to a position of eminence and authority. Luther offers the following précis of Ps. 117: 'all men are liars, because no-one keeps God's law from his heart; nor can he do so, for to be averse to goodness and prone to evil are traits found in all men' (*ML*, 20). And so all men are prone to the hypocrisy inherent in the doctrine of justification by works.

The second fault with this doctrine is that it encourages pride, which used to be called a deadly sin; nowadays, at least in political philosophy, it goes under the name 'voluntarism'. If I believe that I can account for myself before God and measure up to his demand of righteousness through good works, then I arrogate to myself the entire power of raising myself to the level of God. My works are my own and thus in so far as I assume they are good in the eyes of God I am proud of my works, and so I am proud of myself. But pride is a sin: humility is the true Christian virtue. To be a Christian is not to exalt the self before God but rather to sacrifice the self (*ML*, 33). If an individual is to be saved, it is not through her willpower alone: it is through the intervention of God's grace and the gift of faith. The Aristotelian concept of a unique and hermetic agent is thus not applicable here; we struggle against sin not purely through our own efforts but also through the action of God within us. What is at stake in Luther's concept of grace – and its avatars in seventeenth-century metaphysics of action – is thus a *sharing of agency*.

The third fault in justification by works is diagnosed by Paul and elaborated in Luther's commentary on Paul's *Epistle to the Romans*. Paul declares: 'Through the works of the law no man shall be justified before God' (Rom. 3.28). A work is said to be 'of the law' inasmuch as it is the divine law that dictates what a good Christian should do, as found in the ten commandments and the teachings of Christ. However the law itself, in its operation, is radically insufficient in helping humans to attain righteousness. Luther writes;

> Paul proves that the God-given law . . . not only gave no help when it did come, but only increased sin. Our evil nature becomes all the more hostile to it, and prefers to pursue its own devices, in proportion to the strictness of that law. (*ML*, 29)

The law enters into a relationship with sin and temptation whereby its very act of prohibiting certain deeds increases the temptation for individuals to perform such a deed. To liberate ourselves from sin, indeed even to struggle against sin, something other than the law is required: God's grace. Paul differentiates two ways of living: under the law, and not under the law. In Luther's commentary, to live under the law is 'to live apart from grace, and to be occupied with fulfilling the works of the law'; whereas to not live under the law is not to embrace anarchy but rather to live in grace and thus to take pleasure in the law and in doing good but not as an obligation (*ML*, 29).

## *The exposed heart and the action of faith*

The critique of empty works and the hypocrisy of mere ceremonialism gives rise to the concept of the heart as the source of authenticity in any action that conforms to the law. Luther explains the 'law' in Paul's teachings by stating: 'God judges according to your inmost convictions; his law must be fulfilled in your very heart, and cannot be obeyed if you merely perform certain acts' (*ML*, 20). But what is 'your very heart'? When counselling the reading of the *Book of Psalms* Luther says:

> The human heart is like a ship on a stormy sea driven about by winds blowing from all four corners of heaven. In one man there is fear and anxiety about impending disaster . . . and another is puffed up with a confidence and pleasure in his current possessions. (*ML*, 39)

The heart is thus a site of conflicting passions. As such it can give rise to two kinds of speech: in one, the heart is hidden and the passions masked; but in the other, men 'lay bare what lies in the bottom of their hearts'. In Luther's eyes, the Psalms belong to this second sincere form of speech; they contain 'heartfelt utterances made during storms of this kind'. In the Psalms of lamentation, he says, 'You see into the hearts of all the saints as if you were looking at death or gazing into hell' (*ML*, 40). The heart is filled with passions and their conflict, which gives it temporary orientation at best, if not unpredictability. Yet the heart can also be the origin of truth in speech – when speech exposes the heart.

In hypocrisy and its works the heart is absent from the law. What then of justification by faith, what articulation of the heart and the law? Luther defines faith in the following way:

> Faith . . . is something God effects in us. It changes us and we are reborn from God . . . O, when it comes to faith, what a living, creative, active, powerful thing it is. It cannot do other than good at all times. It never waits to ask whether there is some good work to do, Rather, before the question is raised, it has done the deed and keeps on doing it . . . Faith is a living and unshakeable confidence, a belief in the grace of God so assured that a man would die a thousand deaths for its sake. (*ML*, 24)

The grace of God is the gift that brings about faith in us in the first place. If faith is belief in the grace of God, it is belief in its own continuing existence.[4] And that existence, as Luther describes it, is nothing other than immediate immanent action that is perpetually orientated towards the good, with no need of external command or initiation. When Luther says 'it cannot do other than good at all times' he seems to remove any space for deliberation, decision, any time for the initiation or ending of an action and any margin for error. The risk with such a conception of faith is that it is turned some kind of automatic activity. To counter such a risk, Luther adds that faith is not only activity but also a belief. Belief adds a dimension of uncertainty and temporality to faith. To *believe* in God's grace is to at least admit the possibility of God's grace not being guaranteed by some objective law. There is one other reason why Luther needs to affirm that faith is not just a kind of action but a form of belief. If faith consisted of action alone, then it would be too easy to repeat the mistake of conflating it with the performance of works.

This brings us back to the contrast between justification by works and justification by faith. Luther remarks that Paul deals with the objection that if we are justified by faith alone and all works are vain, then we have no need of works. Faith would be nothing more than an attitude, a special kind of belief, which left no traces in the world. In response, Paul shows that faith naturally and spontaneously gives rise to good works. These are good works that are carried out *regardless* of the law; not out of obligation, not out of a concern to exhibit conformity to the law. And yet these spontaneous works *fulfil* the law and *express* the spirit of the law. Nonetheless, he warns, these good works remain but 'outward signs' of faith: 'Like Abraham's circumcision, they are only outward signs proving that his righteousness is contained in his faith' (*ML*, 27). This however raises a difficulty with Luther's doctrine: the works of the hypocrites are also supposed to function as signs of their faith, and yet they are empty. How is it possible to know whether the outward sign corresponds to an inward intention?

## *The emanating work*

When Luther finally provides a list of the 'right kind of works' he accords a slightly different status to them than that of mere outward signs. Rather than naming a set of distinct kinds of action, he lists a number of passions and attitudes: 'peace, joy, love to God and all mankind; in addition, assurance, courage, confidence, and hopefulness in spite of sorrow and suffering' (*ML*, 28). If he were to list distinct kinds of action, such as specific forms of charity, he would be generating a set of rules. A set of rules would run the risk of institutionalization, of giving rise to empty imitations; all the more so the more determinate and detailed they were. In contrast, it is very difficult to imitate 'peace' or 'joy', they must come from within. But neither is the existence of the 'right kind of works' simply a matter of possessing nebulous emotional states and feeling 'joy' or 'love to God and all mankind'. In his comparison between the works of faith and the works of mere ceremonialists, Luther says; 'They trump up their own kinds of work, but these breathe neither peace, nor joy, nor assurance, nor love, nor hope, nor courage, nor certainty, nor anything that partakes of genuine Christian conduct or faith' (*ML*, 28). This negative critique can be transformed into a positive criterion. A work of faith, therefore, is not simply 'peace, joy, assurance', it is a *work that breathes* 'peace, joy, assurance, hope, etcetera'. The work itself is an action that leaves traces in the world, that *emanates* and thus transmits the subjective attitude from which it was born. This is the concept with which Luther reconciles faith and works, this is the concept that completes the critique of institutionalized action – an *emanating work*. Subtracted from all guarantees and predetermined forms, the criterion of success for such a work lies solely in the communication of faith, where faith acts on the heart as the site of multiple passions. This is not to claim that one individual can inspire faith in another by means of a work. This would be in contradiction with Luther's own doctrine of faith as the grace of God. Rather, the success of any emanating work would always be attributed its true author, God.

## Hobbes on religion: Conscience beyond the law

What does Hobbes' critique of the church reveal of the workings of institutions? Does the church simply institutionalize action, such that substances no longer act but institutions?

Hobbes' critique of the church is a direct consequence of his doctrine of indivisible sovereignty. Ecclesiastical power must be subordinate to civil power rather than attempting to rival it. At the beginning of his argument, church and state are treated as separate powers with distinct and rival functions. By the end of the argument, it is no longer a simple question of subordinating powers but one of fusion whereby the church is absorbed into the commonwealth, no longer a distinct body with an alternative function to that of the state, but rather an extension or deputy of civil authority. To reach this position, a full investigation of ecclesiastical power is required, from the supposed sources of its authority, to the origin of its conflict with the state, to the nature of excommunication, preaching and conversion. The investigation creates a new figure of action, *disjoint action*, at the opposite extreme to Luther's emanating work.

### The subordination of powers

Hobbes' initial argument for the suboordination of powers is very simple. It is presented as part of his general analysis of 'things that Weaken, or tend to the DISSOLUTION of the commonwealth', the title of chapter 29 of the *Leviathan*. In that analysis, he lists six seditious doctrines, and the sixth and final doctrine is 'That the sovereign power may be divided' (*L*, 225). A page later, he fleshes out this dangerous doctrine: it 'set[s] up a *Supremacy* against the *Sovereignty*; *Canons* against *Lawes*; and a *Ghostly Authority* against the *Civill*' (*L*, 226). He clearly has neither mixed monarchy nor republicanism but the church in his sights. To divide sovereignty is impossible since civil power cannot be shared among different bodies like pieces of a cake. To grant the existence of a body that has the power to make canons is to grant the existence of another commonwealth. In more specific terms, Hobbes charges the ghostly power and its advocates – the church – of 'challeng[ing] the right to declare what is Sinne [and thus] challeng[ing] by consequence to declare what is law' (*L*, 227). Hence one is in the absurd position of having two commonwealths and one people with the result that a subject can find herself with two different masters and two different commands to obey. This situation is not only absurd but dangerous since it leads directly to 'Civil Warre, and Dissolution'. The options are evident: either the civil power of the commonwealth must be subordinate to the ghostly power, or the ghostly to the civil. In each case there will be one sovereign power alone.

Hobbes has not yet made the argument that spiritual power must be subordinate to temporal power. At this stage he is content to expose the respective claims of church and state to supreme power. On the one hand, the civil authority is 'more visible, and stand[s] in the cleerer light of Natural Reason'. For this reason, it is able to 'draw to it in all times a very considerable part of the people' (*L*, 227). On the other hand, the church, given 'the fear of Darknesse, and Ghosts, [being] greater than other fears' is not in 'want of a party sufficient to Trouble, and sometimes to Destroy a Commonwealth' (*L*, 227). In chapter 38, Hobbes expands on the strength and resource of the church's rival claim to people's allegiance:

> The maintenance of Civil Society, depending on Justice; and Justice depending on the power of Life and Death, and other lesse Rewards and Punishments, residing in them that have the Sovereignty of the Commonwealth; It is impossible a Commonwealth should stand, where any other than the Sovereign, hath a power of giving greater rewards than Life; and of inflicting greater punishments, than Death. (*L*, 306–7)

The problem is that the Church can promise 'Eternal Life' and threaten 'Eternal Death', clearly trumping the offer made by the civil authority. If the commonwealth is generated through the accord of the multitude who seek their greater advantage, who pursue peace and would secure protection from the greatest power, then it seems that the church has the true claim to sovereignty. Yet Hobbes' position in this matter is quite clear: the commonwealth is sovereign, the church subordinate and there shall be one uniform public worship within the commonwealth whose form will be decided by the sovereign (L, 252). How does he arrive at such an opposite conclusion? He engages in a thorough examination of every claim the church might make to exercise supreme temporal power.[5] In the text, this argument is found mixed in with the explication of what a church might be once properly subordinate to the civil authority, but these are two distinct lines of enquiry.

## *The natural church*

The church claims to exercise not just temporal but supreme temporal power on the authority of the scriptures that declare the existence of divine law, which is universal and so applies to all mankind. Hobbes approach here is epistemological: how do we know what is divine law? To qualify as law, words must be made public, they must be promulgated or proclaimed. God declares his law in three ways: reason, revelation and the speech of a miracle-worker who enjoys some credibility. Hobbes then engages in a procedure of elimination. He immediately dismisses supernatural revelation, claiming that God is recorded to have spoken of particular things to particular men, but never to have declared a law by that means (L, 246). The two sources that remain are those of natural reason, and prophecy by a miracle-worker. To these sources correspond God's two kingdoms, natural and prophetic, the natural extending to all those who acknowledge his providence, and the prophetic consisting of the Jewish people whom God chose as his subjects, governing them by positive laws that were given to the prophets such as Moses to announce. This is the second form of divine law to be eliminated from this enquiry: Hobbes will concentrate on the laws corresponding to the natural kingdom of God, that is, on the laws given by reason to all humans.

Before identifying the divine laws given through reason, Hobbes follows the implication that where there is law, there is a judicial apparatus and punishment. In the case of divine law, that punishment is manifest as the adversities with which men are afflicted – some people prosper, others are beset by failure, accident and misery, and this distribution is said to be a function of God's providence. God's right to mete out reward and punishment is derived, oddly, from a possible rational outcome of the state of nature. How does this work? Faced with war of all against all, humans decide to mutually transfer their individual rights to a sovereign protector to guarantee their life and property, but they do so on the basis of all being more or less equal in strength and agility. If it were the case that one among them were so superior to the others as to defeat any coordinated attack, then no such universal transfer of right would be necessary: through his 'irresistible power' he would have ruled the others. Such is the case of God. His right to rule and punish is based on his omnipotence. Shades of Thrasymachus unsettle the theologians – God's right based on his might and not on his goodness! Hobbes naturalizes God by means of this argument, reducing his position to a variant of the hypothetical operations of the state of nature.

The divine laws accessed through the exercise of reason are also none other than the natural laws that Hobbes has already presented, namely, as he summarizes them here, 'Equity, Justice, Mercy, Humility, and the rest of the Morall Vertues' (*L*, 248). These laws are designed to prevent and minimize conflict between humans over past offences, exclusive privileges, private possessions and controversies. They are precisely the same laws that operate in the state of nature to bring about the social contract and thus the construction of the civil authority. By this conflation of divine and natural law, Hobbes achieves one of his main objectives, which was to show that when obeying civil law no one was contradicting divine law. But this is just the first step in demonstrating the superiority of civil authority. So far he has simply rendered the two contenders equal and thus compatible. It is at the very end of his examination of worship that Hobbes subtly trumps divine with civil authority.

In his anthropological analysis of the worship of God, Hobbes again reduces divine worship to a particular variant of a larger category of *cultus* or cult, which is 'that labour bestowed on any thing, with a purpose to make benefit by it'. Where that thing is not an object but someone's mind, then a cult is much the same as 'courting, that is, a winning of favour by good offices' (*L*, 248). 'Amongst men', Hobbes states, 'the end of worship is power' – one form among others of the pursuit of individual interest, and nothing more: this is the result of Hobbes' anthropological flattening of divine worship. He immediately tries to rescue his discourse from the censors by allowing that 'God has no ends' and that we worship him out of duty (*L*, 249). However we are instructed in the very practice of worship by natural reason, and reason 'dictates' to us what is 'to be done by the weak to the more potent men'. Again, Hobbes first tactic is to reduce the divine to yet one more form of the natural, establishing a generic equivalency between the actions of a weak man flattering a powerful man and a Christian believer lighting candles in a church.

## *The dependent church*

His second tactic consists in identifying an aspect of worship that requires the intervention of civil authority to remain consistent. He begins by engaging in a differentiation of worship: it consists of 'inward thought . . . of the power and goodness of another' and 'external signes appearing in the Words and Actions of men' (*L*, 248). Among the words and actions directed towards the other, some are natural, and some institutional. Among the institutional, some are honourable or dishonourable according to specific places and times, and others are indifferent. Regardless of this ultimate distinction Hobbes thus disposes of two categories: natural and institutional worship, which he promptly renames 'arbitrary worship'. Differentiating again, arbitrary worship can be either commanded or voluntary (free); that is to say, commanded when the person who is worshipped dictates how this should take place, and free when it is the worshipper who decides (though again constrained by the recipient's approval). Finally there is public and private worship: 'Publique, is the worship that a Common-wealth performeth, as one Person. Private is that which a Private Person exhibiteth' (*L*, 249). He then comes to the simple objective of this entire differentiating procedure: 'Publique, in respect of the whole Commonwealth, is Free; but in respect of Particular men it is not so'. This implies that it is not God but the commonwealth that decides the forms of arbitrary worship, and these forms must hold for the commonwealth as a whole. As such, particular men are not free to decide on the manner in which they will worship God. In short, Hobbes has already announced his position on the necessity of there being one uniform state church. If any reader were ever to think that in such a climate private worship would be preferable since it is free, Hobbes immediately asserts that it is only free when secret. As soon as such private worship takes place in the sight of the multitude, it is subject to restraint in the form of law and other men's opinions. This is how Hobbes criminalizes the practices of religious dissenters, including the New Model Army lay-preachers and iconoclasts brandishing their slogan 'freedom of conscience'. Freedom in your heads alone, retorts Hobbes, and not in the sight of the law.

If reason supplies the forms of natural worship, and the commonwealth the forms of arbitrary worship, there is no place left for the church alone to dictate the form of worship. The natural use of reason alone supplies us with a list of appropriate qualities to attribute to God during worship – such as existence, infinity, eternity, incomprehensibility – and a list of appropriate actions to perform as signs of honour – such as praying, thanksgiving and sacrificing. Once this list is complete, Hobbes enters into a explicit argument for there being a uniform state church based on the necessity of state unity. For the commonwealth to worship as one, the form of worship must thus be uniform (*L*, 252–3). This is not yet to argue for the subordination of ecclesiastical power to civil power, it is rather to simply assume that it has taken place and to draw the consequences: a state church. But it is immediately afterwards, concerning the 'words (and . . . Attributes of God)' used in worship, that Hobbes trumps ecclesiastical by civil power. In any form of worship, natural or arbitrary, public or private words are used to signify the Attributes of God. However, 'words . . . have their signification by agreement, and constitution of men'. Namely, 'those Attributes are to be held significative of Honour, that men intend shall so be' (*L*, 253). Thus it is neither the scriptures, nor the pope, nor a priest, nor the individual believer who decides the signification of words, but rather a plurality of men. But this is to let the cat in through the door, for Hobbes' eyes a plurality of men as incapable of doing anything, even at the level of semantics, unless united. And men are only united through the contract and as commonwealth and through the sovereign. Hence: 'Whatsover may be done by the wills of particular men, where there is no Law but reason, may be done by the Will of the Common-wealth, by Lawes Civill' (L, 253). It immediately follows that it is the sovereign who ordains what signs of honour are to be used by individuals in their public worship.

Civil authority trumps ecclesiastical authority at the level of the meaning of the words the church must use to communicate with its believers. This is subtle but it is not nothing, for such an advantage holds whether or not the church is actually subordinate to the commonwealth. It is a material advantage, since the church must use language as one of its means. The church is thus dependent on the commonwealth to secure the signification of key terms of worship. Politics passes through semantics.

Hobbes employs a second line of attack in arguing for the subordination of spiritual to temporal authority. This time it is a matter of the authority of scripture. Hobbes begins by claiming the very question *'From whence the Scriptures derive their authority'* is native to the church, arising not in philosophy but in the heart of the church, between different congregations. The question also takes the form of *'How wee know [the scriptures] to be the word of God*, or, *Why wee beleeve them to be so'* (L, 267). In his opinion these are badly framed questions since all Christians believe that God is the first author of the scriptures; this much is not under dispute. However, and this is where the problem lies, the question of *how* we know the scriptures to be written by God admits no answer. The only people who know that God authored the scriptures are those who are privy to supernatural revelation, and for Hobbes such revelation cannot be shared. Therefore we do not *know* that the scriptures are the word of God. The real question is thus 'by what authority are [the scriptures] made law' (L, 267). If, as he has already established, divine law is nothing but the natural law found out by reason, then divine law has no need of a separate authority or mechanism of publication and transmission. The exercise of reason is sufficient to discover 'Morall Doctrine', and its authority is immanent. If, on the other hand, it is by God's authority that divine laws are made such, then they need to be both written and published – otherwise someone could disobey the law and employ the excuse of ignorance. But the writing and publication of laws by God is not manifest but problematic, as argued earlier. Unless a person enjoys supernatural revelation she has no way of knowing that a set of laws were authored and promulgated by God. Consequently, Hobbes argues, this person is not under an obligation to obey such laws *except* by the authority of the person whose commands *already* have the force of law. This person, in Hobbes' philosophy, is none other than the sovereign. By what authority are divine laws made law? The answer is thus by the authority of the commonwealth. The authority of the church is thus suboordinate to civil authority.

In the two cases of the meaning of the words used in worship and the origin of the authority of the scriptures Hobbes employs the same strategy to subordinate ecclesiastical to civil authority:

- First, he naturalizes the supposedly divine activity, whether it be worship or the promulgation of laws.

- Second, he isolates a vulnerability, a weak point in church practice – its use of words whose meaning must be fixed – its inability to prove God's authorship of scripture.

- Third, he shows how it is the commonwealth that intervenes to assist and maintain the church across this vulnerability.

- He thus demonstrates the dependency of the church on the commonwealth, and hence the latter's priority.

## *Fusion of church and state*

Curiously, as soon as he concludes the argument described above, Hobbes repeats it, at the end of chapter thirty-three, as if to show more clearly how he catches the advocates of supreme ecclesiastical authority on the horns of a dilemma. But it is not only a rehearsal of the earlier argument since it brings Hobbes' metaphysics of action into play. It runs as follows:

**1** 'If it not be the Legislative Authority of the Commonwealth that giveth [divine laws] the force of laws, it must be some other Authority derived from God.'

2   That other authority must be 'either private or Publique'.

3   'If private, it obliges onely Him, to whom in particular God has been pleased to reveal it.'

4   'If Publique, it is the authority of the *Common-wealth*, or of the *Church*.' (two different institutions)

5   'But the Church, if it be one person, is the same thing with a Common-wealth of Christians.' (equivalence of the two institutions)

6   Hobbes explains these two different names for the same institution as follows: it is 'called a *Common-wealth*, because it consisteth in men united in one person, their Soveraign', whereas it is called 'a *Church*, because it consisteth in Christian men, united in one Christian Soveraign'.

7   'But if the church be not one person, then it hath no authority at all; it can neither command nor do any action at all.' (L, 268)

The crux of this argument lies in the fifth step, the thesis that the church, if it is one person, is the same thing as the commonwealth. It is important to remember that Hobbes' target, which he identifies at the end of the chapter, is not the gaggle of nonconformist protestant congregations, but the Catholic Church. The Pope claims authority over a congregation that ignores frontiers, hence posing a great challenge to Hobbes' theory of sovereignty as specific to a particular physical territory. The argument from the metaphysics of action is that the church must be one person, otherwise it cannot act as one. In the absence of such unity, one has an aggregate of particular individuals acting in parallel – which happens to be a nice anticipation of Locke's redefinition of the church (L, 321). According to Hobbes the only possible way for Christians to unite in one person is through the mechanism of the social contract, whereby all citizens authorize the sovereign to represent them and act in their name. Hence the church is identical with the commonwealth. For this reason, and this is where Hobbes concludes against the Catholic Church, 'if the whole number of Christians be not contained in one common-wealth, they are not one person'.

Hence, 'nor is there a Universall Church that hath any authority over them' (L, 268).[6]

The most contentious claim in this argument is that the only way the church can unite is through the mechanism of the social contract – one is tempted to object that a church can achieve unity through any number of mechanisms such as social conformity, or members contributing to the common good of the congregation, or explicitly recognizing an institutional code of rules. However the church pretends to have authority over its congregation, and authority, for Hobbes, can only issue from one person, the person to whom power has been transferred by means of the contract: the sovereign. The curious result of this argument is that the church, rather than being subordinated to civil authority, appears to be fused with that authority.[7] The leviathan is Christian in every bone of its body. There is one state church, such as the Church of England, and no religious toleration of dissenting congregations.

In taking aim at the established Church of England, Roman Catholicism and the nonconformist congregations, Hobbes comes to the following distribution of powers within a functioning state church and commonwealth. The church is a body united by the sovereign. The church as institution decides what counts as a canonical book of scripture (L, 267). The church as institution decides what is a genuine miracle (L, 306). But when it comes to thorny theological dilemmas, it is the sovereign who decides (L, 253, 307, 311, 372).

## *The critique of divine inspiration – agency cannot be shared*

Hobbes succeeds in subordinating spiritual to temporal authority by means of the question of authority. Yet this question is posed from a reflective standpoint external to the church. For a believer inside the church there is no question that the scriptures are the word of God. Hobbes disqualifies all immanent sources of authority, and in particular that of supernatural revelation. He does so not by arguing there is no such thing, and that all supposed revelations are hallucinations; that would be too extreme. Rather he argues that it is impossible for agency to be shared. This is an essential element in his philosophy of action and it directly informs his critique of the civil war as driven by the enthusiasm of religious activists and the hysterical passion of the multitude. The divine laws revealed to Abraham or Moses cannot apply to any but God's 'prophetic kingdom', that is the Jewish nation alone (L, 246). And since it was a theocracy, any subject after Abraham and Moses would have to simply obey the civil laws (L, 357). But Moses was in an exceptional position, for 'if every man should be obliged, to take for God's law, what particular men, on the pretence of private Inspiration, or Revelation, should obtrude upon him . . . it were impossible that any divine law be acknowledged' (L, 268). Against the spectre of an uncontrollable multiplication of private revelations and the ensuing chaos of conflicting divine laws, Hobbes disqualifies any inspiration or revelation. Indeed he lists it as one of the 'six seditious doctrines' in chapter 29 (L, 223). In his investigation in the subsequent chapter as to the signification of the term 'inspiration' as used in scripture, Hobbes insists that its use is always metaphorical. Literally the term would suggest the infusion of a substance in the communication of God's will, that is to say, the sharing of God's will through a particular individual, a little like Luther's concept of grace. Hobbes notes that inspiration is not immediate but always takes place through a distinct medium of representation, such as dreams or visions (L, 279). And though he does not make this particular point in this chapter, a distinct medium of representation, as he has previously shown, can always be examined for its authenticity.

Hobbes' critique of inspiration as a rival source of authority, and as direct transmission of God's will, would pose no problems if it were not for the history of the church. The early church had to survive within a Roman empire that was hostile to its very existence. If the church had granted all authority to the temporal sovereign, it would have been immediately abolished. How then can Hobbes explain the survival of the early church? Though not a commonwealth the primitive church is at the very least a functioning community if not one of the most dynamic collective bodies in history. It survives without too much regard for questions of legitimacy and the demands of civil authority, at least until Emperor Constantine. And if Hobbes cannot account for the early history of the church, as it emerges within a pagan state, then he is going to have trouble accounting for its modern legitimacy as 'a company of men professing Christian religion'. So he examines the early church and its practices in detail.

## Excommunication, interpretation and conversion: Powers of the early church

Hobbes' investigation of the church takes its most nuanced turn in the chapter entitled 'Of Ecclesiastical Power'. This is by far the longest chapter in the *Leviathan*, signalling the difficulty and importance of its task. At the outset of the chapter, Hobbes admits that the period of the early church is a different case to that after the conversion of kings ($L$, 338). In the early period, ecclesiastical power lay in the hands of the Apostles, not the civil authority. But in what does ecclesiastical power consist? There are three actions performed by the church that lend it the appearance of possessing civil authority: excommunication, deciding the correct interpretation of the scriptures and converting new members. Hobbes examines each of these actions in turn, and in each case he argues that ecclesiastical power is solely the power of teaching ($L$, 343).

Excommunication is arguably the most visible and dramatic exercise of ecclesiastical power, signifying the expulsion of a former believer from 'the place of divine service' ($L$, 349). For this reason Hobbes is immediately concerned to limit its function and scope. In the time of the Apostles, before the church was joined to civil power, the use of excommunication was merely to avoid the faithful having to eat or keep company with the excommunicated. Its effect was neither terror nor material damages. Without the help of the civil authorities the church could not even prevent the excommunicated from entering their places of worship ($L$, 350). Excommunication only had effect at the level of belief: only those who were faithful and believed in the second coming would be cowed by such punishment, for it condemned them to a life without forgiveness for their sins, and thus to hell. Hobbes then reduces the scope of excommunication by restricting it solely to those dissenters who deny the fundamental teaching of Christianity – that Jesus is the saviour ($L$, 351). This is say that only non-Christians can be excommunicated from the Christian church. The function of excommunication is thus not to stamp out divergent theological opinions, and nor is it to settle institutional conflicts: only members of a congregation can be excommunicated, not an congregation itself (*L*, 352). The reason for somebody's excommunication is always sin, the committing of injustice. As such the true function of excommunication is to act as a deterrent among the faithful. Hobbes concludes his analysis of excommunication by relating it back to the essence of ecclesiastical power: pedagogy. Excommunication is the most extreme disciplinary measure exercised by a teacher, abandoning his pupil (*L*, 353).

The second activity incarnating authority is the interpretation of the scripture. In the time of Moses, the question was simple. He reigned over a theocracy, the prophet and the sovereign were one and the same person, and so the sovereign decided all questions of interpretation (*L*, 356–7). In the time of the Apostles, the question became more complicated. Hobbes allows that before Constantine, not only was each Apostle his own interpreter, but every convert in turn was in a position to make an apostle's writings canonical (*L*, 355, 359). St Paul preached by means of persuasion and reasoning, he testified to the life of Christ without any institutional guarantee. The Apostles, Hobbes argues, never taught anything concerning their title to preach, they simply taught the gospel. When difficulties arose between different teachings, the Apostles came together, took a decision and then wrote letters to the churches informing them of that decision. But this is where a possible objection arises: why would the Apostles gather in councils and synods to decide the interpretation of the scripture if no one were obliged to obey their decisions? These decisions carried no political obligation. Hobbes' solution is to argue that these counsels and synods issued not laws or commands, but 'Precepts' and 'Invitations' (*L*, 361). Any rules offered, on the basis of the New Testament, cannot be 'but Counsell and advice' (*L*, 360).

What then of the most powerful subjective experience that occurs through the action of the church: conversion? Hobbes spends one page alone dismissing the claim to authority found in the practice of conversion. He points out that in the conversion of gentiles it cannot be a question of the authority of the scriptures since the subject does not yet believe that they are the word of God. Nor can conversion be based on the authority of the Apostles as official interpreters of the scriptures, as argued earlier. Conversion as a practice consists solely in transmitting the belief that Jesus is the Christ, the saviour who was resurrected from the dead and will reign over the kingdom to come. This belief is transmitted first through the rational confutation of a gentile's idolatry, and subsequently by testimony to the life of Jesus, which persuades the gentile to faith (*L*, 355). In such an experience there is no obligation to consider the Apostles' interpretation of scripture as law. The conversion leaves intact the subject's obligation to obey the laws of his sovereign. During the period of the early church the New Testament was not even published as a single volume. In this situation, 'Every of the evangelists was interpreter of his own Gospel; and every Apostle of his own Epistle' (*L*, 355). It was Jesus who directed his disciples to interpret the existing canonical scriptures themselves for proof of his being Christ. They had no need, in his eyes, to refer to the official interpretations of the established priests.

The practice of teaching and the practice of conversion were thus one. There were many teachers, and their teaching obliged no one, leaving each free to interpret the scripture in his own guise. Controversies between different teachings did occur, but they were collectively mediated and resolved through deliberation and decision. These decisions were not binding. What is a practice that brings about subjective change without reference to an external or institutional authority, without obligation? It is an action: action, as Aristotle defines it, is what changes the subject. And yet in the seventeenth-century metaphysics of action, through mechanism and nominalism, it is no longer substances that act but institutions. Here in the examination of the institution par excellence, Hobbes, the grand absolutist, admits the existence of coherent action outside, or before, the commonwealth. The name of this action is teaching. The force of teaching is such that when a commonwealth is instituted and its subjects are Christian it must watch over and control the doctrines fit for public education. Teaching affects men's opinions, and 'mens actions are derived from the opinions they have of the Good, or Evil, which from those actions redound unto themselves' (*L*, 372). To ignore the circulation of opinions spread by teaching is thus to ignore a possible cause of rebellion against the sovereign.

Perhaps this exceptional form of pedagogical action is confined to the Christian church in the time of the Apostles, and perhaps its scope does not surpass conversion and worship. If ecclesiastical authority is submitted to the sovereign in the time of Christian commonwealths, from Constantine onwards, this kind of action should not take a significant place. And yet the problem cannot be circumscribed so easily.

## *The figure of disjoint action*

The early Christian church was not authorized and deputized by the Roman civil authority. Rather it was seen as seditious and as a menace to the stability of the Roman empire. Hobbes recognizes the illegality of the early church in the form of the following problem: how can a believer obey both God and the civil authority when the two are in conflict? In other words, what may a Christian do to avoid persecution by authorities for not obeying the law? These questions emerge in the context of Hobbes' argument that Christ left the ministers of his church with no legal power or authority. He cites Paul: 'Servants obey in all things your Masters according to the flesh; and not with eye-service, as men-pleasers, but in singlenesse of heart, as fearing the Lord' (Col. 3.22), and then comments 'This is spoken to them whose Masters were Infidells; and yet they are bidden to obey them *in all things*' (L, 343). A Christian subject in an infidel country such as the Roman Empire is thus bidden to obey the sovereign. What then happens if there is a conflict between the pagan civil authority and Christian divine law? For instance: 'what if a king . . . forbid us to believe in Christ? . . . What if we be commanded by our Lawfull Prince to say with our tongue, what we believe not; must we obey such command?' (L, 344). Hobbes' answer is double. On the one hand, faith and belief are beyond the reach of the law and the sovereign's commands. Faith can neither be created on command nor dissolved on command (L, 390). On the other hand, 'Profession with the tongue is but an external thing, and no more than any other gesture whereby we signify our obedience' (L, 344). In this, Hobbes bases himself on 2 Kgs 5.17 where the Prophet Elisha pardoned the Syrian, Naaman, for the practice of a pagan external cult: 'In this thing pardon thy servant, that when my master goes into the house of Rimmon [a pagan God] to worship there, and he leaneth on my hand, and I bow myselfe in the house of Rimmon'. Hobbes comments, 'a Christian, holding firmly in his heart the Faith of Christ, has the same liberty . . . allowed to Namaan the Syrian' (L, 344). Here within the practice of worship and obedience to the sovereign a Lutherian distinction is created between two realms: the external realm of gestures and speech, and the internal realm of the heart. In the situation of a Christian believer having to obey a pagan law, it is possible for these two domains to become disjunct; that is to say, an individual may perform an act of worship in which she does not believe. At the same time in her heart she engages in an alternative and properly Christian form of worship, thus 'holding firmly' to her faith. The action of the believer is thus split into two; there is the external action, the performance of conforming to law, which does not meet with 'inward approbation', and then there is the internal action of faith.

It is the external action, the performance of conformity, that most clearly matches Luther's category of the empty work, yet its contents are inverted. In the hypocrites' action, the external form of the work is Christian, but the inward intention is unchristian, aiming solely at temporal gain. In the Christian immigrant's action the external form is unchristian, being pagan, yet the inward intention remains Christian. Like Luther's conception of faith, the true act of worship is born in the heart, and it is contrasted to a realm of empty ceremony and indifferent forms. Unlike Luther's faith it remains inward and does not and cannot give rise to emanating works. This inward faith is divorced from the external realm. It is incarnated not only in the Christian immigrant in a pagan land, but also in other split figures such as the dissenter-subject, or the Muslim immigrant in a Christian land. The investigation of ecclesiastical power thus adds an element to the seventeenth-century metaphysics of action; the figure of split or rather *disjoint action*, a crucial condition of the stability and uniformity of the commonwealth.

Hobbes then frames one last objection to his position, and it appears to be devastating. Christ says, 'Whosoever denyeth me before men, I will deny him before my Father who is in Heaven' (Mt. 10.32–33). This is where the figure of disjoint action is shown to imply a separation of agencies. Hobbes' response is to argue that any action a subject performs in obedience to his sovereign yet against his faith in Christ is to be attributed to that sovereign, and not to the subject:

> Whatsoever a subject . . . is compelled to in obedience to his Soveraign, and doth it not in order to his own mind, but in order to the laws of his country, that action is not his but his

soveraigns; nor is it he that in this case denyeth Christ before men, but his Governour, and the law of his countrey. (*L*, 344, cf. 389)

This position amounts to extending the agency of the sovereign over the entire body of citizens; any action in conformity with the law – and not just those of worship – is thus performed not by the individual citizen but by the sovereign. Later on, he clarifies 'the Subject . . . is in that case, but an Instrument, without any motion of his owne at all' (*L*, 389). As set out in detail in the following chapter, this is Hobbes' answer to the first query of the question of political action – who can act? The sovereign alone can act, and the sovereign can act through individual subjects, who are thus divested of their agency in the case of lawful actions. This is the first part of what we will come to know as the Hobbesian chiasmus of agency.

The doctrine of disjoint action holds not only of Christian immigrants in pagan countries, but also of pagans and religious dissenters within a Christian commonwealth. Hobbes imagines a third objection to this doctrine whereby it is accused of being 'repugnant to true, and unfeigned Christianity' (*L*, 344). He answers this accusation by asking what should we expect of a subject of a Christian commonwealth who is a believer in Islam. If the latter is commanded by his sovereign to attend service at a Christian church on pain of death what should he do? Disobey his sovereign and suffer death or externally conform and internally remain true to his own religion? To counsel the former course of action, Hobbes argues, is to open the door to all private men disobeying civil authority in matter of religion. In the interest of public order, Hobbes thus opens the possibility of internal dissent, or private paganism.

What is the consistency of the internal action of faith, of the heart? In the chapter on ecclesiastical power, when distinguishing between the laws of the commonwealth and the rules or counsel and advice proffered by the Apostles, Hobbes asserts: 'Internall Faith is in its own nature invisible, and consequently exempted from all humane jurisdiction' (*L*, 360). Not only is it exempt, but it is literally absent from the domain of the law. A Christian sovereign cannot oblige a subject to believe (*L*, 389). The law can produce only forced actions (*L*, 390). Yet this is to proffer but a negative outline of consistency, where internal faith simply marks the limit of the law. Hobbes does award some positive consistency, or thickness, to internal faith by naming its author, and in doing so he follows Luther's doctrine of grace: 'Beleef, and Unbeleef never follow mens commands. Faith is a gift of God, which man can neither give, nor take away by promises of rewards, or menaces of torture' (*L*, 343). Faith is an action: the action of believing Jesus is the Christ, the action of inward worship and the action of obeying the divine laws. And yet, though faith is an action undertaken by a believer, since it is a gift of God, the individual believer alone cannot take full responsibility for it, but shares his agency with that of God. What is beyond the sovereign's power is ultimately both private and more-than-private, being shared with a transcendent outside.

Hobbes is the great distributor of discrete agency: within the commonwealth, the sovereign acts alone; within the state of nature, individual subjects act alone; in the passage to the social contract, individuals make their rational calculations alone. However here, in his treatment of faith, he does admit the sharing of agency – with the caveat that it occurs only within a restricted domain that is divorced from the realm of public action. Conscience can be joined to the public realm, but solely in cases where the believer is orthodox, resides in a Christian commonwealth, and that commonwealth has instituted a uniform code of worship. In such a situation alone can the believer-citizens translate their inner faith into public worship. But surely, one could object, this is most often the case in those polities aimed at in Hobbes' *Leviathan*? It so happens that this is most definitely *not* the case in the closest possible example of the workings of a commonwealth – contemporary England. England is riven with religious dissent.

In different passages, the inward realm of faith as distinct from external actions goes under different names. In chapter 43, Hobbes re-examines, for the fourth time, the question of civil obedience in a conflict between divine and civil law. This time his tactic is to reduce to an absolute minimum the article of faith to which a Christian must remain true on pain of forfeiting eternal salvation – that article is 'Jesus is the Christ'. If it is possible to obey the sovereign's command without denying this article, then it is just to do so. To hold to this article of faith, Hobbes argues, it is sufficient to have the 'will to obey him' or an 'Endeavour to fulfil the law' (*L*, 404, 413). For it is the case that 'God accepts in all our actions the will for the deed'; that is, he 'accepteth it for the performance is selfe' (*sic*; *L*, 413). There where the domain of the sovereign ends, solely having power over mens' external actions, begins the exclusive knowledge of God. Apart from the individual in question, there is but one access to the inward action of faith, and that is God's, for 'God knoweth the heart' (*L*, 378, 348). This position reconciling split obedience has the curious consequence of turning individual conscience into a form of absolute, into a form of the thing-in-itself. In the individual's rational calculation that leads to the social contract, private conscience is placed as the foundation of the sovereign power. Yet conscience is not accessible to that sovereign power. Only the mind of God enjoys access to the heart.

## Conscience and its vicissitudes

It is in his early work, *On the Citizen*, when arguing for the identity of divine law and natural law, that Hobbes gives the most contemporary name to this inward realm of the heart: 'the laws of nature are a matter of *conscience*, i.e. the just man is the man who makes every effort to fulfil them' and 'God accepts willing for doing in good and bad actions alike' (*C*, 64–5; my italics). At the end of the *Leviathan* he confirms the use of this term in his doctrine of disjoint action. While listing the errors of vain philosophy that lead to the kingdom of darkness, he states it is an error to extend the law, which is the rule of actions only, to the very thoughts and consciences of men by examination. To do such is to embark upon an inquisition (*L*, 471).

But what is conscience for Hobbes? It is worth tracing the fortune of this term in the *Leviathan*. In chapter eight, that part of Hobbes' anthropology devoted to 'the Ends or Resolutions of Discourse', the original meaning of conscience is given. When two or more individuals know the same fact then they are said 'to be conscious of it, one to another': in short 'conscience' names the state of shared knowledge that is recognized as such (*L*, 48). It is for this reason, Hobbes allows, that it 'ever will be reputed a very Evill act, for any man to speak against his *Conscience*; or to corrupt, or force another to do so'. Consequently it has been entirely legitimate and acceptable to listen to what is called the 'plea of conscience'. The problem is that the meaning of the term has degraded to mere metaphor, in which it simply refers to an individual's secret facts and thoughts, and then still further to a distorted sense wherein

> men, vehemently in love with their own new opinions, (though never so absurd), and obstinately bent to maintain them, gave those their opinions that reverenced name of conscience, as if they would have it seem unlawfull, to change or speak against them; and so pretend to know they are true, when they know at most, but that they think so. (*L*, 48)

The degradation of the meaning of conscience is epistemological; the term no longer refers to knowledge of fact but to mere opinion. It is also social, 'conscience' no longer signifying collective but individual knowledge. It is precisely the degraded and contemporary use of the term conscience that concerns Hobbes when he places second in his list of seditious doctrines: '*whatsoever a man does against his Conscience, is Sin*' (*L*, 223). Given that a man's conscience is his judgement, this thesis is a simple variant of the first seditious doctrine that states that every individual is judge of good and evil. Speaking of sedition, it happens to be the case that conscience is a key political vocable in the English revolution. It can be found in the Leveller tracts, the *Solemn Engagement*, the *Case of the Army Truly Stated* and in the Putney Debates. Colonel Rainborough, the Leveller-agitator, names conscience along with freedom as the grounds of his action (*PL*, 32).

The term occurs again much later in the *Leviathan*, in the complicated chapter on ecclesiastical power. When minimizing the material consequences of excommunication, Hobbes admits that Paul does instruct us to reject heretics, but he claims Paul is simply advising the faithful not to meddle in theological debates; that is, 'not to make new articles of faith, by determining every small controversy, which oblige men to a needless burden of *conscience*, or provoke them to break the union of the Church' (*L*, 351; my italics). Here conscience is identified as not just the place of the single central tenet 'Jesus is the Christ' but also of an accumulation of derived and minor beliefs. It is the finitude of conscience, its limits that determine two possible outcomes for an exaggerated theological multiplication of articles of faith: either an excessive burden for conscience, or a split in the church. Either there is too much to believe in; or an individual decides to believe in one set of articles to the exclusion of any others, and then takes this exclusivity to be essential, thus initiating conflict. It is not Peter but *conscience* that is the rock of the church, in that it is the site of the central tenet 'Jesus is the Christ'. It is this belief that Christ identifies as the rock when handing over the keys. Yet conscience, being finite, is fragile. And yet it is also a force pregnant with the power to divide the church. It would be wise to treat it carefully.

## *Are 'we' all primitive Christians at heart?*

Treat conscience with care: this is precisely what Hobbes advocates in his analysis of the the church in England and how it might go forward. In the last chapter of the *Leviathan*, he embarks on a rapid history of the relation between conscience and the Roman Catholic Church's ascent to temporal power. In the time of the Apostles, the conscience of the Christian believer was free (L, 479). The first 'knot' tying conscience into a form of obligation occurred when the Presbyters assembled and issued decrees on the nature of Christian faith, excommunicating those who disobeyed. The second knot was tied when a hierarchical level was added to the church, the presbyters of the chief city of a region naming themselves 'bishops' and extending their jurisdiction over the other presbyters of the provinces. The third knot was tied with the addition of a final level to the hierarchy, with the Bishop of Rome arrogating to himself, by virtue of the status of the imperial city, power over all other bishops, naming himself Pope. But for Hobbes history does not proceed from better to worse, as it does for Plato: what is built up can come down, and thus 'the *Analysis*, or *Resolution* is by the same way; but beginneth with the knot last tied' (L, 479). One senses Hobbes' delight as he recounts the progressive untying of the three knots: first Queen Elizabeth dissolved the 'power of the Popes' in England. Second, 'the Presbyterians lately in England obtained the putting down of Episcopacy' – note it is a little rich to attribute this action to the Presbyterians, since it was rather the action of Rump Parliament, from which most political Presbyterians had been purged (L, 479). Nevertheless the third and final knot was undone when 'the Power was also taken from the

Presbyterians' (*L*, 479). Given the analysis above of the exceptional status of teaching in the early church compared to action under a Christian commonwealth, the astonishing result of this untying of knots is that:

> We are reduced to the Independency of the Primitive Christians to follow Paul, or Cephas, or Apollos, every man as he liketh best: Which, if it be without contention, and without measuring the Doctrine of Christ, by our affection to the Person of his Minister . . . *perhaps is the best*. (*L*, 479–80; my italics)

These are already two heavy caveats: the condition of the primitive church is the best if it does not lead to conflict, and if believers do not follow divergent teachings on the basis of a cult of personality. But then Hobbes gives his reasons why this is a preferable state of affairs. Given his massive critique of the Roman Catholic Church as the 'Kingdom of Darkness', such reasons may seem superfluous – it is evident that the 'Independency' of the early Christians is preferable to that of subjects who are led to believe that the Pope has supreme temporal power. But Hobbes has to give extra reasons for this anomalous and exceptional status of the Christian religion in England. The position he has argued for so far in the *Leviathan* is not that of a complete absence of hierarchical organization. Rather, he advocates a state church, with uniform code of worship; just as Queen Elizabeth sought to establish with the Act of Uniformity. A state church is a far cry from each individual following 'Paul, or Cephas, or Apollos, every man as he liketh best'. But the outcome of the English revolution has confronted Hobbes with a different situation. As I explain in the following chapter, the Engagement Controversy of 1650–2 concerned whether former royalists should swear an oath of loyalty to the newly established republic. The Hobbesian position in this debate was that one should accept the de facto sovereign. Perhaps, for Hobbes, one should also accept the de facto church.

But there is a significant difference between *accepting* the actual situation and *granting* that it might be the best possible situation. Of the two reasons Hobbes gives for the present situation of the church being the best, the first concerns the treatment of conscience: 'there ought to be no Power over the consciences of men, but of the Word itself, working faith in every one, not always according to the purpose of them that plant and water, but of God himself, that giveth the increase' (*L*, 480). Note that from the perspective of the church, of those who plant and water, the direction and growth of faith is unpredictable. Hobbes' use of the parable of sowing not only identifies the dynamism of the church's present existence, but it also shifts the register of his discourse from evaluation to prescription, to pointing the way forward. Due to historical events the church finds itself in the exceptional position of existing according to a correct understanding of the singularity of its power: the power of teaching. Here fact and value coincide: the *actual* situation of the church after the English revolution, deprived of all institutional hierarchy, is the *best*. Hobbes is not a critic but an apologist for the contemporary church. To recommend that this status be maintained is also to recommend that the church understand and accept its current 'primitive' state as the best. This would imply a thorough transformation of its institutional beliefs and practices. Hobbes is in great danger of losing his historical reputation as the grand atheist: not only is he an apologist but here he becomes reformer of the church.

The second reason for the current state of the church being the best concerns the believer's use of reason with regard to her own salvation. 'It is unreasonable in them', explains Hobbes,

> who teach there is so much danger in every little Errour, to require of a man endued with reason of his own, to follow the Reason of any other man, or of the most voices of many other men; Which is little better, than to venture his Salvation at crosse and pile. (*L*, 481)

'Crosse and pile' means 'heads and tails'; it refers to a game in which players bet money on the toss of a coin. It is unusual for Hobbes to speak of the matter of faith and salvation in terms of reason, but as Locke shows in the *Letter on Toleration*, it is perfectly coherent with reason as natural law to calculate salvation as the maximum possible benefit an individual can secure. The subject revealed by the current church in England is the subject of the primitive church, devoid of hierachy, conferring the business of his salvation to no superior. This subject is thus the same as the subject of the state of nature, who reasons according to natural law so as to secure his own protection. As Hobbes' analysis of the workings of the passions within society shows, at the beginning of *On the Citizen*, the state of nature is contemporaneous with the commonwealth. It is neither chronologically prior to the covenant, nor a simple logical presupposition as some interpreters of social contract theory would have it. As such, the subject of the state of nature, which is the subject of the primitive church, is the same as the subject of the Leviathan.

## *Evacuation of the 'who': Disarticulating conscience and commonwealth*

It is this operational identity between the subject of the primitive church and all subjects within the commonwealth that is confirmed in the final passage in which the term 'conscience' is used. The 'Review and Conclusion' to the *Leviathan* can be read as addressed at least in part to Hobbes' fellow countrymen caught up in the engagement controversy; that is to say, to former royalists faced with the new republic's demand that they swear an oath of allegiance. To require approbation of past actions, he advises, is to sow a seed of the destruction of the state 'when there is scarce a common-wealth in the world whose beginnings can in conscience be justified' (*L*, 486). It is appropriate to take this proposition at the letter: in conscience, there is scarce a commonwealth in the world whose *beginnings* can be justified. This sentence is famous but its interpretation is hard, for every commonwealth formed through the social contract is absolutely justifiable in conscience according to Hobbes' own doctrine: such is the individual's calculation of the utility of the existence of the commonwealth, securing public safety. And so here Hobbes is not referring to his own doctrine but aiming at historical accounts of the 'beginnings' of commonwealths, referring, for instance, to William's conquest of Saxon England. For Hobbes there can be *no historical* articulation between conscience and commonwealth at the beginnings of a state. That is to say, if one made a historical claim that the right to rule is founded on the righteousness of the original war that secured sovereignty, then one is giving license to every 'successful Rebellion that Ambition shall at any time after raise against them, and their Successors' (*L*, 486). For Hobbes the right to rule depends on possession of power, not on how power was acquired.

As long as one holds on to power then one has the right to power. Shades of Thrasymachus again. But Thrasymachus' question to Socrates, we remember, is who? Who says what is justice? Who is the ruling authority in the city? And Hobbes, with this doctrine of *post factum* justification, evacuates the place of the 'who'. If no line of kings can claim divine right, or right by virtue of victory in a just war of conquest, if no popular assembly can claim right by virtue of bringing a revolution to its endpoint, then it is *possession alone* that grounds right to rule, and anyone through the contingency of historical events could happen to be in possession of power – such as the Rump Parliament sitting in the House of Commons on the date of publication of the *Leviathan*.

Again, to claim to historically justify the origins of rule in a righteous war is indeed to articulate conscience and the commonwealth in the beginnings, but such a discourse is impossible for Hobbes from the standpoint of an existing government for it would legitimate any future successful rebellion. This argument requires three extra steps to attain clarity.

1  If a claim basing the right to rule on a just war opens the door to *any* armed rebellion claiming justice, then from Hobbes' standpoint there must be absolutely no distinction between such claims; it is not the case that some are justified and others mistaken. Yet, from the standpoint of particular regimes that do claim their right to rule on the basis of a just war, it is precisely such a historical claim that endows the regime with individuality.

2  According to Hobbes' civil philosophy, the right to rule is based on the laws of nature through the creation of the social contract (*L*, 255). However this theory provides for the legitimacy of government in general, not for that of a particular government. The particularity of a regime can be taken into account by Hobbes' theory in terms of its relative soundness: does it allow or does it censure the seditious doctrines that tend to weaken a commonwealth? But such an analysis of the 'infirmities' or soundness of a commonwealth does not historically individuate it, it simply places the regime on a scale of evaluation ranging from 'solid' to 'on the point of dissolution'.

3  If Hobbes says the right to rule is based on possession of power, then any rebellion, *once* successful, is legitimate according to his own doctrine. This certainly appears to be the case with his endorsement of the Rump Parliament's rule over the newly established Commonwealth of England.[8]

The fundamental consequence of this argument is that the 'who' of power is evacuated in favour of the efficacy of power. It does not matter who is the ruling authority, whether monarch or legislative assembly, whether an individual with a centuries long lineage or an assembly democratically elected by a popular army. What matters is the solidity of the possession of power: the mutual equivalence of protection and obligation.

Hobbes position is 'there is scarce a common-wealth in the world whose beginnings can in conscience be justified'. This statement identifies a disjunction between conscience and the beginnings of the state, which is no less than a disjunction between conscience and history. The sum of these disjunctions is an evacuation of the 'who' of power; that 'who' cannot be individuated by a historical process. In the engagement controversy, the Hobbesian position on history becomes clear: conscience thus suffers no historical tie to a particular state, no loyalty. An individual's only concern with the state is expressed in the rational calculation of her own safety. If, at a particular historical conjuncture, a sovereign is no longer capable of assuring public safety – and this is the grand fragility of the leviathan – then an individual, in all conscience, *could* change her mind about the validity of this particular social contract. As such, no individual is exclusively joined to any commonwealth in particular. It is thus not just the citizen-dissident, but *all* subjects who are fundamentally split from the institution. Hobbes thinks to reinforce the leviathan by fusing state and church, rendering their respective foundations of natural law and divine law indistinct, but in doing so he fuses the subject of the state with the subject of the church. Unfortunately for the stability of the commonwealth, this move amounts to admitting a subject whose conscience is not only inaccessible to the sovereign, but also forms a kind of fifth column, in that it shares agency with God.

What is an institution in Hobbes? An ahistorical state church.

The consistency of an ahistorical state church depends on the conscience of individuals, from whom it is disjoint. The disjunction of the inner realm of conscience from the outer realm of the law and public action may appear to restitute Luther's distinction between the heart and the law, faith and works. Yet Luther manages to rearticulate faith and action in his concept of the emanating work. In contrast, the Hobbesian institution, perpetually severed from the individual consciences at its base, can never be an emanating work.

## Locke on religious toleration: The investment model of faith

No philosophers could appear more opposed on the seventeenth-century question of religion than Hobbes and Locke. Faced with the wars of religion that devastated Europe and the religious factionalism that contributed to the English Civil War, Hobbes advocates the fusion of church and state and the imposition of a uniform code of worship. Locke, on the other hand, advocates religious toleration and the multiplication of liberal churches. And yet, if their investigations into the ecclesiastical institution are followed long enough, the same figure of action emerges: disjoint action, with conscience split from external performance. Despite all expectations, Hobbes' enquiry into citizen-dissidents, and Locke's reimagining of the church as liberal association, give rise to exactly the same structure of the subject: split from its public manifestation, free of all essential ties to an institution.

Midway through his career Locke changed his mind on the question of religious worship: from counselling strict uniformity to advocating tolerance. This change in orientation is well-known and documented in the scholarly literature.[9] Initially, in both a letter to a correspondent and in his *Two Tracts on Government*, published in 1660–1, Locke wrote against toleration as an impracticable policy, given the play of forces and interests in the political arena, a policy that would lead to civil war.[10] In 1667, Locke wrote *An Essay Concerning Toleration*.[11] In this text he champions religious toleration and changes his analysis of worship. The text that will concern us here is the mature expression of his views: *A Letter concerning Toleration*, written in the winter of 1685–6, published in Latin in Gouda, Holland, in 1689, and then immediately translated into English and published by William Popple without Locke's assistance in the same year.

At the outset of this text Locke's target is the practice of religious persecution. In particular he aims at its use by established churches enjoying a position of hegemony. Persecution takes the form of the 'exercising of compulsive force', of the 'persecut[ing], torment[ing], destroy[ing] and kill[ing] of other men upon pretence of Religion' and the 'exercise of all manner of cruelties'. More specifically the practices at which Locke takes aim include 'depriv[ing] [men] of their estate, maim[ing] them with corporal punishments, starv[ing] and torment[ing] them in noisom Prisons, and in the end even tak[ing] away their Lives' (*LT*, 23–4). The ostensive aim of these practices, their raison d'être, is to stamp out and dissuade 'conscientous Dissent from Ecclesiastical Decisions, or Separation from Publick Worship' (*LT*, 24). Ultimately the fantastical end of such practices is the 'extirpation of sects', which consists in converting heretics on the pain of torture to the practice of the orthodox cult, and forcing the heterodox to publically adopt a faith in which they do not believe (*LT*, 25).

## *The analysis of persecution*

Locke makes four arguments in his critique of religious persecution: the argument from *hypocrisy*, the argument from *charity*, the argument from *uncertainty* and finally the argument from *dominion*. The argument from hypocrisy rehearses the lines of Luther's critique of empty works. Those who engage in religious persecution are all the more zealous in their pursuit of heresy, and the salvation of others, as they are blind to their own sins and the sins of their own congregation. They forget the primary duty of a Christian, which is not to enforce conformity to 'an external Pomp' but rather to pursue virtue and eradicate vice from their own lives. Here Locke channels Christ's teaching 'let he who is without sin be the first to cast stones' (Jn 8.7). As in any argument from hypocrisy it is incumbent upon the critic to offer a definition of true rather than feigned virtue. Locke argues that the goal of true religion is to order men's lives according to the rules of piety.

The essence of Christianity lies in the effort to lead a moral life, not in the establishment of orthodoxy.

The argument from charity relies on the authority of the Apostles, who teach that when faith acts, it is with love, not with the sword. To be a Christian is to exercise charity and good will towards others, even to those who are not Christians. And yet it is questionable whether those who practise religious persecution do it out of a spirit of 'Friendship and Kindness'. If such was their spirit, Locke claims, they would spontaneously devote their energies first and foremostly to the eradication of their own sins. And yet they do not, as established by the argument from hypocrisy. Ergo the practice of persecution, though supposedly advancing the cause of the church, is unchristian. Again, as with the argument from hypocrisy, this argument indicates by implication the true manner in which a Christian church watches over the faith and spreads the gospel: through love and teaching; 'prepared with the Gospel of Peace, and with the exemplary Holiness of their Conversation' (L, 25). Here Locke's analysis is hardly distinguishable from Hobbes' examination of ecclesiastical power in the primitive church.

The argument from uncertainty makes a brief appearance and it is the odd one out, relying on an approach familiar to us from the *Essay concerning Human Understanding* rather than from Locke's political works. The point is simple: what is pursued in persecution are 'convictions of conscience' concerning both articles of faith and ceremonies. However, given the sources we have concerning faith and ceremony, we will not know which among these 'nice and intricate matters, that exceed the capacity of ordinary Understandings' are correct until the day of judgement (L, 24). Locke writes:

> Which of the Parties contending about these things is in the right, which of them is guilty of Schism or Heresie, whether those that domineer, or those who suffer, will then at last be manifest, when the cause of their Separation comes to be judged of. (L, 24)

The final adjudication of disputes in which all causes are manifest occurs, of course, on the day of judgement. Until that day, given our mortal and 'ordinary understanding', we should suspend judgement. In the *Essay*, Locke makes the same argument without any hyperbolic reference to the Last Judgement:

> The necessity of believing, without Knowledge, in this fleeting state of Action and Blindness we are in, should make us more busy and careful to inform our selves than constrain others. At least those, who have not thoroughly examined to the bottom of their own Tenets, must confess, they are unfit to prescribe to others; and are unreasonable in imposing that as a Truth on other Men's Belief, which they themselves have not searched into, nor weighed the Arguments of Probability, on which they should receive or reject it. (*EHU*, IV, 16, §4)

In the place of divine judgement we find another hyperbolic reference, to the work of the Cartesian philosopher, who 'examin[es] to the bottom of [his] own Tenets'. Locke suggests that only if such an examination were complete and successful would it be permissible to impose one's beliefs on others as true. Failing the manifest exercise of divine judgement, failing the completion of the Cartesian philosopher's examination, we should 'confess our unfitness' to judge and condemn other people's beliefs. This argument, unlike those from hypocrisy and charity that base themselves on scripture, has a negative ground: the absence of certain knowledge. It risks scepticism in circumscribing humans within a 'fleeting state of Action and Blindness', and the subjective position it suggests, one of doubt, one of weighing arguments, is not in accordance with the confident denunciation of persecution in the name of true Christianity (*EHU*, IV, 16, §4).

One phrase in the passage cited earlier identifies the fundamentally political stakes of religious persecution, and thus anticipates the fourth argument: in any conflict over religious orthodoxy the two combatants can always be analysed into the categories of 'those who domineer, or those who suffer'. This introduces the fourth argument, the argument from dominion. It states that if the arguments from hypocrisy and charity are correct, and if the motivations behind the practice of persecution do not belong to Christian virtue, then they most definitely belong to the pursuit of earthly power. Here Locke echoes Luther's condemnation of the hypocrite's empty works. The use of force and the sword in the policing of orthodoxy may well generate a 'numerous Assembly joined in the same Profession' but it is 'altogether incredible' to pretend that such will be 'a truly Christian church' (*L*, 25). In other words, force can succeed in producing and securing a collective body, however, it cannot assure the Christian identity of that body through faith. It misses its target.

Locke's four arguments thus present us with a diagnosis of failure: the failure of a certain form of political action, religious persecution. Religious persecution fails to achieve its ostensive goal, which is to prevent the 'divorce of sects' and to strengthen and expand a united Christian church. It fails because it uses the wrong means: force and compulsion rather than preaching. It fails because it sets to work the wrong agent: the civil magistrate and not the pastors of the church. Finally, it fails because the wrong intentions are at work: not the desire to spread the faith, but the desire to enjoy dominion and empire. Yet at the same time, according to Locke's fourth argument, religious persecution does succeed in securing its latent goal: reinforcing the power of a dominant faction. Yet if such domination is bought at the price of perpetual civil conflict leading to political instability and chaos as seen in the Thirty Years War that devastated Europe in the first half of the seventeenth century, then it leads to disaster. Such a disaster would be imputed to the government for failing in its primary duty to secure public safety.

However, in the *Letter* the main problem is not civil conflict animated by religious motivations – that is rather Hobbes' problem, and also Locke's in the *Essay concerning Human Understanding*. In the *Letter* the most evident problem is the unchristian practice of religious persecution. Locke's solution occupies the opposite end of the spectrum to that of Hobbes: he does not fuse but separates church and state. Rather than one state church, he advocates a plurality of tolerant churches. Rather than having the sovereign decide the forms of public worship he recommends that this matter be left to each individual church to determine. And yet despite Locke's radical difference from Hobbes, the same figure of disjoint action reoccurs.

## *The separation of civil and religious authority*

Locke separates church from state by distinguishing their respective objects, their powers and their agents. The object of the state is to secure the civil interests of its subjects, namely their life, liberty and property. The power of the state is exercised through the civil laws and their enforcement in the administration of punishment. The privileged agent of the state is neither the executive nor the legislative branches of government but the local magistrate. The object of the church, on the other hand, is the 'public worship of God' (*LT*, 28, 30). The power of the church is not a punitive power. It does dispose of specific laws, stipulating such matters as the time and place of assembly, distinction of officers and rules for the admission and expulsion of members (*LT*, 28). Yet, for the enforcement of such laws, it may use neither compulsion nor force. To keep its members mindful of their duty a church may employ 'Exhortations, Admonitions and Advices' alone. If all else fails and a stubborn and recalcitrant member persists in breaking the church rules, then he should be 'cast out and separated from the Society' (*LT*, 28). Excommunication thus remains the ultimate exercise of ecclesiastical power, yet it cannot touch a person's body or estate, just as in Hobbes' analysis (*LT*, 30).

But what is the agent of the church? Here an asymmetry appears in Locke's treatment of church and state. There is an ecclesiastical equivalent to the civil magistrate: Locke speaks briefly of 'Bishops, Priests, Presbyters [and] Ministers' when he details the clergy's duty of toleration. He exhorts the clergy to spread the message of charity and toleration as duties proper to any Christian. Yet the bulk of his arguments concerning the inadequacy of civil magistrates to act on religious matters foreground another agent of the church: the individual believer. In contrasting the jurisdiction of the civil magistrate with that of the church, Locke states that the care of one's soul is an inalienable responsibility; no man can entrust this task to another man. Elsewhere he declares – and this is a constant refrain throughout the *Letter* – 'the care of each Mans salvation belongs only to himself' (*LT*, 47). In his original definition of the church and its objective he says:

> A church then I take to be a voluntary Society of Men, joining themselves together of their own accord, in order to the publick worshipping of God, in such a manner as they judge acceptable to him, and effectual to the salvation of their Souls. (*LT*, 28)

The goal of the church – public worship of God – is determined and conditioned from an individual level. Worship of God is undertaken to secure the salvation of believers' souls. The agent of the church is thus not so much the pastor or the priest, members of a minimal organizational hierarchy, but the individual worshipper.

What is at stake when Locke says 'the care of each Mans salvation belongs only to himself' (*LT*, 47)? He explains that nothing is more important for an individual than the salvation of her soul, nothing can outweigh eternity. The salvation of one's soul is the 'highest obligation' (*LT*, 47). Not only is it the highest value for any individual, but it is also the individual who is the securest seat for the evaluation of such a task. In other words, whatever clamour zealots might make about an individual's practice of unorthodox ceremonies, no one is more genuinely concerned for this individual's salvation than herself. Locke puts it in negative terms; the civil magistrate 'is certainly less concerned for my Salvation than I am' (*L*, 37). The value of salvation is thus central *for* the self, and at the same time it is centered only *by* the self. Salvation provides the individual with an absolute orientation – nothing is more important – and it also provides the individual with an exclusive task: no one else could care as much about this as myself.

It is not just on the terrain of value, but also on that of knowledge that an individual's salvation is her own business. Making use of the argument from uncertainty Locke advances that given centuries of religious and theological controversy no one knows what exactly is the 'one only narrow way that leads to heaven' (*LT*, 37). This is a strong claim. It means that in religious matters nobody knows exactly what they are doing. In such a situation, we have an epistemic duty:

> Those things that every man ought sincerely to enquire into himself, and by Meditation, Study, Search, and his own Endeavours, attain the Knowledge of, cannot be looked upon as the Peculiar Possession of any one sort of Men. (*LT*, 36)

In a remarkable anticipation of Kant's definition of enlightenment, Locke argues that if knowledge of the way to heaven is not in the possession of other institutionally qualified persons, then it only belongs to 'every man' in himself. That is to say, given the complete absence of distinction between persons in the matter of knowledge of God, given this democratic levelling, given that it is the individual's 'highest obligation', the question of how to enter heaven can only be a matter of individual enquiry. Locke's position implies that each and every Christian should personally engage with the difficult questions of sin and grace, penance and redemption.

The thesis *the care of each Man's salvation belongs only to himself* has an epistemic dimension and an evaluative dimension. It also reveals a psychological criterion or guarantee of authenticity: the will, or conscience. Conscience marks a limit to the force of law: 'Laws are of no force at all without Penalties, and Penalties in this case are absolutely impertinent; because they are not proper to convince the mind' (*LT*, 27). Echoing Hobbes' argument, Locke states that outward force is impotent to persuade the understanding to believe any particular article of faith. In a hyperbolic formulation he declares, 'God himself will not save men against their wills' (*LT*, 35). This declaration places individual will as a kind of absolute, as in Hobbes, an irreducible sine qua non, an unavoidable and necessary condition of religious practice. He then reinforces this position by restating Luther's conception of justification by faith:

> If I be not thoroughly persuaded thereof [of the correct articles of faith and form of worship] in my own mind, there will be no safety for me in following it. No way whatsoever that I shall walk against the dictates of my conscience, will ever bring me to the mansions of the Blessed ... Faith only, and inward Sincerity, are the things that procure acceptance with God. (*LT*, 38)

Faith is ascribed to a sphere of inwardness in contrast to the realm of 'outward force'. It is faith alone that is efficacious in procuring salvation. The form that faith takes is assent to a number of articles. And the seat of faith is the individual conscience, beyond the reach of the law. By saying *the care of each Man's salvation belongs only to himself* Locke posits a centre of value and evaluation, an autonomous centre of epistemological enquiry, and a guarantee, a ground of authenticity and efficacy in the form of assent. Each of these determinations is historically gathered under the name of *conscience*. Individual conscience is thus the ground of religious practice. This implies that conscience is the ground of the church as institution. The crucial question for this chapter's investigation is how Locke conceptualizes the relationship between conscience and church.

## *Who is on the inside, who on the outside? Conscience, church, magistrate*

Locke *spatializes* the relationship by means of Luther's distinction between the inner sphere of faith and the outer sphere of works. Once Locke separates church and state and details the duties of toleration, he comes to the question 'what is to be done?'; that is to say, how does a church proceed when practising toleration? He immediately distinguishes between 'outward Form and Rites of Worship' and the 'Doctrines and Articles of Faith', and he adds that the outward forms are justified by faith (*LT*, 39). For Luther an individual is justified by faith not works. For Locke, a religious rite is justified by an individual's faith. The agent of justification is the same, faith, but its object has changed, from the individual sinner to a particular religious ceremony. And this is not to reinstate Luther's idea of the emanating work. Locke subjects the status of outward forms and rites to further analysis because they constitute the very target of religious persecution. What breeds enmities among Christian brethren, he writes, are 'Circumstances' and 'frivolous things' such as the manner of dress, the possession of a mitre (*LT*, 36).

Strictly speaking, from the standpoint of the civil magistrate, the status of outward forms and rites is that of 'indifferent things' (*LT*, 39–40). They only acquire a sacred status due to the religious use they undergo. The ceremonies of baptism and the eucharist acquire symbolic value within the sphere of the church: in themselves the washing of an infant in water and the consumption of bread and wine are meaningless activities. As elements of the worship of God they cease to be indifferent inasmuch as they have been ordained by God for such a purpose. Belief thus has the power to invest certain objects and acts with signification. This power of transformation is limited to the practical sphere of an institution, since from an another point of view, that of the civil magistrate, the activity of dripping cold water on a baby's head remains entirely innocuous.

At this point Locke clarifies and develops the distinctions he makes between faith and worship, indifferent things and sacred rites. His goal is to display how repugnant and counterproductive it would be for a civil magistrate to impose supposedly correct forms of worship upon a church. If this occurred believers would be forced to perform rites they did not believe in, that did not please God. As such they would incarnate the figure we know from Hobbes as disjoint action. And yet from the magistrate's civil standpoint, however repugnant for a dissident, these forced rites would remain indifferent things (*LT*, 40). So Locke distinguishes among the outward forms and rites of worship between those that are actually part of the worship, and those that are mere circumstances. For example, for Christians the time and place of worship, the clothing and postures of the worshipper are mere circumstances since they are not expressly commanded by God (*LT*, 41). There are other parts of worship that are believed to have been 'instituted by God himself' (*LT*, 40). This distinction is crucial since it shows that Locke does not embrace an absolute dichotomy between the inner sphere of faith and the outer sphere of worship: some rites *are* invested by faith. This is a shabby copy of Luther's fusion of inner and outer in the emanating work, but it does allow Locke a vague vision, within the constraints of his liberalism, of how religious practice might be collectively animated.

Finally Locke nails the relation of conscience and institutional form into an inner-outer schema with a telling analogy and a distribution of jurisdictions. He sets out the duty of toleration for the clergy, requiring them to preach charity towards dissenters who basically 'mind their own business' (*LT*, 34). He then reinforces the point by appealing to the common practice of non-interference in 'private Domestick Affairs':

> In the management of Estates, in the conservation of bodily Health, every man may consider what suits his own conveniency, and follow what course he likes best. No man complains of the ill management of his Neighbour's affairs . . . But if any man do not frequent the Church . . . this immediately causes an uproar'. (*LT*, 34)

The analogy between the realm of faith and 'private domestic affairs' reinforces the image of the inwardness of conscience as closed or protected place, as a zone of non-interference, a zone that cannot be appropriated by an institution, or exposed to an outside. It also neatly aligns Locke's meditation on religious toleration and the church with liberalism's atomization of society – but that is a conclusion to come.

The civil and spiritual jurisdictions are distinguished by the distribution of moral actions: 'Moral actions belong therefore to the Jurisdiction of both the outward and inward Court; both of the Civil and Domestick Governor; I mean, both of the Magistrate and Conscience' (*LT*, 46). This passage is explicitly concerned with the distinction between church and state as the solution to the problem of religious persecution since Locke continues by saying, 'Here therefore is great Danger, least one of these Jurisdictions intrench upon the other, and Discord arise between the Keeper of the publick Peace and the Overseers of Souls' (*LT*, 46). The metaphor of 'outward and inner court . . . Magistrate and Conscience' thus redistributes, refigures the relation between state and church. In doing so, it reduces the church to conscience: the church has an outward public existence – such are the forms of worship – and it certainly publically judges actions in sermons and in the excommunication of wayward members. However, here, in the question of the judgement of action, the church, a collective and public body, is reduced to the 'inner court' of conscience. This is but one piece of evidence for my hypothesis, laid out in full in the following section: Locke's redefinition of the church and his articulation of the institution with conscience *volatizes* all collectivity, reducing it to a temporary and contingent aggregate of individual consciences.

## *A church is a voluntary association*

When separating church from state Locke defines the former as a 'free and voluntary society'. He explains that this means no one is born into a church, and that one does not inherit one's faith in the same way one inherits land or goods from one's family (*LT*, 28). An individual is not subject to any form of obligation, nor is bound in any way, with regard to a particular religious institution. Rather an individual is free to choose and join any church. But if there are many churches in the tolerationist view of religion, what would impel an individual to choose one church over another? It would be the individual's belief that a particular church provides a 'Profession and Worship that is truly acceptable to God'. This implies that it is in this church that the individual has the best 'hopes of salvation'. A church is also a voluntary association, and this is crucial, inasmuch as a member is free to leave the congregation if she should so will. The reason for an individual to leave a church would be the discovery of 'any thing either Erroneous in the Doctrine, or incongruous in the Worship of that Society to which he has join'd himself' (*LT*, 28). Such a discovery would diminish an individual's hopes of salvation and so she is free to leave. By implication, the individual is also free to join another church with a different and better doctrine and worship. In Locke's eyes, the only bind to which a church member is subject is the duty to procure her best possible chances of salvation. If it appears that her 'expectation[s] of eternal Life' might be disappointed, it would be too much of a risk not to leave that church and join another.

Every single member of a church – little matter how many years they have been in the church, whatever office they may be responsible for, and whatever denomination the church might be – enjoys this same freedom to leave and join another congregation at any moment. The very existence of a church as an institution is thus reduced to being nothing but an accumulation, an aggregate of those individual wills at any given moment that assent to its particular form of practice. At any one time, a flux of members could be joining, and another flux leaving the church. Perhaps one could object that a church is not reduced to an aggregate of individual wills in Locke's thinking, since it does present one and the same form of worship for those individuals to assent to. The institution would thus possess some kind of solidity, some material and symbolic stability, even if its membership numbers perpetually fluctuated. Yet Locke has argued that all rites are indifferent things unless invested by individual faith: dripping water on a baby only becomes baptism through individual belief. A set of rites may well exist independently of any particular set of believers, but it is only through the individual and inner assent of believers that rites acquire any signification.

What we have here is in the contemporary idiom a 'bottom-up' rather than a 'top-down' definition of an institution. It appears to be an exemplarily democratic conception of a church, yet there is no 'demos', no conception of the collective that accompanies it.

The individual is alone in his calculation of his expectations of eternal salvation. This is the sole bind of the individual to the institution: a calculation. There is no mention of any relationship of charity or fraternity an individual might have to other members of the church. Since an individual is free to join or leave any church on the grounds of an individual calculation, he is also free from any binding religious or cultural identity: Baptist or Anabaptist, now Church of England, now a Quaker, once a Presbyterian, now a Ranter. An individual may assume one identity, and for a long time if she stays in one church, but inasmuch as the church remains a voluntary association, and its rites have not been expressly guaranteed by God in person, she could at any moment withdraw from that particular church and slip off that particular cultural identity, like one more costume among others.

## *The subject of toleration*

It is for this reason that it is appropriate to speak not so much of the individual believer as of the *subject* of toleration. Subject is the term used in the history of philosophy to qualify the conception of personhood or individuality that emerged in seventeenth-century philosophy from the cogito onwards. The following determinations, extracted from the foregoing interpretation of Locke's *Letter*, can be assigned to the subject of toleration:

- A subject is stripped of communitarian envelopes.
- A subject may enjoy direct and exclusive access to a transcendent totality via the shared agency of faith.
- A subject is pure agency.
- A subject is equal to all other subjects.
- A subject is the site of the action of reason.

A subject expresses its agency, it acts rationally, by means of the operation of giving or withdrawing its assent to an institution. It may perform external actions while withdrawing its conscience from those actions, deeming them meaningless, as in the case of Hobbes citizen-dissident. It may quit one church and join another so as to maximize its chances of salvation, as in Locke's conception of membership of a voluntary association. The operation of rationality in each case is that of switching assent to an institution on or off. In short, the subject of the institution in both Locke's and Hobbes' investigations of the church, is nothing more than an individual, or atomic, switch.

This last determination is a summation of the other five properties of the subject. Its emergence in the *Letter on Toleration* can be traced to the idea that an individual enters willingly into a particular church solely on the basis of a rational calculation of his or her chances at gaining eternal salvation through the practice of that churches' rites and articles of faith. In the language of classical economics, such a calculation makes the subject of toleration a 'global utility maximizer'. The utility is global because although churchgoing may involve temporary sacrifices – taking up time that could be otherwise consecrated to the pursuit of sensual pleasure or earning money – it aims at a long-term utility that vastly surpasses any goods to be attained through work or libertinism in this world. Locke's voluntary churchgoer is a preference-switcher and as such forms an ancestor to Adam Smith's concept of 'economic man' as a utility-maximizer in the *Inquiry into the Wealth of Nations*.[12] The subject maximizes her utility by choosing the church that offers the best possible chances of attaining salvation, and by immediately changing churches as soon as it appears that a rival church may be making a better offer. This is the figure of the subject that emerges from Locke's investigation of the church: the atomized switch.

## Conclusion: The volatized collective

One of the tasks of the next chapter is to show how Hobbes' concept of disjoint action applies not only to the church but also to the citizen's position in the commonwealth. The same identity will be demonstrated in Locke's work between the figure of the subject at stake in the *Letter concerning Toleration* and that in the *Second Treatise on Government*, where the citizens's consent to government is the origin of political obligation.

To situate the contribution of this chapter, recall that the overall project is to identify and investigate different models of the practical – that is to say, the ontological – conditions of collective political action. Locke's and Hobbes' investigations of the church as institution give rise to very particular ontology of collectivity. On a symbolic level, a church consists of a particular set of rites and articles of faith. On an ontological level, the church consists of the aggregated preferences of multiple subjects. For both Hobbes and Locke the ground of the institution lies in voluntary decisions taken by individuals. But for Locke this is not just the case at the original historical moment of genesis; throughout the life of the institution its being consists of the assent of a multiplicity of individuals. At any one time, some individual members may be leaving the institution, and other new members joining it: a number of switches are being flicked off, and another number switched on. Hobbes' supposed absolutism would thus simply be one setting among others determining the flexibility and rapidity of subjective switching: the switches are all fixed in the 'on' position. For Locke each and every individual switch can be flipped on or off at any moment.

In Locke's thinking of religious toleration the collective becomes a temporary aggregate. Its solidity depends on statistical correlations between the average rate of switching on and that of switching off. The conservatives' fear that a liberal position on religion and political obligation would result in the disintegration of social fabric and a balkanization of church and commonwealth, though excessive, hides an important ontological diagnosis: the correlate of the freedom of the subject of toleration is multiplicity.

The concept of preference-switching is a thin notion of liberty compared to the iconoclasm and lay-preaching that spread through the New Model Army as it marched through the counties of England in pursuit of the royalist army. For Locke, subjects are free only in so far as they are unbound, disintricated and stripped of any regional or collective identification. In short, there is no collective experience of liberty to be had. To switch is to momentarily recreate a state of indeterminacy, a situation analogical to that in the *Essay* of the infant's mind as tabula rasa. In a state of indeterminacy there are no other individuals with whom to join in action.

To the figure of disjoint action corresponds the subject as atomic switch. To the subject as atomic switch corresponds the collective as statistical aggregate of switching rates.

It seems that Luther's legacy has been perverted. The separation of faith from works has been institutionalized into a split between conscience and the public performance of authorized religious rituals, but the union of faith and works in the concept of the emanating work has been lost. No aggregate of atomic switches could ever form an emanating work. Yet in Hobbes account of the historical untying of the institutional knots of the church in the English Revolution, laying bare and reawakening the primitive church, the shared agency of faith as a gift from God re-emerges into the light. As we each follow Paul or Cephas or Apollos, 'reduced' to the independency of the early Christians, the sharing of agency is no longer confined to private conscience beyond the reach of the law. Agency is shared between persons in the practices of religious conversion and teaching: these are emanating works. And so Luther's legacy has been divided, but it survives. In Hobbes' work, at least in that part where he confronts the concrete consequences of the English revolution on the church, action is not entirely institutionalized.

In the previous chapter it is shown that in both Locke's and Hobbes' nominalist philosophies of action it is no longer substances but institutions that act. The present chapter has led an enquiry into institutions: Hobbes' concept of a uniform state church fused with the commonwealth and Locke's church as a voluntary association. The result of this enquiry is that at the base of institutions and their actions we find the operation of disjoint subjects and a volatized form of collectivity. When institutions act, subjects act, at base.

What then of political action?

# CHAPTER FIVE

# Hobbes and Locke on politics: Sovereign action and contractual action

There is no respite for England, no rest from political troubles in the eyes of Hobbes and Locke when they write their works on politics. Each of their constructions is designed to contain or eliminate such troubles. On the way, they both dismiss the politics of the English revolution under the headings of hysterical passion, enthusiasm and conflict over the interpretation of actions. Models of political action can be extracted from their writings by posing the five queries, those queries identified in Chapter two's anatomy of the Leveller-agitator failure. This extraction is the first task of this chapter and it results in the twin models of sovereign action and contractual action. These models have enjoyed long legacies in European politics. The second task of the chapter is to show their limits and impurities, and by so doing open up space for alternative understandings of action, such as that found in the Leveller-agitator alliance.

Let us begin at the beginning, in the state of nature.

## The very hypothesis of a state of nature

The state of nature is a hypothesis produced by subtracting institutional authority, political obligation and written law from society. In Locke's and Hobbes' eyes this subtraction enables them to analyse human interaction in the raw, in a situation in which actions are neither right nor wrong. Natural actions would thus appear to be neutral: sheer mechanisms of passion, belief, deliberation and execution assembling one person with other elements of a situation. In line with the metaphysics of action outlined in Chapter three, it would appear that in the absence of institutions, Locke's and Hobbes' nominalist approach to action cannot apply. In its place, solely an ontological or mechanist description of action would be valid. To speak of action in the state of nature would thus be to map the motion and impact of bodies. Something vaguely like this can be found in Hobbes when he speaks of the passions in the state of nature and how they affect human interactions. However neither Hobbes nor Locke entirely subtract action from rules. One form of law remains, one set of rules: the laws of nature, precepts discovered by reason. Consequently, neither of our two philosophers go all the way in reducing action to mechanist description. Indeed, on the basis of the state of nature, both of them develop institutional models of action in line with their nominalism.

Nevertheless it is possible to employ the same interpretative tactic in the analysis of their political thinking as in the analysis of their treatment of religion. One can show how their models of action are not monolithic but incomplete, including elements of other alternative models of action. Not everything in Hobbes corresponds to sovereign action, not everything in Locke corresponds to contractual action. The grounds of such impurities always turn out to be ontological. Sooner or later it is a question, beyond the power of the institution, of the environment of political action. It is the ontology of that environment that necessitates the emergence of alternative models of action to the institutional, whether sovereign or contractual. The name for that environment in Chapter three was the practical indeterminacy of use. In this chapter it assumes the name of the variability of human affairs.

## *The operation of the laws of nature and their subject*

In classic social contract theory the role of the laws of nature is ambivalent, as noted by generations of commentators. On the one hand, the first law of self-preservation is the very foundation of Hobbes' 'war of all against all', of Locke's 'ill condition'. On the other hand, the provisos attached to it – self-preservation can be secured better by cooperation, by peace, or self-preservation does not legitimate harming others – immediately provide the exit route, they lay the foundations of the social contract (*L*, 91; *ST*, §6). These rules for action, which are supposed to be independent of any particular form of society or morality, contain the modern state in germ form. They seal the fate of collective action. It is the guarantee of the state alone that allows actions be concatenated in society without dissolving into chaos. This is the fundamental political intuition at stake in both Hobbes' and Locke's versions of social contract theory. One action cannot be joined to another action without an institutional guarantee. One cannot transfer ownership of property to someone and receive money in return without the backing of the law. Individual actions are thus collectivized on the basis of the potential intervention, upon violation of contract, of the known and predictable force of written law. No collective action without a judge. No society without a state. It is on this basic point that the Leveller-agitator model of action differs: it offers an alternative account of how actions can be collectivized.

The laws of nature play three roles: they bring about the state of nature, they furnish an exit from the state of nature and they ground political obligation. As a ground for political obligation they provide a measure, they furnish norms for the judgement of the government's actions. This is only implicit in Hobbes, but Locke draws all the consequences. If a government does not act to secure public safety, if it actively threatens people's lives and property, then the people may exercise a right to resistance:

> The Community perpetually retains a Supreme power of saving themselves from the attempts and designs of any Body, even of their Legislators, whenever they shall be so foolish or so wicked, as to lay and carry on designs against the Liberties and Properties of the Subject . . . [a] Society of Men . . . will always have a right to preserve what they have not a power to part with; and to rid themselves of those who invade this Fundamental, Sacred and unalterable Law of Self-Preservation, for which they entered into Society. (*ST*, §149)

This is a clear illustration of the contractual model of political action: the community retains its position as holders of a contract.

The people can rightfully break the contract if the other party, the government, does not fulfil its obligations, namely protecting the people's liberty and property.

According to Hobbes, the laws of nature provide a measure of government in an entirely different manner. As mentioned in Chapter four, in the Engagement Controversy, Cromwell's republic demanded that its former enemies engage their allegiance to the newly established commonwealth.[1] In the controversy that erupted over this demand, some writers argued against any such engagement. They claimed that such a pledge would be tantamount to sacralizing the de facto power of usurpers and conquerors, and removing all grounds of right from government. As Quentin Skinner has shown, Hobbesian arguments were employed on the other side of the controversy by those termed 'engagers'. Hobbes, in the 'Review and Conclusion' of the *Leviathan*, summarizes his political theory as establishing 'the mutual relation between Protection and Obedience'. On this basis, he argues that a government's legitimacy lies not in the history of the actions that brought it to power, but simply in its present capacity as possessor of power to protect the people (*L*, 491). And the government's principle function of protection is grounded and measured by the first law of nature: that of self-preservation as rationally calculated by each individual. Hence, by the measure of natural law, one can be a rightful subject to a legitimate conqueror (*L*, 485).

Hobbes' opponents and the royalists in the Engagement Controversy were quick to point out the difficulties inherent in such a position. As Skinner puts it, 'when citizens are not adequately protected [by their sovereign] their obligations automatically cease'.[2] Marchamount Nedham embraced this logical consequence of running a Hobbesian line in arguing for engagement: a subject's allegiance will immediately switch if a new government conquers power; there is no ground for historical loyalty to a defeated regime.[3] The apology for de facto power volatizes political obligation in that it becomes a mere function of the subject's rational calculation of the present government's capacity to protect his life and property. The natural law of self-preservation thus furnishes a draconian, immediate and material measure of the legitimacy of the actual government. In Hobbes' theory of political obligation there is ultimately no room for process, for the concrete actions that brought a particular government to power and that could be judged as rightful or illegitimate. In Hobbes' model of political action the function of the sovereign is necessary and its reach is absolute, but the historical identity, the particular nature and the individual policies of a sovereign are utterly contingent and indifferent.

Locke's right to resistance, and the Hobbesian position in the Engagement Controversy have direct consequences for the figure of the subject at the base of the social contract. These consequences can be identified by way of a requirement Rousseau laid down for the social contract theory. He stated that before one speaks of the act by which a people forms a government, 'it would be best to examine the action by which a people is a people'.[4] Locke's and Hobbes' differences are illuminated by the ways in which they meet this requirement, but at base the solution is the same. Locke explicitly grants unity to the people independent of the formation of the commonwealth. In his treatment of the dissolution of government under invasion he distinguishes between the consistency of society and the consistency of government (*ST*, §211). Hobbes appears to provide a perfect contrast: without the unity of the sovereign the people are a disordered multitude. Following Rousseau, one could object to Hobbes that the very action of forming the social contract presupposes a united people. But for Hobbes, and this is his modernity, the basis of the social contract is *not substantial but operational unity*. Every individual makes the same rational calculation concerning her self-preservation. The actions of every individual concord in that they are all ruled by the same laws: the laws of nature. But this is precisely what is at stake in Locke's model of the institution of government: the operations of the laws of nature.

What is the subject of this operation? In Chapter four, the analysis of Locke's definition of a church gave rise to the concept of the subject as 'atomic switch'. The thesis is that when institutions act, it is subjects who act at base. The action of the subject is an operation of switching consent to the institution on or off. On the basis of Locke's right to resistance and Hobbes' volatization of political obligation in the Engagement Controversy, this thesis can be confirmed with regard to their models of the commonwealth. The state of nature can be understood as another name for the subject-position of being withdrawn from the institution, for the position of looking from the outside in, judging society and its institutions according to their utility. In the state of nature, all actions are subtracted from civil law but submitted to natural law. Each action is thus initiated on the basis of a rational calculation of it augmenting or diminishing the probabilities of self-preservation. At this level no collective action exists. Other people only enter into my consideration when I calculate with whom I should act, and against whom I should act. Both the Lockean and Hobbesian subjects of the commonwealth are at base atomic switches.

## *Deciding the outcome of actions*

It is all very well to rationally calculate one's actions, but what is more important is the actual outcome of such actions.

In the state of nature individual actions fail locally, and once added together they lead to global failure. They cannot be collectivized. In this at least, Hobbes and Locke are in agreement. Without cooperation, without a social contract, no person can hope to secure the means to her survival: there is no property law, there is no security. As soon as one acquires food it can be stolen. Fear thy neighbour! Action fails at a local level because it does not achieve its goal, which is always that of maximizing self-preservation. At a global level, actions concatenate to generate an unlivable state of affairs that Hobbes baptized 'the war of all against all', unmediated and irreconcilable conflict. Locke differentiates the state of nature from the state of war, but he nevertheless identifies it as an 'ill condition' of uncertainty that drives 'mankind' into society to secure 'the preservation of their property' (*ST*, §127).

Actions in the state of nature fail because of their global environment, but what about actions within the commonwealth: what decides their outcome? Locke identifies the 'inconveniencies' of the state of nature as being the inability to decide controversies between individuals, and the incapacity to effectively punish violators of the law of nature: '*Want of a common Judge with Authority, puts all Men in a State of Nature*' (*ST*, §19, §127). Society, in contrast, secures the execution and enforcement of the law. For both Locke and Hobbes the judge's decision concludes controversies and puts an end to social conflict (*L*, 125). The outcome of actions within the commonwealth is thus decided by judgement: the judgement of the civil magistrate or the sovereign (*ST*, §89). The judge intervenes with controversial actions alone, and neither Hobbes nor Locke explicitly treat the outcome of non-controversial action. However, both take an explicitly nominalist position on the nature or moral value of actions, as already outlined in Chapter three. It is the positive instituted law that enables the attribution of moral value to actions since in the state of nature they have none (*L*, 89–90). One can extrapolate that the outcomes of non-controversial actions may be determined in function of the civil law.

There is another kind of action whose outcome must be determined: action that begins within the commonwealth only to exit it, the act of resistance. For Hobbes any act of resistance immediately turns its agent into a rebel, expels him from the commonwealth, and plunges him into the state of nature, an enemy of the state. Back in the state of nature, his actions lead to global failure. Hobbes ends the second part of the *Leviathan* with a warning as to the natural chain of consequences that are entered upon by rebellious action. God's 'natural punishment' of rebellion is 'slaughter' (*L*, 254). Locke, in contrast, is famous for championing the right to resistance. He reserves the people's right to dissolve a government if it fails to guarantee property. As in Hobbes, an agent of resistance cannot appeal to any social institution to decide the nature or outcome of her action. Her only recourse is an 'appeal to Heaven'. This enigmatic appeal has two functions. One is to invite divine attribution of moral value, the other is to pray for success, to ask for divine intervention in securing the outcome of the action. The crucial paragraph that fuses these two functions is found in Locke's chapter on conquest. In its struggle against an invader, a conquered people could repeat an appeal to heaven generation after generation, until justice is achieved, till they have 'recovered the native Right of their Ancestors' (*ST*, §176). The appeal to heaven is thus the anchor of a long practical process. Locke anticipates the objection that such a doctrine will give rise to 'endless trouble'. His counterexample is deceptively simple: 'He that troubles his Neighbour without a Cause, is punished for it by the justice of the Court he appeals to' (*ST*, §176). And then he makes the grand analogy between human and divine justice:

> He that *appeals to Heaven*, must be sure he has Right on his side; and a Right too that is worth the Trouble and Cost of the Appeal, as he will answer at a Tribunal, that cannot be

deceived, and will be sure to retribute to every one according to the Mischiefs he hath created to his Fellow-Subjects; that is, any part of Mankind. (*ST*, §176)

The implication is that if one does have justice on one's side, then one will not have caused needless trouble, one will not be punished but rather rewarded. That is to say, Heaven will intervene and decide the success of one's rebellion against the invader. Locke refers to the story of Jephthah in Judg. 11.27: '*Jeptha* . . . was forced to appeal to Heaven. *The Lord our Judge* (says he) *be Judge this day between the Children of* Israel, *and the Children of Ammon*, and then prosecuting, and relying on his *appeal*, he leads out his Army to Battle' (*ST*, §21). Outside the purview of any civil judge, an action of resistance is arraigned and tried in the court of divine justice. The definitive assignation of its moral value is at the same time the determination of its practical outcome: to be in the right is to succeed. Cromwell was famous for his trumpeting of providence as the sole explanation of the New Model Army's victories over the royalists. The Leveller-agitators also claimed the favours of providence in the preamble to *An Agreement of the People*: 'God having so far owned our Cause as to deliver the Enemies thereof into our hands'. Little matter the awkward fact that God often allows the wicked to prosper.[5]

What determines the outcome of an action that exits the commonwealth so as to institute another, as in a civil war? In Locke, in Cromwell and in the Leveller-agitators it is divine judgement that decides the outcome of such an action. Yet the appeal to providence is limited in that it offers no account whatsoever of the actual mechanisms, the 'secondary causes' in seventeenth-century terms, behind the success or failure of a particular action. Under a providential interpretation of events, the success of an action signs its justice. It is one thing, however, to invoke providence after the fact – such is an apology. It is quite another to 'appeal to heaven' before the fact – such is hope.

In the state of nature, and in the commonwealth as instituted by social contract, rational calculation provides the rule for action, that is, an action is the end product of rational calculation. In the state of nature the outcome of an action is decided by its immediate ontological environment: the existence or non-existence of neighbouring and hostile actions. In the commonwealth, or in the situation of exiting the commonwealth so as to institute another, the outcome of an action is decided by judgement, human or divine. One decision to initiate the action, one decision to end it.

## *The missed turning*

For seventeenth-century metaphysics, decision, calculation and judgement may become the object of a science: it is for this reason that it is possible, in both Locke's and Hobbes' eyes, to develop a science of action and morality.[6] Yet in both philosophies, action is not regulated by calculation and judgement alone. The very hypothesis of a state of nature is pregnant with other determinations of action. The state of nature is generated by a process of subtraction; a logical process that removes social custom, positive law and morality from individual action. On occasion, this process goes further and removes natural law and judgement from the face of action. For instance, Hobbes admits that in some situations in the state of nature, natural law is solely obeyed *'in foro interno'* rather than in actual practice, because strict obedience would lead to the individual 'mak[ing] himself a prey to others, and procur[ing] his own ruin' (*L*, 110). An individual adopts the law of nature as the rule of their action only in the case of judging there is 'sufficient security, that others shall observe the same Lawes unto him' (*L*, 110). In Locke, the laws of nature can also be momentarily suspended: one of the chief 'inconveniences' of the state of nature is that of 'the irregular and uncertain exercise of the Power every Man has of punishing the transgressions of others' (*ST*, §127). To punish transgressions is to execute the law of nature; if punishment is impossible, the law of nature loses the force of law (*ST*, §130). As in Hobbes, the suspension of the law of nature always depends on an individual's immediate environment, on neighbouring actions, on hostile intentions. These are ontological determinations. Of course, the individual still determines, by rational calculation, at what moments the rule of natural law is suspended. Nevertheless the form of action is momentarily subordinate to an ontological determination, namely, to the contingent and local arrangement of other neighbouring actions.

If, by means of the very hypothesis of a state of nature, the process of subtraction were carried further to remove all natural law, calculation and judgement from action then Locke's and Hobbes' philosophies would remain capable of explaining patterns of human interaction. Both embrace mechanism as an account of the motion and encounters of diversely sized bodies. There are resources in their philosophies for thinking action in terms of its ontological environment; that environment consisting simply of other neighbouring actions. But this turning was missed in the history of philosophy. Their thinking of action was nuanced, ambivalent and complicated, divided between different conceptual frameworks, a mechanism of passions or a science of morality. Yet only one framework emerged from their philosophy to dominate the subsequent tradition: the nominalist and institutional framework of calculation and judgement.

In the analysis of this framework, it will turn out that both the Lockean and Hobbesian models of political action are impure, bearing both *counter-models* and *inverse-models* of action. It is in these concealed inverse-models that a thinking of the local and plural context of each action emerges. In Hobbes, it arises – in the interstices of the sovereign – under the name of prudence.

## Hobbes' model of sovereign action

Let us recall that the Leveller-agitator model of political action emerges within five queries about political action, each clearly present in sequences of the English revolution:

- Who can act?
- Who can act on what grounds?
- Who is right about what is to be done?
- Why do we succeed or fail?
- If you and I split, were we ever united, and to what end?

Outlining Hobbes' and Locke's models of political action in line with these queries sheds light on their peculiar constitution.

## *The sovereign alone can act*

In Hobbes' model, the sovereign alone acts in the field of politics, whether the sovereign be a monarch, executive council or legislative assembly. The sovereign is one, indivisible, exceptional and his action is total, covering the entire political field. As outlined in the section above, the Hobbesian position on the Engagement Controversy reveals that the only question of importance to a rational subject is whether the present government can guarantee his security right now. Consequently history is erased from political obligation: there is no place for loyalty and the government does not gain its authority through its past actions. In this framework, the question 'who can act?' is left empty of any positive content. In the *Leviathan*, it is replaced by the question 'what can act?' This section explores Hobbes' response to that question, wherein it is shown that what can act is the sovereign as a unified, indivisible and exceptional institution that enjoys a total reach over the commonwealth's territory. Hobbes' task is to explain just how such an institution could be constituted.

The theory of the constitution of the sovereign begins from the principle that a multitude of people cannot act. It is the most fundamental claim in Hobbes' theory of action. To revisit the essential passages already mentioned in Chapter four, in the *Leviathan* Hobbes states: 'If the church be not one person, then it hath no authority at all; it can neither command, nor do any action at all' (*L*, 268). In *On the Citizen* he stipulates:

> One must not attribute to [a crowd] a single action of any kind. Hence a crowd cannot make a promise or an agreement, acquire or transfer a right, do, have possess, and so on, except separately, or as individuals, so that there are as many promises, agreements, rights, and actions, as there are men. For this reason a crowd is not a natural person. (*C*, 76, 94)

The grounds of this claim are not made clear. This is a stumbling block for our investigation. Why is unity a precondition of action? A number of hypotheses are possible. On the one hand, it could be the case that this is a purely metaphysical axiom and forms part of the basic model of action outlined in chapter three. On the other hand, it could be a political principle where unity is shorthand for the indivisibility of sovereign. As such it would form part of the polemic against republicanism and its recommendation of mixed constitutions.

However, it is more likely that the condition of unity is related to the Aristotelian distinction between voluntary action and passion. A multitude cannot act because it is fundamentally passive; an external agent always instigates any movement on the part of a crowd. This is precisely what is at stake in Hobbes' diagnosis of the English civil war: seditious doctrines are responsible for the unruly passions of the mob. No one should be allowed to read ancient Greek and Roman authors for it is they who seed the ideology of republicanism that equates all kings with tyrants (L, 225–6). Hobbes' most dramatic description of passion become madness in a crowd concerns sedition:

> For [a multitude] will clamour, fight against, and destroy those, by whom all their life-time before they have been protected, and secured from injury. And if this be Madnesse in the multitude, it is the same in every particular man. For as in the middest of the sea, though a man perceive no sound of that part of the water next to him; yet he is well assured, that part contributes as much, to the Roaring of the Sea, as any other part, of the same quantity: so also, though we perceive no great unquietnesse in one, or two men; yet we may well be assured, that their singular passions, are parts of the seditious roaring of a troubled Nation. (L, 55)

The danger for a commonwealth lies not in one or two discrete individuals, who on their own may well appear to be not particular 'unquiet'. Rather it lies in the joining up of such individuals, whereby they become parts of a *continuum* of sedition, as if there could ever be discrete 'parts' to the sea. In this astonishing passage the seditious passion of the multitude leads to a breakdown of discrete order into a continuum that cannot be verified at a local level, but only manifests itself at a global level: 'the roaring of a troubled Nation'. Here Hobbes establishes a clear link between the absence of unity in a multitude and passion.

Yet there is a small problem. Chapter three's investigation of Locke's derivation of the idea of action showed that the very idea of a self-contained agent initiating action presupposes unity. Hobbes is not going to be able to ground unity in activity and multiplicity in passivity. But even apart from that problem, under his mechanist account of action there is no hard and fast distinction between action and passion, activity and passivity. There are no actors who spontaneously and independently initiate chains of events. On a political level, the sovereign does not act alone and separate from the people, he acts through the consent of everyone, and in turn everyone acts through the sovereign. What are the grounds then for the principle that only a unified person can act?

The most evident grounds Hobbes provides for his principle of unity, at least in the case of the sovereign, are practical and thus political: it is better for the sovereign to be one and indivisible. Otherwise power would be shared between different bodies – such as a legislative assembly and an executive, as in Locke; or between a civil government and the church, which Hobbes sees as Rome's position. In Hobbes' eyes, to divide political power is to dissolve the commonwealth since rival powers tend to destroy each other (L, 225). In such an untenable situation, 'Every Subject' he claims 'must obey two Masters' (L, 227). One of Hobbes' most direct references to the English 'Civil War' concerns precisely such division:

> If there had not been first an opinion received of the greatest part in England, that these Powers were divided between the King and the Lords, and the House of Commons, the people had never been divided, and fallen into this Civil Warre; first between those that disagreed in Politiques; and after between the Dissenters about the liberty of religion. (L, 127)

If power is divided among three bodies, instituting a mixed government such as recommended by republicanism, the commonwealth will be subject to three factions. Each would claim as a representative body to 'bear the Person of the people'. Cooperation between institutions is impossible in Hobbes' eyes. The reason for this is simple: to act politically is to command a subordinate to do something or to pass a law that all subjects must obey. The structure of authority presumes a minimal order, a hierarchy, where one instance possesses power, and the lower instance must obey the former's commands. For a commonwealth to remain united, that order of power must have a maximum term, and there can only be one maximum, the sovereign (*C*, 88).

For the stability of the commonwealth the sovereign must be indivisible. Yet the sovereign is not a natural person. In *On the Citizen*, Hobbes explains how a crowd, despite its lack of unity, can make an artificial person: 'if the same crowd individually agree that the will of some one man or the consenting wills of a majority of themselves is to be taken as the will of [them] all, that number becomes one person' (*C*, 76). In the *Leviathan*, this procedure is elaborated by means of the theory of authorization. According to that theory, an artificial person, the 'actor', is one who is considered to represent the words or actions of another man, the 'author' (*L*, 111). The artificial person is termed an actor inasmuch as he impersonates or bears the person of the author. In other words, the actor is said to act in the name of the author. In turn, the author is said to own the actor's actions. The actor acts by authority, where that authority is a right to perform an action (*L*, 112). Further, when an actor makes a covenant, he binds not only himself but also the author of his acts.

This theory of authorization is linked to unity as a precondition for action in the following manner:

> A multitude of men, are made *One* person, when they are by one man, or by one Person, represented; so that it be done with the consent of every one of that multitude in particular. For it is the *Unity* of the Representer, not the *Unity* of the Represented, that maketh the Person One. And it is the Representer that beareth the Person, and but one Person: And *Unity*, cannot otherwise be understood in Multitude. (*L*, 114)

In the action of authorization that creates the commonwealth, it is the unity of the sovereign, whether monarch or assembly, that confers unity upon the multitude. This is not to say that the operation of authorization presupposes unity in that it requires a unified recipient. It is not the case that authorization picks out a pre-existing single monarch or assembly to be sovereign of the people. The sovereign is nothing prior to the operation of authorization: there are no monarchs, no legislative assemblies before their authorization by the people. As identified above, there is no substantial unity in Hobbes, only operational unity. The operation of authorization constitutes the unity that is the precondition of action. The mark of the unity of the commonwealth lies in the single artificial person of the sovereign.

If the operation of authorization lies at the base of the social covenant, whenever the sovereign acts, each and every one of his subjects also acts. The direct authors of every act of the sovereign are you and me as subjects, as unified by our representer (*L*, 148). This doctrine has extreme consequences:

> Nothing the Sovereign Representative can do to the subject, on what pretence soever, can properly be called Injustice or Injury; because every Subject is Author of every act the Sovereign doth . . . and therefore it may, and doth often happen in Commonwealths, that a Subject may be put to death, by the command of the Sovereign power; and yet neither do the other wrong. (*L*, 148; cf. 124, 172)

The sovereign can never commit injustice against one of his subjects, because when he acts, the subject is also acting, and one cannot act against oneself. Harming oneself is against the law of nature. By the same stroke rebellion is rendered not just illegitimate but impossible: an individual cannot act against the sovereign because in doing so she would be acting against herself, and harming oneself is against the law of nature. What a neat trick Hobbes has pulled off!

In the ordinary run of affairs every action of the sovereign is simultaneously an action each subject owns as author of the sovereign. Hobbes then inverts the equation of sovereign with subject. In his argument subordinating ecclesiastical authority to the sovereign any action on the part of a person in a position of civil authority, such as a magistrate or a bishop, is at the same time the act of the sovereign. Hobbes writes: 'For every act done, is the act of him, without whose consent it is invalid' (*L*, 373). Someone might object that many historical examples can be given of the Christian church electing its own bishops. In turn Hobbes insists that such elections were valid only via the authority of the sovereign. In the chapter on civil law he states that 'in all Courts of Justice, the Sovereign . . . is he that judgeth' through the person of any subordinate judge (*L*, 187). Authorization and delegation: not only are all acts of the sovereign immediately the individual's, but any governmental action an individual carries out is also the sovereign's. The author of each and every political action is the sovereign. In so far as a person acts publically and with civil authority he is a stand-in, a placeholder.

What is at stake is a bidirectional ownership of action between the individual and the sovereign, a chiasmus of agency. Its result is simple: no one acts in the field of politics save the sovereign. The chiasmus of agency locks down the political field.

## *The sovereign acts on the grounds of protecting the people*

The second enquiry into political action asks who can act and on what grounds? For Hobbes the sovereign acts on the grounds that he guarantees protection for all those subjects who authorize his actions. Protection is guaranteed by instilling a fear of punishment into subjects who might otherwise break their covenants and cause dysfunction in social interaction (*L*, 117). The sovereign guarantees public safety by 'keeping men in awe' of his 'visible power' such that they observe reason rather than obeying the urgings of their passions. This immediately provides an answer to the fifth enquiry of political action: If you and I split, were we ever united, and to what end? All subjects are united under the sovereign, through common authorization of his powers, and to the end of protection. If it should so happen that the commonwealth is invaded and dissolves, then subjects will split. Each individual will be freed of obligation to the sovereign, since the latter would no longer be capable of assuring her safety (*L*, 153–4).

In acting as a safeguard for the self-preservation of each and every subject, the sovereign enjoys an exceptional position: 'The Sovereign of a Commonwealth, be it an Assembly, or one Man, is not Subject to the Civill Lawes' (*L*, 184). The sovereign is not obliged to obey his own laws because, as Hobbes stipulates in *On the Citizen*, one cannot be under obligation to oneself (*C*, 84). In the *Leviathan*, he adds the argument that if the sovereign were subject to the civil laws, this would set up the laws as a higher power, as a judge, and thus it would amount to as making a new sovereign. In turn that higher sovereign's application of the laws would also be submitted to higher judgement, and so on, generating an infinite regress and the dissolution of any fixed hierarchical order (*L*, 224). The sovereign is thus free in the strict Hobbesian sense; that is to say, there are no legal impediments or external constraints upon his actions (*L*, 224). Indeed the sovereign enjoys a state of nature in his relationship with other sovereigns. His position is exceptional: seal and guarantor of the existence of the commonwealth, he nevertheless, unlike any of his subjects, openly shares out his existence between two zones, society and nature. In the state of nature he is free, yet in society he is constrained.

In society the sovereign is subject to the laws of nature. His power is not quite absolute; there are limits to what he can command. Hobbes identifies an objection to his account of absolute power: what if the sovereign commands an individual to kill herself, or to give evidence against herself of a crime? The rule for this question is found in the individual's original purpose in making the covenant and giving up power to the sovereign. There are certain things that cannot be transferred by contract, namely an individual's right to self-preservation and to defend herself by force from force (*L*, 98, 153). Thus if sovereign commands a subject to harm or kill herself, then in that case alone the subject is free to disobey (*L*, 151). The sovereign is also constrained in that he cannot promise to give away part of his power nor abdicate: such promises are automatically void (*C*, 100). Finally, although the sovereign is not a partner in the covenant but rather its product, he does have a definite task to fulfil (*L*, 122). Though the sovereign's position is exclusive, his power indivisible and absolute and his actions above the civil law, traces of the contractual model do remain in Hobbes' model. The sovereign can act on the grounds of ensuring protection: this is what subjects receive in exchange for obedience. As soon as the sovereign fails to assure protection he is no longer sovereign (*L*, 153, 230). The commonwealth is dissolved, all subjects freed, you and I no longer united but split and exposed in our condition as atomic switches.

## *The sovereign alone is right about what is to be done*

The question 'who is right about what is to be done' finds an immediate answer in the Hobbesian model. Only the sovereign could ever be right about what is to be done. There are no private grounds for moral judgement in Hobbes; to believe so is to hold a seditious doctrine (*L*, 223). For this reason it is impossible to oppose any other judgement about the right course of action to that of the sovereign. Subject to constraints, as mentioned earlier, the sovereign's power is not, strictly speaking, absolute. However, he does enjoy an exclusive monopoly over the question of what is to be done, and this offers us a snapshot of what is meant by absolutism.

## *Can the sovereign succeed or fail?*

The elimination of all independent grounds for judgement appears to leave no place for the fourth query of political action: why do we succeed or fail? This is the question of practice, and it should take hold however much power the sovereign has, since it aims at what actually happens when the sovereign acts, regardless of his exclusive determination of the right course of action. The sovereign's power cannot be so extensive as to actually control all the consequences of his actions. Surely he is subject, like any other agent, to the contingencies and variability of the reception of action. This at least is one of our fundamental metaphysical convictions today; what actually happens in the *event* of action is outside anybody's control, accidents do happen, results are unpredictable. This is why it is so difficult for us to understand Hobbes' apparent erasure of the question of success and failure.

Look at the list of political actions undertaken by the sovereign. Whether king or parliament, the sovereign establishes the civil law as the law of property, thus guaranteeing and regulating economic exchange. He governs doctrines, censors and polices public discourse, especially religion. He administers justice. He administers an army and funds it. He can declare a state of war or peace with other nations. He appoints all officers of state, awards titles of honour, coins money, disposes of the estate and persons of infant heirs and enjoys pre-emption in markets (*L*, 167–9). The branches of governmental activity are divided into: finance and internal revenue, the military, education, the judiciary, internal security and prisons and foreign affairs.[7] In each action, and in each area of government a public minister acts in the name of the sovereign. But surely a minister could mistake the sovereign's command? Each of the actions listed above can evidently go wrong, and in so many ways. Socrates' objection to Thrasymachus would seem to hold: the sovereign, however absolute, must be capable of making a mistake.

Here Hobbes provides the simple answer that would have cinched the argument for Thrasymachus – who says that an error has been made? Who is the judge of failure? It is here that Hobbes' nominalist account of action has its greatest impact on his thinking of politics. If substances no longer act, but institutions alone act, and if no action can be named if not by an institution, then there is no separate ontological determination of an action's fate. In the hierarchical structure of Hobbes' commonwealth, the being of an action is registered and verified at different institutional levels. Between those levels, at the level of the interlinking of means and material consequences, its being disappears from view. All laws are commands on the part of the sovereign (*L*, 183). In turn, 'all Lawes are general Judgements, or Sentences of the Legislator' (*L*, 197). To act politically is to command and to judge, and then to judge the effect of one's commands.

In the commonwealth there are no independent standpoints from which the results of the sovereign's action can be measured. Hobbes stipulates that the commands of the sovereign may be neither censured or disputed by his subjects (*L*, 144). The sovereign has a monopoly on judgement: we have not come to the end of this doctrine's consequences. In the interests of the stability of the commonwealth, the sovereign may judge all of his actions to be successful, whatever happens. Everything, every little hiccup and accident, was foreseen – it is all part of the grand plan. A one-dimensional sphere of action has been created in which every single time something is done, not only was it the right thing to have been done, but it also succeeded. The workings of the Hobbesian commonwealth resemble a perfect machine.

This cannot be right. If the state of nature is not a distant period of history but the underside of contemporary society, as Hobbes' analysis of the passions in *On the Citizen* suggests, then the troubles of the state of nature will always affect and disrupt the workings of the commonwealth: it cannot be smooth sailing in perpetuity for the Hobbesian ship of state. The key lies in Hobbes' analysis of the workings of the civil law. It is in the vulnerabilities of the law and in their remedies that general criteria can be found for determining the success and failure of sovereign action.

The sovereign is the author, the exclusive interpreter and the prosecutor of the civil law. Law is a specific address from the sovereign to the subject, an address that establishes a relationship of obedience whereby the subject will keep certain rules for social action. These rules are supposed complete in their coverage of all kinds of interaction, and in their coding of those interactions into just and unjust, legal and criminal. Distributive laws determine the rights and the liberty of action of subjects while penal laws determine penalties for infractions of the law (L, 197). For infractions to be punishable, the law must be made known to all subjects, it must be publicized. The civil law, together with its enforceability, is the sole guarantee and cement of a stable collective for Hobbes:

> Law was brought into the world for nothing else, but to limit the natural liberty of particular men, in such manner, as they might not hurt, but assist one another, and joyn together against a common enemy. (L, 185)

Without the law, no collective: this is Hobbes' fundamental intuition, this is what is passed down in his model of political action. But for the law to function correctly four structural vulnerabilities must be addressed, vulnerabilities concerning its *source*, its *agents*, its *meaning* and its potential *miscarriage*.

The law is vulnerable in its source in that there is confusion over the existence of rival sources of civil law. For instance, as Hobbes laments in the first dialogue of *Behemoth*, the Catholic Church would have its canons treated as civil law. On the other hand, certain authors argue that members of parliament – 'private men' – or subordinate judges are authors of the common law. Such sources are to be dismissed as illegitimate: it is the sovereign who stands as the exclusive authority at the source of the law. However, there are other legitimate sources of the law: divine positive law as revealed in the scriptures; natural law as revealed by reason; and unwritten customs as revealed by history. In each of these cases, Hobbes has resort to a mechanism of inclusion and containment. 'The Law of Nature', he declares, 'and the Civill Law, contain each other and are of equall extent' (L, 185). In turn, only those customs that are reasonable are legitimate laws, and their reasonability is decided by the sovereign. The authority of customary laws lies not in the length of time for which they have existed, but rather in the sovereign's will through his 'tacit consent' (L, 184, 197). In the case of divine law Hobbes argues that the Jewish people's submission to Moses when he revealed the divine law must be understood as the effect of their prior submission to him as their civil sovereign (L, 199). If, on the contrary, divine revelation was seen as the source of law, a terrible risk would be run: none other than the atomization and dissolution of society;

> For if men were at liberty, to take for God's Commandements, their own dreams, and fancies, or the dreams and fancies of private men; scarce two men would agree upon what are God's Commandements; and yet in respect of them every man would despise the Commandements of the Commonwealth. (L, 199)

Hobbes is at pains to show how the declaration of any divine positive law, claiming the authority of God, must have the second sanction of the sovereign, since not just anyone but only certain people have the authority to declare 'what be these positive Lawes of God' (L, 197). Any claim to divine authority must thus be enveloped and approved by the civil authority. It appears that Jesus would not have done so well in Hobbes' commonwealth.[8]

Hobbes also asserts an identity between divine laws and natural law: 'the Law of Nature (which is undoubtedly God's law)' (L, 198). If this identity is transitive, divine law is identical to natural law, which is in turn identical to civil law. From the standpoint of the sovereign, it is civil law and civil authority alone that provides the access, the sanction and the authoritative source of all types of law.[9] The structure here is one of external exclusivity and thus completion, joined to internal inclusivity and subordination. All those divine laws shall be recognized as divine that are declared to be so by a prophet who has been authorized by the civil authority. All unwritten customs shall be recognized as legitimate that have been determined as reasonable by the sovereign. It is a structure of embedded envelopes or regions, one inside another. No region of law stands on an equal footing with another, but rather each exists within a vertical hierarchy in which the sovereign is always the last instance. The vulnerability of the law in its source is thus remedied by the condition of the sovereign's authority.

If the sovereign acts by establishing and enforcing laws then the body of action takes on this hierarchical structure. A change at one level of the hierarchy results in a separate change at another level of the hierarchy. The passage of legislation in parliament results in an increase in the amount of taxes a citizen is obliged to pay. Each of these changes, on separate levels, can be verified and compared to ensure that an action has been properly carried out, a law enforced, a command executed. At the top level of the hierarchy rests the sovereign, unique point of enunciation of the law. All other positions in the hierarchy are subordinate. As remarked earlier, the top position is exceptional, in that the sovereign is 'not Subject to the Civil Lawes' (*L*, 184). The sovereign, as source of law, may repeal any law of which he may fall foul, thus instantly changing the law to suit his situation. Elsewhere Hobbes states: 'For all Lawes, that bind, are understood to be Lawes by his authority that has power to repeal them' (*L*, 196). Hence the anchor of the law is a separate point, an agency, that can alter laws. But not only is the point of enunciation of the law separate, it is also indifferent to the content of what it authorizes. In the case of a commonwealth by conquest, Hobbes notes that the new sovereign may choose to govern a vanquished province by means of the written laws that were already in place, under the former sovereign. These laws immediately become 'the Civill Lawes of the Victor, and not of the Vanquished Common-wealth' (*L*, 185). This proviso separates authority from authorship: 'For the Legislator is he, not by whose authority the Lawes were first made, but by whose authority they now continue to be Lawes' (*L*, 186). Here falls the republican myth of the founder-legislator such as Solon or Lycurgus, author of the ideal republic – the sovereign, albeit source of law, does not necessarily have to compose specific laws for his commonwealth. The point of authority that binds subjects to the law is indifferent to the content of those laws. It is thus not the creation of the law that marks the unique status of the sovereign, but rather the power to repeal, negate and alter laws, which may already exist. In Hobbes' construction both the subject *and* the sovereign, at base, are thus indifferent to the historical content of the commonwealth.

Though Hobbes does not explicitly speak of the success or failure of political action, he does place three additional conditions on the correct operation of the civil law: the condition of *full verification*, the condition of *correct interpretation* and the condition of *perfectibility*. Each of these conditions corresponds to one of the three remaining vulnerabilities of the law, vulnerabilities that lie in the identity of its agents, the interpretation of its meaning and miscarriage in its application.

For the law to be enforceable it must be known to subjects of the commonwealth, it must be publicized. And it can only be known, and thus binding, to those subjects having 'the means to take notice of it', that is excepting 'natural fooles, children or madmen' (*L*, 187). The sovereign's declaration of the law may take place in many media – 'either by word, or writing, or some other act' – each media embodying a mnemotechnics of the law, enabling the population to remember the law, in direct inheritance of Solomon's advice that 'a man . . . bind the ten Commandements upon his ten fingers' (*L*, 189). To declare the law to the subjects of the commonwealth the sovereign needs these media. However, they introduce a great risk: fraud. It is possible for 'private men' to publish laws suiting their own 'unjust designs', thus impersonating the sovereign. Given this risk, the publication of the law must be accompanied with sufficient seals and signs of its genuine authorship. All subjects of the commonwealth must encounter a limit to their ignorance here: they must know who the sovereign is, and by what official signs he may be recognized. This is the second condition of the law's correct operation: the condition of verification of the authorship of the law.

The third condition is that in the application of the law its true intention or meaning be correctly interpreted (*L*, 190). Laws cannot immediately take effect within society and perfectly shape all individuals' actions; rather, 'All Laws, written and unwritten, have need of Interpretation'. Interpretation is the site of the third great vulnerability of the law. Due to the 'divers significations of many words' it is quite possible for civil laws to be misinterpreted (*L*, 191). The letter of the law, consisting of 'bare words', may well be ambiguous, and thus through argument it can be shown to have many meanings. Nevertheless, Hobbes insists that there is but one unique sense of the law, and it is identical with the legislator's intention. In turn, the legislator's intention must always be supposed to be equity. However, in the application of a law to a particular case, the determination of equity may well give rise to alternative interpretations and arguments. For this reason Hobbes takes extreme care to identify all rival interpreters of the law and disqualify them, reserving interpretation to the 'Judge constituted by the Sovereign Authority' alone (*L*, 191). Henceforth neither moral philosophy, nor commentaries on the laws, nor even sentences passed by previous judges are relevant. It is the acting judge alone who interprets the law as representative of the sovereign.

To interpret and apply the civil law in the name of the sovereign is to act politically.

But what does a judge actually do in particular? In judging a particular case, she takes two things into account: the fact of the matter, for which she must carefully listen to witnesses and assess evidence; and the right of the matter, for which she must pay attention to 'the Statutes and Constitutions of the sovereign' as cited in the lawyers' pleadings. It is the question of right which allows the judge to determine whether the action, if a crime, should be called a 'Murder, Homicide, Felony, Assault' (*L*, 195).

In particular cases, the law turns out to be too general to provide clear grounds for a reasonable sentence. For instance, Hobbes mentions the law ordaining that if a man be expelled from his home by force he may be returned to that home by force. Yet what happens with a case where a man forgets to lock his door and on his return is kept out of his house by force? According to the letter of the law he has no recourse, since the law does not mention nor cover such an eventuality (*L*, 194). In such a situation the judge must supplement written law with the law of nature, and suppose that the sovereign's intention in making the original law was also to contain such cases. To supplement the law, the judge must decide where equity lies in the absence of explicit indications. Hobbes also recognizes that ambassadors and even public ministers find themselves in similar situations. When swift decisions are called for, it may be the case that the sovereign's instructions are incomplete or even absent. In such a case the ambassador or minister must take as their instructions the dictates of reason, and decide what would be most in concordance with the sovereign's interests (*L*, 188). These situations in which the law is incomplete mark the fourth vulnerability of the law.[10] The remedy for this vulnerability is the judge's capacity to supplement and thus perfect the law.

In granting this capacity Hobbes lets the cat in the door. In this space of action beyond written rule, in which the judge or minister must immediately make up their own rule for action, we witness a return of the Aristotelian conception of action under the heading of prudence (*phronesis*). As mentioned in previous chapters, prudence is the kind of reasoning used by actors in uncertain or exceptional situations – situations in which the indeterminacy of usage comes to the fore. Prudence, Aristotle repeats, is not a science; it involves approximation. There is thus no room for prudence in the workings of a machine, much less a perfect machine, and yet here it is in the heart of the commonwealth. Hobbes, in line with Aristotle, recognizes that in the exercise of prudence there is room for error: 'there is no Judge Subordinate, nor Sovereign, but may erre in a Judgement of Equity' (L, 192). The structural incompletion of the law can thus lead to miscarriages of justice. However, prudence does not set its rules in stone: judges can rectify their errors. If a judge should find herself faced with a similar case to the one in which she erred, Hobbes encourages her to give a contrary sentence more in accord with equity. In other words, coherence and precedent should be sacrificed to justice as a better judgement of equity: 'No man's error becomes his own Law' (L, 192). The problem lies not in making mistakes, but in failing to recognize those mistakes: once recognized they can be fixed.

The fourth vulnerability of the law, its excessive generality faced with singular cases, is made up for by its perfectibility in the hands of individual judges.

The civil law as the sovereign's command operates smoothly if the following four conditions are kept:

- Condition of exclusive authority: the sovereign alone is the source of law.
- Condition of verification: only those published laws bearing the official seal of the sovereign are binding.
- Condition of exclusive interpretation: the sovereign and his agents alone may interpret the law.
- Condition of perfectibility: the sovereign and his agents alone can identify and correct errors in the application of the law.

If these four conditions are not met, the law will not operate correctly: there will be confusion over rival sources of law, impostures of the sovereign, incorrect interpretations of the law and miscarriages of justice. These are all instances of failure in the sovereign's action. The ambition at the outset of this examination of Hobbes on civil law was to identify general criteria for the success or failure of sovereign action. We needed to find the properly Hobbesian response to the fourth query of political action: *why do we succeed or fail*? This task has been accomplished: it is quite clear that the four conditions for the correct operation of the law can be interpreted as general criteria for the success of sovereign action. Interestingly enough, each of these four conditions simply amounts to a further dose of sovereign power, as *exclusive* and *ubiquitous*. The success or failure of the sovereign's action can thus be managed, or at least modified, by an intensification of the sovereign's action. The more the sovereign acts, the more he reinforces his control over the operations of the law, the more successful that operation will be.

If the law is successful in its operation, the commonwealth holds together. Ultimately there is no other criterion for the success of the sovereign's action than that of the unity of the commonwealth. If the people are united under a sovereign and form a commonwealth, then his action is successful. If the people become a disorganized multitude again, such as in a civil war or an invasion, then the sovereign's action has failed. This criterion is massive and blunt: complete success or complete failure measured by the very existence or inexistence of the commonwealth. It is a global criterion, and it only admits two states: a return to the state of nature, or the existence of a commonwealth, and no intermittent degrees.

This global criterion can be translated onto a local level. Chapter 29 of the *Leviathan* lists six seditious doctrines that 'tend to the dissolution of the commonwealth'; doctrines, for instance, that reserve rights to one's property against taxation, or rights to individual religious inspiration. Each of these doctrines is classified as a risk to the stability of the commonwealth, as harbouring the potential to create disorder and rebellion. One of the chief tasks of the sovereign is the government of doctrines. The very existence and publication of sedition is thus a localized mark of the sovereign's failure to control, censor and suppress such doctrines. Again the criterion is blunt: the existence or non-existence of such doctrines within the public domain marks the failure or success of the sovereign's action. Yet the criterion is local in that particular sources of such doctrines may be identified – Hobbes naming papists, Presbyterians and universities as the chief springs of seditious doctrine in the lead-up to the English civil war.[11]

In the absence of control over the circulation of doctrines, the sovereign runs an increased risk of sedition and rebellion: the higher the number of doctrines circulating, the higher the risk. The success or failure or political action can thus be measured not only globally but also by degrees of risk. The same measure of risk is applied in the operation of the civil law, subject as it is to the four vulnerabilities. Each vulnerability presents a risk, each remedy reduces that risk and contributes to the smooth operation of the law. From the standpoint of the sovereign, the success of his action is measured by the minimization of risk to his rule, and the minimization of risk depends on the extent of his control: control over public doctrines, control over the execution and enforcement of the law. The existence of seditious doctrines can be controlled through legislation concerning religious uniformity in preaching and educational uniformity in universities. Such legislation constitutes a command passed down the hierarchy of government from sovereign to the local magistrate. Changes on one level can then be compared and verified against changes at another level. The success of a decree can be measured in terms of the number of prosecutions of religious dissenters.

According to the doctrine of authorization, each and every subject of the commonwealth is not the recipient but the author of all such actions. In the body of the leviathan, politics is always a matter of *self-control*.

In turn, from the standpoint of the subject, the success or failure of the sovereign's action depends solely on his capacity to assure the protection of the public.

Both the sovereign's and the subject's criteria for success and failure are formal: they hold no place for a historical project on the part of a people nor for a political process other than the global formation or dissolution of a commonwealth. All they sanction is the more or less smooth operation of the law, sole condition of the existence of a human collective, of a commonwealth.

## *The reception of action in conscience*

The actual reception of a political action is evacuated in Hobbes' theory. The myriad consequences of actions in social interactions and people's lives disappear. The being of action is replaced by the verification of local existences in narrow registers – are seditious doctrines still being preached from the pulpits of Maidstone or not? Has the printing press responsible for the Leveller pamphlets been seized or not? Little matter what people think about the affairs of the commonwealth and why amidst recent events and daily life they have been brought to think that way. All that matters is the measurable impact of the sovereign's actions: the smooth operation of the law, the non-existence of sedition.

However, as outlined in Chapter four, in his treatment of religious dissent and the limits of ecclesiastical power, Hobbes is obliged to recognize the ontological dimension of the reception of political action in the form of individual consciences. Hobbes asserts that sovereigns 'have all manner of power over their Subjects, that can be given to man, for the government of men's *external actions*' (*L*, 377; my italics). Yet this power meets its limit in that a Christian king cannot oblige his subjects to believe (*L*, 389). The law itself reaches its limit in private conscience: only God can know the heart of men. Of course, the commonwealth could easily accommodate a discord between internal conscience and external actions: all subjects could find themselves in the exemplary position of the Christian immigrant in a pagan kingdom, obliged to perform rites in which they do not believe, subjects of disjoint action. As long as external actions remain in conformity to the law the commonwealth is intact.

Yet individual conscience is not just a borderland to be tolerated, a site of dissent that is manageable as long as it stays private. For Hobbes individual consciences, as shown in Chapter four, are actions, and they lie at the very foundation of the commonwealth – this is the figure of the subject as atomic switch. It is in private conscience that each individual calculates their chances of survival and decides to enter into the formation of the commonwealth. This crucial act of conscience is not buried in the mists of time, nor is it a mere logical presupposition: it can become quite active within the heart of the commonwealth, in at least two kinds of situation. The first, mentioned earlier, is when the sovereign oversteps the limits of his power and commands a subject to harm herself: on the basis of the natural law of self-preservation all subjects are free to disobey such a command. The second situation is that of invasion by a foreign power and the sovereign no longer assuring the people's protection: here individual consciences decide to withdraw their consent and give it to the victor instead. Conscience is thus not merely the inward and opaque site of private beliefs but rather a source of action, switching allegiance on or off. This is a permanent possibility: it is coextensive with the existence of the commonwealth.

Hobbes must thus recognize that the social field in which the government operates consists, among other things, of individual consciences. Each and every action of the sovereign takes place within a social context. For instance, in *Behemoth*, Hobbes speaks of the necessary reformation of the universities, an act that will transform the milieu of higher education (*B*, 58). This milieu is made up of individual consciences. The reformation of the universities will have its impact in those consciences, indeed it is designed to do such. Yet from the standpoint of the law, individual consciences are private, opaque and beyond reach. In his model, Hobbes can only account for the action of individual conscience under two modes: authorization of the sovereign, or de-authorization of the sovereign – no other determination is available. That other determinations might exist, that a model of political action might need to take them into account in thinking the reception of action, is signalled by two moments alone in Hobbes' own construction. The first, mentioned earlier, is the return of prudence that occurs when judges and public ministers are called to act beyond the letter of the sovereign's commands. Prudence operates in an unpredictable and irregular field – individual consciences make up much of that irregularity, as Hobbes recognizes: 'A state can constrain obedience, but convince no error, nor alter the minds of them that believe they have the better reason' (*B*, 62). The second moment in the *Leviathan* that gives a glimpse of an alternative model of action is in Hobbes' consideration of the contemporary state of the English church, as detailed in the previous chapter. The events of the English Revolution have forcibly returned the church to its primitive condition, in which we are all free to follow Paul, or Cephas, or Apollos (*L*, 479). Each of these preachers acts politically through teaching, and through the practice of conversion. To teach or to convert is to join one conscience to another by way of witness.

Hobbes would operationalize political action, assigning it to one total and exclusive agent, and mapping it out onto hierarchized levels wherein its efficacity can be measured through the registration of simple local existences: unauthorized interpretations of the civil law, seditious doctrines, private men's judgements of the sovereign's actions. The reception and consequences of action, which at an ordinary individual level he recognizes to be long and complicated, are simplified and reduced to a question of verification by an institutional procedure. The being of an action is thus evacuated. But the body of the leviathan, as the famous frontispiece shows, is composed of a million private consciences, whose action is permanent, whose judgement of global efficacy may fall at any moment, and whose beliefs remain opaque to the sovereign. His actions are not only authorized but also received by those consciences. This is what Hobbes' model of sovereign action leaves open to be thought – outside the law, outside the institution and its judgement, the being of action takes place in the *joining together of consciences.*

The institution of the sovereign – however exclusive, indivisible and ubiquitous it may be – is also constitutively incomplete and thus so are its actions. Not all of the sovereign's actions are determined by judgement, and not all actions issue solely from the sovereign.

## Locke's contractual model of political action

> *Reason* and common equity, which is that measure God has set to the actions of Men, for their mutual security. (*ST*, §8)

Hobbes insists on the unity and indivisibility of the sovereign. In complete contrast, Locke divides government into two different institutions: the legislative and the executive. He defines political power and the scope of political action as follows:

> *Political Power* then I take to be *a Right* of Making Laws with Penalties of Death, and consequently all less Penalties, for the Regulating and Preserving of Property, and of employing the force of the Community, in the Execution of such Laws, and in the defence of the Common-wealth from Foreign Injury, and all this only for the publick Good. (*ST*, §3)

## *A consensual state of nature*

To set out the foundation of such a right, Locke has recourse, like Hobbes, to the hypothesis of a state of nature in which all individuals enjoy liberty and equality, and in which their actions are ruled by the laws of nature. The difference between our two authors lies in Locke's insistence on the state of nature not being a state of war (*ST*, §19). On the contrary, he argues that it is precisely the institution of absolute power, as in Hobbes' sovereign, that introduces a state of war. In the state of nature, on the other hand, social interaction for mutual benefit is possible. On a physical and anthropological register, Hobbes places equality between individuals as the ground of perpetual conflict over resources, fear and uncertainty. On a moral and political register, Locke places equality between individuals as the ground of an obligation to mutual charity and justice. He cites Richard Hooker's argument in *Ecclesiastical Polity* whereby things that are equal enjoy the same measure: hence if I would 'receive good . . . at every Man's hands' then I should reciprocate and take care to 'satisfie the like desire . . . in other men' (*ST*, §5). Locke identifies the whole scope of the law of nature to be not so much individual self-preservation, as in Hobbes, but 'the Peace and *Preservation of all Mankind*' (*ST*, §6). As such the first teaching of the law of nature identified by Locke in the *Second Treatise* is that 'no one ought to harm another in his Life, Health, Liberty or Possessions' (*ST*, §6). The first reason for this law is that all humans are the creation of God and thus his property, being his alone to dispose of. Second, there is no ground among equals that would grant one individual authority to destroy another. Locke does qualify this law by stating that no one should harm another 'when his own Preservation comes not in competition' (*ST*, §6). This leaves the door wide open to Hobbes' *war of all against all* in which each individual's preservation is always in competition with another's. The distinction between our two authors' versions of the state of nature thus requires another more material postulate: Hobbes presumes scarcity of resources and density of population whereas Locke posits abundance of resources and a scattered population – 'in the beginning all the World was America' (*ST*, §49).

Despite admitting a slight chance of competition, Locke clearly distinguishes the state of nature from the state of war: in the case of conflict both states are devoid of any superior authority to appeal to for arbitration. A state of war, however, adds a 'declared design of force upon the Person of another', that is a declaration of enmity and a plan to destroy another. Locke immediately identifies one case of such a design: one man seeking to institute his absolute power over others. Little matter whether Locke has Hobbes or Filmer in his sights in this polemic; his tactic is to outline the legitimate form of political action by drawing a portrait of an illegitimate model of absolute power. He argues that to exercise absolute power over another man is to take away the latter's freedom, and to ignore the latter's consent. To ignore the subject's consent is to signal that one will 'use [her] as [one] please[s]' (*ST*, §17). The despot's use of subjects becomes arbitrary: without stipulated limits, such usage could end in death. For this reason, from an individual's perspective, any attempt to institute absolute power over him is equivalent to the declaration of a state of war.

Locke's argument ostensibly concerns the difference between the state of nature and a state of war, yet he is already setting out the conditions of the social contract. In the chapter on slavery, he states that even if an individual's consent were sought in the institution of absolute power, as Hobbes might be understood to argue, an individual cannot give away power over his own life since he does not possess such power himself in the first place. Each individual is the creation and property of God alone, the corollary being that there is no right to dispose of one's life. The social compact thus cannot imply subjection to absolute power: it must maintain freedom – that freedom which Locke declares to be 'the foundation of all the rest'. At the level of utility, government is instituted and men 'put themselves into society' to secure their preservation and so for that very reason government cannot take the form of absolute power (*ST*, §17). Like Hobbes, he seeks to square the circle of modern political philosophy and reconcile individual freedom with political obligation, but he will do so in a different shape, that of the contract, and this will allow him to disqualify absolute monarchy as inconsistent with the very nature of civil society (*ST*, §90).

Locke's analysis of the state of nature is designed to identify the origins of political power. This implies three tasks. First, political power must be grounded in the laws of nature. Second, the desire to enter society must be explained if social interaction for mutual benefit is already possible in the state of nature. Finally, the shape of the social contract must be explained. Locke accomplishes the first task by endowing every individual in the state of nature with an executive power to enforce the laws of nature. Any individual may punish any other individual who violates those laws (*ST*, §87). No judicial authority nor written laws are established in the state of nature; nevertheless, an offender is an individual who indicates by their actions that they 'live by another Rule, than that of *reason* and common Equity' (*ST*, §8). In Locke's state of nature, social interaction for mutual benefit is possible. To violate the law of nature is thus to behave against recognized norms, to remove oneself from the proto-community and to become 'a noxious creature' (*ST*, §10). Locke identifies the individual's executive power to punish offenders as the source and measure of the magistrate's actions in civil society (*ST*, §11). It furnishes a measure inasmuch as it does not consist of an 'Absolute or Arbitrary power' to dispose of criminals in any manner whatsoever. Rather, one punishes solely to prevent further offences and to exact compensation for damages according to the dictates of reason (*ST*, §8). In the actual formation of '*Political Society*', Locke stipulates that 'every one of the Members hath quitted this natural Power, resign'd it up into the hands of the Community' (*ST*, §87). Thereafter the community assumes this power and takes up the position of a neutral umpire with the requisite and exclusive authority to decide all controversies.

As for the second task, the inconvenience of the state of nature lies precisely in the absence of an established authority to decide controversies. Individuals quit the state of nature to achieve 'comfortable, safe and peaceable living one amongst another, in a secure Enjoyment of their properties, and a greater Security against any that are not of it' (*ST*, §95). In short, individuals enter society to preserve their property, a task rendered most difficult in the state of nature due to three obstacles (*ST*, §124–5). The first obstacle lies in the law of nature being unwritten and hence unfixed. It may be accessed by the use of reason alone and thus, due to individual ignorance, its proper application to particular cases cannot be trusted. The second inconvenience is that every individual is both a judge and an executioner, especially concerning their own cases in which they will be biased. There are no neutral observers to be appealed to and so there is a high risk of miscarriages of justice. Finally, even when a correct sentence has been passed, individuals often lack the power to enforce it upon an offender. It may appear that for Locke individuals form a political society solely to regularize and guarantee the punishment of criminals. But such a measure in turn serves the greater goal, which is the preservation of property, understood in wide sense to include lives, liberties and estates.

The final task of the analysis of the state of nature is to explain the shape of the 'social compact'. Each individual consents to constitute a community in agreement with all other individuals. In doing so each gives up her position as judge and executor of the law of nature, reserving the power to enforce the law to the community alone. As such, an individual accepts the obligation to obey the decrees and determinations of the majority of the community. Echoing Hobbes, Locke states that the individual thus 'authorizes the Society, or . . . the Legislative thereof to make Laws for him as the publick good of the Society shall require; to the execution of which his own assistance is due' (*ST*, §89). This action turns the community into 'one Body, with a power to Act as One Body' (*ST*, §96). The social compact, as in Hobbes, is thus the sole form in which action is collectivized: all subjects authorize and thus own the actions of the government; the same chiasmus of agency is at stake. The civil magistrate is the proxy of every subject who ever entered into society.

## *Conditions of contractual action*

The crucial dissimilarity with Hobbes' model of sovereign action lies in the position of the government. For Locke, it is not placed above the law in an exceptional position. It is not a product of the contract, but rather a partner to the contract. The citizen also remains an active partner in the contract: free to judge the government's performance at will, free to withdraw from the contract, free to quit the commonwealth and join another, free to exercise a right to resistance if the government should begin to exercise absolute power. As the condition of political obligation the social contract can be activated at any moment. For this reason *all* political action in Locke's commonwealth may be said to take the form of the contract.[12] This form is given in a set of five conditions that enjoy an analogical relationship to those of ordinary legal contracts. They include: the formal equality of contracting members;

freedom to choose and enter into one or another contract; entrance for mutual benefit and the equalization or commonalization of interests through the exchange of services; stipulated conditions including identity of parties, duration of contract, and means; and a clause of non-performance entailing dissolution of the contract.

Locke begins his construction of the state of nature with a postulate of formal equality: all individuals are politically equal in that none enjoys jurisdiction or authority over another (*ST*, §4). He soon qualifies this postulate by stating that at a social level it is inequality that reigns, some people enjoying precedence over others for various reasons of age, birth and merit (*ST*, §54). Nevertheless, in the formation and maintenance of the social compact each individual puts herself under the same obligation and expects, in return, the same recourse to the civil law in the case of controversy. The contract enshrines *isonomy*, the ancient Greek virtue of equality before the law.

The social compact is said to be a voluntary agreement in which each individual freely chooses her government. When the government acts, it thus does so as the crystallized will of the people, as in Hobbes. But unlike Hobbes, the will and freedom of each subject remains permanently active. A crucial condition of entering the social compact is to subject one's property to the laws of the commonwealth (*ST*, §120). Henceforth anyone who would enjoy such property in turn, by inheritance, or purchase, must do so under the condition that such property continues to be submitted to the laws of the land. In analysing the form of consent to government given by individuals, Locke distinguishes between express and tacit consent. An express declaration of consent is said to permanently bind a subject to a commonwealth. To determine the nature of tacit consent, and how far it binds an individual, Locke seizes on the moment of transfer of property. To acquire property that has been subject to the laws of the commonwealth is to give tacit consent to the jurisdiction of the government. However, 'the *Obligation* any one is under, by Virtue of such Enjoyment, *to submit to the Government, begins and ends with the enjoyment*' (*ST*, §121). Here membership of the commonwealth depends on the ownership of property:

> Whenever the Owner, who has given nothing but such a *Tacit Consent* to the Government, will, by Donation, Sale, or

otherwise, quit the said Possession, he is at liberty to go and incorporate himself into any other Commonwealth, or to agree with others to being a new one, *in vacuis locus*, in any part of the World, they can find free and unpossessed. (*ST*, §121)

This astonishing privilege is not reserved to land speculators alone: every individual, upon coming of age, may inherit property from her parents. This is precisely the moment in her life in which an individual may choose to give consent and join the social compact. Previously she was subject to her father's tutelage (*ST*, §117). The act of consent is thus concretized, individualized and multiplied in Locke's account of the social contract. It is not given by the entirety of a community together, either hypothetically or in a distant past, but each individual's consent is 'given separately in their turns' (*ST*, §117). Not only is the moment of consent localized for each subject, but they are also said to be faced with options; not just whether to join the commonwealth their parents were subject to, but also to choose between alternative commonwealths, or even to set up a new commonwealth (*ST*, §118). The subject as an atomic switch is foregrounded in Locke's theory of the commonwealth. A contract joins a limited number of people and creates a finite body. The finitude of that body implies the existence of other possible bodies, of other possible contracts. Precisely as in business, the subject, through the disposition of property, is free to choose the contract that suits her.

Each partner in the contract enters into political society not just for sake of individual benefit but for mutual good (*ST*, §163). This mutual good is realized by an equal exchange of services: all give up their natural power to enforce the law of nature. In turn, all receive security in their protection of their property through the operation of the civil law and the established judiciary. One gives up much of one's natural liberty and in turn one receives 'many conveniences, from the labour, assistance, and society of others in the same Community' (*ST*, §130). There is no disproportion between the executive power an individual gives up and the power exercised by the government as a result of the contract: neither is arbitrary, neither is absolute – 'no body can transfer to another more Power than he has in himself' (*ST*, §135). Exchange establishes a measure between individuals and the government. Furthermore, the equalization of interests in the contract must be maintained by setting up institutional safeguards. Those who detain legislative power must be prevented from setting up interests of their own distinct from that of 'the rest of the Community' (*ST*, §143). Monarchies do the opposite: they encourage one man to think of himself as having a distinct interest from that of the people (*ST*, §139).

The social contract, like any contract, also includes a number of clauses stipulating its duration, the identity of partners and its means. In the case of an express declaration of consent its duration is permanent. In the case of tacit consent, its duration depends on an individual's possession of property under the laws of the commonwealth. Once all such possession ceases, so does the consent. In terms of the identity of partners, the people alone choose the form of government and appoint the legislative. From that point onwards no other body can make laws save that legislative (*ST*, §141). The agents of government must be of sound body and mind and independent of any constraints, 'For what Compact,' Locke argues, 'can be made with a Man that is not Master of his own Life? What Condition can he perform?' (*ST*, §172). The means for satisfaction of the contract shall be the creation, promulgation and enforcement of civil laws. Such laws must be written and established and known by the population such that they are 'received and allowed by common consent to be the Standard of Right and Wrong, and the common measure to decide all Controversies' (*ST*, §124).

Finally, like all contracts, the social contract contains a clause of non-performance upon which it may be dissolved. Locke explains:

> For all power given with trust for the attaining an *end*, being limited by that end, whenever that *end* is manifestly neglected, or opposed, the *trust* must necessarily be forfeited, and the power devolve into the hands of those that gave it, who may place it anew where they shall think best for their safety and security. (*ST*, §149)

In other words, government always answers to the people, and the people retain a right to resistance. This may appear similar to Hobbes' allowance that upon dissolution of a commonwealth through invasion, its former subjects are freed of their obligation to the sovereign. However the people in Locke's model need not await the entire destruction of the commonwealth before they are freed of obligation. It is their right to judge at any moment whether the government is fulfilling its part of the contract. If the government should attempt to exercise absolute power, then it will have broken the terms of the social contract and the people will be justified in engaging in rebellion, regardless of the presence of any foreign aggressor. The right to resistance is the people's sole protection against an absolute ruler (*ST*, §93). As mentioned above, absolute power removes a people's freedom and unleashes a reign of arbitrariness. It introduces a state of war and relationships of force. Locke states: 'In all States and conditions, the true remedy of *Force* without authority, is to oppose *Force* to it' (*ST*, §155). The use of force without authority may not occur in the shape of a full-blooded assault on the people but rather in the more local form of an unlawful usage of an arrest warrant. In this case, the subject has the right to resist (*ST*, §206). Locke is at pains to insist that in such local cases the exercise of the right to resistance will not disturb the entire government (*ST*, §208).

The doctrine or the right to resistance is thus clearly designed to keep the government within the limits of the law; that is to say, within the terms of the social contract. It is directly opposed to Hobbes' doctrine of the sovereign being above the law.

The normative ground of the right to resistance is the law of nature concerning self-preservation, as outlined earlier. The ontological ground of the right to resistance is the consistency of society as distinct from the consistency of the government (*ST*, §211). The exercise of absolute power by the government does not necessarily dissolve the entire social contract throwing all individuals back into the state of nature: society remains. The people may choose to 'constitute to themselves a new Legislative, as they think best, being in full liberty to resist the force of those who, without authority, would impose any thing upon them' (*ST*, §212).

When the right to resistance is exercised in the form of a full-scale rebellion, there is no established judge on earth who has the judicial authority to decide between the two contestants, the people and the government. It is precisely in this matter of the decision of controversies that Hobbes employs his doctrine of a maximum or absolute power. For whatever conflict between civil parties, there is always a higher authority to be appealed to. Yet in Hobbes there is no possibility of conflict between the people and the government, for resistance is not just futile but impossible. According to the chiasmus of agency, to attempt to harm the sovereign is to attempt to harm oneself. Any act of force against the government immediately precipitates its agent into the state of nature, and in the state of nature there is no authority to decide controversies. In contrast, through his distinction of two levels of consistency, society and government, Locke can maintain that during an act of resistance its agents remain part of society and thus can make an appeal to an authority to decide the controversy between them and the government. The problem is that there is no higher terrestrial authority. The government has fallen from the position of civil authority to that of a simple contender in a conflict. Locke's solution is to stay firm on the postulate that in every conflict the parties appeal to a higher authority to decide its outcome. In place of an earthly authority he offers a celestial authority. Those who exercise their right to resistance make 'an appeal to Heaven' (*ST*, §168). At a structural level this is precisely Hobbes' move – install a maximum authority, enveloping all other authorities, who will decide in the last instance. Yet unlike Hobbes' sovereign, the divine court of judgement is inaccessible, its mechanisms mysterious and the terrestrial results of its judgements open to interpretation.

Locke's enshrining of the right to resistance is the signature of the contractual model of political action. It brings to the forefront the people's position as an equal and active party within the contract. Each action on the part of the government is clearly positioned as one party's fulfillment of the terms of the contract. The other party, the people, made up of each and every individual, fulfils its part of the contract by aiding the government in the execution of the laws that it passes (*ST*, §130). The people participate in the work of the government by conforming their actions to the rules it establishes. Throughout the *Second Treatise*, as Peter Laslett notes in his edition, the fundamental question for Locke in political matters is *who shall judge?*[13] Once the social contract is in place, it is the constituted civil magistrates, ultimately authorized by the people, who shall judge all matters of controversy. Counterbalancing this role, it is also the people that shall be a judge, in turn, of the government's performance. This occurs in their exercise of the right to resistance (*ST*, §240). It is the people who decide whether the government is attempting to exercise absolute power. And the exercise of absolute power is defined as a breach of trust leading to the dissolution of the contract (*ST*, §239).

In Locke's model of contractual action, the subject retains an active political intelligence in all periods, not just in exceptional periods of resistance. The subject judges all actions of the government; she is perpetually on the lookout for tendencies towards tyranny or the ruin of the commonwealth (*ST*, §210, §230). In Locke's ship of state every sailor's eyes, while rigging the sails, are fixed on helmsman and horizon. The subject is an equal counterbalancing party to the contract, the subject is both judge and participant. Locke's is what we now call a 'stakeholder society'. Every political action is measured for its adequacy to the terms of the contract, every political action balances out two parties.

## *The form of government: Division of powers*

Each model of political action has implications for the form of government. Hobbes' model of sovereign action vaunts the indivisibility of the sovereign; whether assembly or monarch, there is but one authority, one source of law, one source of judgement and decision. In Locke's contractual model, there are two separate branches of government: the legislative and the executive. In all 'well-framed governments' these powers are in 'distinct hands' (*ST*, §159). Locke argues for the prudence of such a division: if one body were to wield both legislative and executive power, the temptation would be overwhelming to exempt itself from the law, and thus pursue a private interest separate to that of the commonwealth (*ST*, §143). Grounds for the distinction between the legislative and the executive may also be found in the very being of the law. Once it is published for the law to exist as law and not just as an mere document, it must be endowed with continual force, or a 'perpetual Execution'. Hence the requirement for a 'Power always in being' that will ensure the execution of the laws (*ST*, §144). Locke adds a third power, the federative, which corresponds to the power each individual exercises in his relationships with other individuals in the state of nature. The commonwealth and its citizens entertain just such a relationship with 'the rest of mankind'. As in Hobbes, 'the whole Community is but one Body in the State of Nature, in respect of all other States or Persons out of its Community' (*ST*, §145). The federative power of a government regulates such relationships and is thus concerned with declarations of war and peace, alliances and all other such transactions. At an institutional level, however, its function is included within that of the executive.

Locke awards supreme power to the legislative. It is the people's original decision to confer the legislative power on all, a few or one man that determines the form of government: democracy, oligarchy or monarchy (*ST*, §132). Its function is to make laws to rule men's actions within the commonwealth. In making laws it determines 'the Rights, and fence[s] the Properties of those that live under it' (*ST*, §136). Locke defines the laws as 'the bonds of society, [their role is] to keep every part of the Body Politics in its due place and function' (*ST*, §219). He continues by explaining, 'when that totally ceases, the *Government* visibly *ceases*, and the People become a confused Multitude, without Order or Connexion'. This is a Hobbesian lapsus since society is supposed to have a separate consistency to that of government in Locke's model. For the laws to function as the bonds of society they must be written and published. Consequently the legislative should not govern through extemporary decrees. It should also establish known judges. In this manner the people will know their duty and the rulers the limits of their power. Those limits are determined by the original transfer of power, which excludes any absolute and arbitrary power (*ST*, §135). As a result the legislative may not exact taxes, which is to seize individual's property, without the people's consent. The legislative and the people are thus equally placed before the law, equally limited or ruled in their actions, equally cognizant of their role.

The function of executive power is to enforce the law but it also makes decisions in situations that are not covered by any existing law: this is the exercise of *prerogative*. Like Hobbes, Locke notes that the law is perpetually incomplete; it cannot provide for every single case or situation that may arise within a commonwealth. Discretionary power must therefore be allotted to the executive to act in particular cases. The law is not only incomplete but inflexible; in some cases its strict application may do harm, and so the executive also retains the power to mitigate sentences and pardon offenders. Incomplete and inflexible, the law is also slow: the executive cannot wait for the legislative to assemble, deliberate and formulate new laws to face unprecedented situations. The legislative fails to achieve the 'dispatch requisite to execution', whereas the executive can act quickly and in all discretion (*ST*, §160). In each of these situations – incompletion, inflexibility, tardiness – the executive makes up for the operational weaknesses of the legislative, it compensates for them. The executive thus acts outside the written law without prescription. As in Hobbes so with Locke; in the midst of the model of contractual action we have an example of Aristotelian action. No rules are being followed but guidelines are being improvised in a practical context of variation and uncertainty. This would be nothing less than the return of prudence in the heart of institutionalized action, rendering the latter constitutively incomplete. But Locke always has recourse to natural law as a general rule-giving framework for action in the absence of civil law. As such the fundamental rule governing all exercises of prerogative remains the preservation of all members of society (*ST*, §159).

Although the executive power acts in situations where the legislative power cannot, it remains subordinate to the latter. This stipulation is subject to two tensions. First, the executive is permanently in exercise, whereas the legislative meets periodically (*ST*, §153). Secondly, as such, it is the executive that possesses the power to convoke and dismiss the legislative power, setting the terms of parliament and fixing the dates of elections. It also retains the power to regulate the proportion between each voting district or electoral borough and the number of representatives the latter sends to the legislative assembly. These are no small powers to be held by the executive. Locke explicitly admits the role of prudence in the executive's determination of when to call parliament. He also places this action under the general rule of 'mak[ing] use of this Prerogative for the publick good' (*ST*, §156). But the fundamental relationship between the legislative and the executive, the one that keeps the executive in check, is one of accountability. The executive, Locke stipulates, 'may be at pleasure changed and displaced' by the legislative (*ST*, §152). It may even be punished if found guilty of 'any mall-administration against the laws' (*ST*, §153). The legislative thus retains the superior position of judging whether the executive has exercised its prerogative for the public good. In Locke's conception of government all 'Ministerial and Subordinate powers' are 'accountable to some other Power in the Commonwealth' (*ST*, §152).

The form of government derived from the model of contractual action involves two separate bodies. Each body's operation compensates for and shores up that of the other body. The actions of the twin branches of government are measured by stipulated limits to their power, by published laws, and by the overall law of the preservation of all members of society. The relationship between each organ of government and the people is one of accountability: indeed, in so far as the people remain a contractual party and thus judge of the entire government, the supreme power remains with them (*ST*, §149). The figure corresponding to this form of government is not that of the pyramid, all powers being resumed in one, but rather that of a balance, where the power resumed in the legislative is weighed and measured by the power remaining in the people. The contractual model of action hence furnishes a permanent matrix for the critique of government, for protest against arbitrary rule, and for the eventual rectification of policy and reform of institutions. In so far as we would reform our government and correct its actions, we are Lockean.

In the sections that follow it will be a question of how Locke repeatedly attempts to differentiate contractual action from a counter-model, that of absolute arbitrary power, which in some regards resembles the Hobbesian model of sovereign action. The second question concerns what kind of society Locke derives or sees as adequate to his model of political action. It turns out that contractual action forms a framework for very particular kinds of social interaction.

## *The counter-model: Despotic action*

Locke runs a polemic against absolute power throughout the entirety of *The Second Treatise*.[14] He argues that it is arbitrary and inconsistent with civil society. Hobbes' conception of political action is designed to contain and decide all social conflict. Locke's does the same, while also preventing the establishment of absolutism. Indeed a sketch of another entire model of action, despotic action, emerges in Locke's arguments against absolutism. The contractual model of political action thus contains what I call a *counter-model*.

Locke makes three arguments against absolutism. We are already familiar with the first: the ground of all political authority is the consent of the people. In turn, the source of all political power in the state of nature is the individual's power to execute the law of nature. However the law of nature does not authorize absolute power over oneself, nor over other human beings. For this reason, no such power could ever be transferred from individuals to the community by means of the social contract.[15]

The second argument turns on the rational calculation of interest. An individual agrees to enter into the social contract to escape the 'ill condition' of the state of nature, in which his property is perpetually insecure. However, it would be strictly against his interest to ever grant absolute power to the government for protection, since that would place him in a worse predicament than the state of nature (*ST*, §137). As Locke famously puts it, perhaps in reference to Hobbes:

> This is to think that Men are so foolish that they take care to avoid what Mischiefs may be done them by *Pole-Cats*, or *Foxes*, but are content, nay think it safety, to be devoured by *Lions*. (*ST*, §93; emphasis in original)

The third argument elaborates this image of the absolute monarch as lion. To exercise absolute power is to exercise arbitrary power. Power is wielded in an arbitrary manner when nothing sets any limits to its exercise. Arbitrary power can thus confiscate the individual's property, lay hands on her body and eventually her life. To be subject to such power is to be reduced to the condition of a slave. But to be a slave, in Locke's analysis, is to forfeit one's life to another's control, and thus to install a relationship based on force rather than reason. Moreover, to be a slave is inconsistent with civil freedom (*ST*, §22). There are two immediate consequences: first, absolute monarchy is inconsistent with civil society; second, an absolute monarch enters into a state of war with his or her subjects (*ST*, §90, §24, §172).

Locke identifies the form of governmental action that accords with absolute power: it is rule by 'extemporary Arbitrary decrees' (*ST*, §136). He reinforces this identification by describing it as, 'Absolute arbitrary Power, or Governing without *settled standing laws*' (*ST*, §137; emphasis in original). Elsewhere he critiques the idea that the original of absolute power lies in patriarchal power, arguing that a father's authority could never ground a 'sovereign power of commanding' (*ST*, §69). The sovereign, of course, is Hobbes' preferred term for government. Whether or not Locke happened to have Hobbes alone, or Hobbes and others, or others rather than Hobbes in mind when he wrote his critique of absolute power, it remains the case that the contractual model of political action contains a counter-model of *despotic action*. From the standpoint of contractual action, the very existence of despotic power renders any possible contract null and void, whether political or commercial. 'What compact can be made', exclaims Locke, 'with a Man that is not Master of his own Life? What Condition can he perform?' (*ST*, §172). In his critique of conquest as a ground of absolute power, Locke argues that if the king or conqueror may take goods, money or land away from his subjects at pleasure, 'then all free and voluntary *Contracts* cease, and are Void, in the world; there needs nothing to dissolve them at any time but power enough' (*ST*, §194; emphasis in original). Government through sovereign command and extemporary decree is thus antithetical to contractual action; never the twain shall meet. Judged in a contractual framework, the absolute monarch's commands are actions without measure, without counterbalance. This is not to say that despotic actions have no recipients, but the nature of absolute power determines the nature of its recipients: no longer citizens or subjects, they are slaves. As slaves they cannot hold the sovereign to account. In the contractual model, by implication, to act is to measure.

It is not the case that there is no place for commands or decrees in Locke's model. As outlined above, he carves out a substantial space in the business of government for the exercise of executive prerogative. He is consequently quite careful to limit this exercise since he admits, in the chapter on tyranny, that executive power is 'an Arbitrary Power in some things left in the Prince's hand' but, and this is the crucial stipulation for him, it is a power used 'to do good' (*ST*, §210). This immediately opens another can of worms as to who will judge whether or not executive power has really been used for the public good – and this is where Locke's second safeguard comes into play, as indicated earlier. The executive power is held accountable for its actions by the legislative power, which is the supreme power.

## The inverse-model: Prudence

Given the existence of these safeguards it is curious that Locke should term executive prerogative 'an Arbitrary Power'. The context is that of identifying abuses of power that lead to tyranny, including the employment of prerogative 'contrary to its end'. Yet taken at the letter, Locke's formulation identifies prerogative, whether used contrary to its end or not, as an arbitrary power. Why?

A clue can be found in Locke's lengthier treatment of prerogative in chapter 14. When listing the tasks of the executive, and justifying the need for electoral reform, Locke treats us to the first properly ontological description of the context of political action in *The Second Treatise*:

> Things of this World are in so constant a Flux, that nothing remains long in the same state. Thus People, Riches, Trade, Power, change their Stations; flourishing Mighty Cities come to ruine, and prove in time neglected desolate corners, whilst other unfrequented places grow into Populous Countries, filled with Wealth and Inhabitants. (*ST*, §157)

Such continual change in human affairs leads to certain boroughs becoming rotten, bearing more parliamentary representatives than their shrunken population should allow. Subsequently the representativity of parliament is compromised. The executive must correct the distribution of electoral circumscriptions in line with the true geographical distribution of the population. Locke maintains this ontological line of argument when he explains why it is that the executive detains the power of convoking parliament, rather than the timing of its sessions being determined by a fixed rule: it is a 'case where the uncertainty, and variableness of humane affairs could not bear a steady fixed rule' (*ST*, §156). Finally, in his justification of the executive acting beyond the letter of the law, Locke explains 'it is impossible to foresee, and so by laws to provide for, all Accidents and Necessities, that may concern the publick' (*ST*, §160). It is the environment of political action that necessitates the existence of a permanent executive ready to act. The very nature of public affairs consists of accidents, new necessities and continual change: here the indeterminacy of practice again comes to the fore.

Chapter three already showed how such indeterminacy can upset a nominalist, even pragmatist, approach to the thinking of action. This thesis is confirmed in Locke's political philosophy where the institutional model of action gives way to an entirely different model in the exercise of executive prerogative. That is to say, the quality with which the executive should act, one eye on the variations of affairs, the other on public safety, is *prudence*. Just like sovereign action, contractual action hides an inverse-model, that of prudential action.

After admitting that prudence is not a science, and that there are no rules about how to apply rules for action, Aristotle infamously fails to define prudence. In his final attempt to capture its nature he intentionally commits an ad hominem fallacy: prudence is that knowledge we assume the prudent statesman possesses, such as Pericles. To endorse such an assumption is to set up a master whose knowledge cannot be defined by philosophy. This is an extremely foreign tactic for the likes of Locke whose antipathy for un-circumscribable masters has already been noted. Nevertheless, Locke adds a further piece of the Aristotelian conception of action when he describes the difficulties of the federative power, that part of government devoted to international relations. 'Prudence and wisdom' is required of those hands that exercise federative power since these matters cannot be 'directed by Antecedent, standing, positive Laws' (*ST*, §147). Here it is not a question of accidents and changes in public affairs but of other agents' actions; 'what is to be done in reference to Foreigners, depend[s] much upon their actions, and the variation of designs and interests' (*ST*, §147). This is a fragment of Aristotle's theory of factionalism, according to which the *polis* consists of multiple actions and reactions. For Aristotle, the city-state as a whole is a reception-zone for action. This zone consists of nothing but other actions, vectored by 'the variation of designs and interests'. In the exercise of prudence, the executive has to take into account in planning its actions not only the singularity and complexity of the situation in which it finds itself, but also the probable intentions and multiple interests at work in other agent's actions.

For Locke it is important to restrict the place of prudence within his global model of contractual action. The exercise of prudential action in external matters is acceptable because it takes place in the state of nature. In internal matters, executive prerogative is certainly exercised, but the calculation of other agents' designs and intentions should be entirely unnecessary. The relations between the different organs of government are determined by accountability alone. Moreover the executive is the sole political agent acting on immediate matters, in lieu of the legislative's slow framing of laws. Yet if one digs a little deeper such calculations do start to creep into internal affairs. The legislative has the power to hold the executive to account for its acts, and may even dismiss it if necessary. The executive is aware of this impending judgement during its own operations. Given such a situation some degree of calculation of each others' designs and intentions may enter into the relationship between the two. In the chapter on prerogative, Locke recognizes the extreme possibility of an irresolvable conflict between the two organs of government:

> The old Question will be asked in this matter of *Prerogative*, But *who shall be Judge* when this Power is made right use of? I Answer: Between an Executive Power in being, with such a prerogative, and a Legislative that depends upon his will for their convening, there can be no *Judge on Earth* . . . The People have no other remedy in this, as in all other cases where they have no Judge on Earth, but to *appeal to Heaven*. (*ST*, §168)

Yet between an irresolvable conflict, and a minor disagreement over the way the legislative holds the executive to account, a whole range of conflictual situations could arise. Accountability is not enough to ensure a smooth working relationship based on subordination. The executive has too many exceptional powers that affect the very working of the legislative for it to simply remain in a subordinate position. It is not just a deputy for the legislative assembly. For this reason it is accurate to state that are at least two agents, two political actors, within a Lockean commonwealth. As such, the executive's exercise of prudential action must also take into account the legislative's designs and intentions in the realm of internal affairs. It is not easy to restrict the place and scope of prudential action once admitted within the heart of the institution.

Prudence is not a science, it does not follow rules but determines how to act in the absence of rules, making up guidelines on the fly, with only the public good as a landmark. This is why Locke describes the exercise of prerogative as 'arbitrary', whether it be used contrary to its end or not. All prudential action involves element of improvisation, and all successful improvisation gives rise to the supposition of mastery. Mastery for Locke – and this is one of his blindpoints – can never be anything other than despotic.

## *Zones of resistance*

In the passage in which Locke entertains the possibility of the abuse of executive prerogative, he develops a narrative of the slow subversion of the bases of a liberal state: a split between pretences and actions, between the use of prerogative and the public good, favouritism in the appointment of magistrates, 'experiments made in Arbitrary Power', and the rise of Catholicism secretly encouraged (*ST*, §210). The context, within the chapter on tyranny, is that of an apology for the right to resistance. Locke is arguing that the right to resistance will not cause great inconvenience to all sitting governments. The only moment in which resistance may cause a great disturbance is when the government is actually perceived by the majority of the people to be in breach of the social contract, and in such a case the disturbance is evidently merited (*ST*, §209). Locke's line of argument at this point is to naturalize resistance: how could an individual not exercise his or her right to resistance given the government's behaviour? He writes a rebel's log for Plato's ship of state:

> If a *long train of Actings shew the Councils* all tending that way [the introduction of arbitrary power], how can a Man any more hinder himself from being persuaded in his own Mind, which way things are going; or from casting about how to save himself, than he could from believing the Captain of the Ship he was in, carrying him, and the rest of the company to *Algiers*, when he found him always steering that course, through cross Winds, Leaks in his Ship, and want of Men and Provisions did often force him to turn his course another way for some time, which he steadily turned to again, as soon as the Wind, Weather, and other Circumstances would let him? (*ST*, §210)

What is curious about this passage is that it does not place the subject in the position of the atomic switch, judging the government and withdrawing its assent from the institution. Here the citizen is engaged in the work of interpretation, adding together a number of different incidents and actions, dismissing appearances, distinguishing between momentary disruptions and the true long-term course of government. Interpretation has a different temporality to judgement; it pieces together parts of a puzzle over time, rather than acting punctually. It may precede judgement, but it involves different operations of the understanding, such as gathering and weeding information, assigning different levels of importance, distinguishing degrees of probability or veracity. And in the interpretation of the government's direction, just as in prudence, the subject cannot follow any rules or institutional procedures.

This would be of little importance if it were only exceptional subjects, such as Lord Shaftesbury, who took it upon themselves to interpret the government's direction. But all Lockean subjects as parties to the social contract are potential subjects of resistance, pending their interpretation and judgement of the government's actions. What is beginning to emerge here, as a direct consequence of the contractual model of action, is a space of political action which is neither that of civil society nor of the state of nature nor even of the state of outright war but a state of resistance, in which the contract is beginning to fall apart, institutional rules no longer hold, and a divorce is occurring between semblances and reality. To be accurate, it would be best to term this space of interpretation and prudence not so much a state of resistance as a *zone of resistance*, since its exact borders are difficult to define.

It is in Locke's critique of conquest as an origin of absolute power that the idea of a zone of resistance finds its fullest development. It is also in his examination of conquest that the contrast and overlap between Locke and Hobbes receives the clearest light.

In chapter 20 of *Leviathan*, Hobbes treats the case of 'commonwealths by acquisition' rather than 'commonwealths by institution'. He classifies under the former term all those governments established by force. The sole difference between a commonwealth by institution and a commonwealth by acquisition is that in the former individuals choose their sovereign 'for fear of one another, and not of him they Institute' whereas in the latter they choose the sovereign whom they are afraid of (*L*, 138). For Hobbes, even though a covenant may proceed from fear of death it is valid: the social covenant itself ultimately proceeds from fear of death

(C, 38). For this reason it is quite possible for a legitimate government to be founded on conquest. The simple equation of obedience with protection should make this evident, as in the Engagement Controversy, mentioned earlier. The obligation to obedience on the part of the vanquished is not sourced in the victor's actual conquest, but rather in their submission to his power, their acceptance of defeat (L, 141). Their status thereafter is that of servants to a master, and the master retains the right to use all that the servant possesses: 'His goods. . . .his labour . . . his servants and . . . his children' (L, 142).

Locke's position is that a forced consent is not a real consent, and so a conqueror does not govern by the consent of the subdued people (ST, §186). In an almost direct reference to Hobbes' example of a covenant obtained on fear of death, Locke claims that if a robber were to force me to 'seal Deeds to convey my Estate to him' with a dagger at my throat, this would give him no title to my property (ST, 176; cf C, 38). On these grounds he proceeds to a stringent and critical delimitation of a conqueror's pretensions to power. In an unjust war, the conqueror gains no right to govern over anyone (ST, §176). In a just war, the victor gains no right to govern over the free men who fought for him (ST, §177). The conqueror does gain despotic power over enemy combatants, but not over those who were not engaged in the war, who did not agree to its pursuit, who did not aid and abet. Nor does a conqueror gain power over the children of enemy combatants, nor over the possessions of the enemy combatants. Consequently any despotic power gained by conquest is as limited as its original, the war of invasion: it is geographically and numerically circumscribed and it is short-lived.

To circumscribe the claims of conquerors, Locke lays out two fundamental personal rights: the first is that of personal liberty, the freedom to dispose of one's person as one wills; the second is the right to inherit one's father's goods (ST, §190). These two rights will turn out to be mutually inclusive. On the basis of the second right, if a conqueror makes a claim to the property of enemy combatants he immediately infringes the right of the latter's children to their inheritance. Consequently if one were to live as a descendent of a subdued people, under the yoke of a conqueror, one would have the right to repeat the appeal to heaven, resist the government, and claim back one's property (ST, §191). It is in this sense that Locke enlarges the zone of resistance in his examination of conquest: here resistance may be carried on down through the generations (*ST*, §176). A family tradition of rebellion could form part of my inheritance. Resistance does not necessarily imply a short interval in which a people switches from one frame of government to another, but may involve a long played out campaign that lasts for decades, complete with setbacks and interruptions. In such a temporality, the subject is evidently not party to a social contract with the conqueror's government, yet nor is she in a global state of nature. Rather, the subject of long-term resistance is in a state of war, and as such must exercise prudence in the calculation of other agent's designs and interests. Resistance is a form of prudential action in that it is not dictated by the civil law, nor does it follow specific rules, but works to re-establish the rule of law. Resistance takes place amidst the breakdown of contractual action, but it cannot be labelled 'non-contractual' since it works to re-establish a new contract, to frame a new legislative.

Another site of prudential action has thus emerged in Locke's contractual model, rendering it incomplete and dependent on its inverse-model. This is striking: perhaps a general rule could be extrapolated from this case, to be confirmed in other examples – *there where a model of action is not entirely itself it depends upon other models.*

Upon further examination the difference between Locke's and Hobbes' positions on conquest becomes blurred. From a Hobbesian perspective, if a conquering sovereign can de facto provide protection to a population in the shape of a functioning state of law, then it is in a individual's interest to submit as subject to that sovereign. Yet for Locke the individual quits the state of nature for much the same reasons as in Hobbes: insecurity of property, uncertainty of livelihood. And she seeks to gain just what a Hobbesian individual would gain: self-preservation. When faced with a conqueror's offer of protection, a Lockean individual could thus quite easily acquiesce and become a subject of that conqueror.

If this is the case, the difference between Locke and Hobbes does not turn on the question of an individual's freedom. As the chapter on the church revealed, exactly the same figure of the subject lies at the base of the institution for both Locke and Hobbes: the subject as atomic switch; that is to say, the subject that operates by switching its consent to the institution on or off. The key difference between our authors lies rather in property rights. What is inadmissible in a conqueror's claims for Locke is the infringement of property rights. A legitimate government gains the consent of the people on two conditions: the people were in a state to choose their government, *and* they were also 'allowed their due property' (*ST*, §192). Locke then argues that even if a conqueror were to gain rights over the persons and estates of the conquered, it would be impossible for him to gain absolute power. The reason he gives is that the very existence of property negates arbitrary rule: 'The nature [of property] is, that *without a Man's own consent it cannot be taken from him*' (*ST*, §193; emphasis in original). Property is a bulwark of freedom; it is the material instance of freedom.

The upshot is that despite appearances Locke has exactly the same position as Hobbes on government by conquest, equating obedience with protection – he just raises the bar far higher on the nature of protection. First and foremost protection guards a person's property such that it can be properly transmitted to his or her children. The subject in Locke is not just a switch that might give its assent to an institution, but a switch that has a perpetual investment in some form of property, in the widest possible sense of the term. As diagrammed by the two fundamental rights, the subject takes on existence in the form of the freedom to dispose of its own person, to acquire and dispose of property. The atomic switch is a disposer of property, whatever institution it belongs to.

In Locke's counter-model of despotic action, the subject retains no power to judge the sovereign's actions as right or wrong. As such it escapes polecats and foxes in the state of nature only to be devoured by a lion in the commonwealth (*ST*, §93). Yet this is not an accurate portrait of Hobbes' commonwealth, since as we have seen limits are drawn to the sovereign's power by natural law, and the subject may withdraw their obedience if the government is dissolved through invasion. As remarked previously, in the basement of sovereign action we find an element of contractual action. Through the equivalence of obedience and protection the subject is released from their obligations when the government fails to perform its part of the contract. This marks a definite convergence of Locke's and Hobbes' models, but as if in awareness of an uncomfortable proximity Locke ridicules any last minute opt out clause:

> To tell *People* they *may provide for themselves*, by erecting a new Legislative, when by Oppression, Artifice, or by being

delivered over to a Foreign Power, their old one is gone is only to tell them they may expect Relief, when it is too late, and the evil is past Cure. (*ST*, §220)

For Hobbes the subject may act as a switch only when the commonwealth is dissolved. For Locke this is far too late, the damage has already begun *and* finished. In his model, a subject can act as a switch and begin to exercise resistance even on the basis of a single unlawful act on the part of the magistrate (*ST*, §206–8). It may be the case that illegal actions and exercises of arbitrary power increase in frequency, and subsequently acts of resistance gather pace and strength, though the commonwealth be not yet dissolved, thus generating a zone of resistance.

Though Locke stakes all on the difference between contractual and despotic action, one element of his counter-model does creep into his model, and that is arbitrariness in action. It is found in the exercise of executive prerogative, where the government cannot wait to pass new legislation but must act by decree in a situation where there are no specific rules to be followed. This arbitrariness turns out not to be an element of despotic action, but rather of Aristotelian prudential action. The latter is not so easy to contain and turns up in at least four places in Locke's model: executive prerogative, the exercise of federative power, the relation between the executive and the legislative and the potential emergence of a zone of resistance.

The composition of Locke's model of contractual action is complex: it includes both a counter-model of despotic action and an inverse-model of prudential action, a place for the contained use of arbitrary power, and a zone of resistance.

## *Contractual action as a frame for social action: Acquiring property*

Society retains consistency independently of government. Yet government also renders society possible through the provision of laws. Some authors understand a liberal political system to be one that provides a neutral frame for a whole range of social practices and cultures. This is not the case with Locke. Contractual action privileges certain forms of social interaction.

As Laslett notes, Locke's distinction between the state of nature and political society is not an absolute division; much of the activity occurring in a natural state is what goes on in society.[16] It is precisely to regulate the conflicts arising from such activity that standing laws and neutral judges are required. In Locke's state of nature there are two activities to which individuals consecrate their time: the acquisition of property, and the punishment of violations of natural law.

'In the beginning, all the World was America' – this is the economic premise of Locke's theory of property; there is no scarcity, land is widely available, and through God's grant it initially belongs to all mankind (*ST*, §49). The task he sets himself is that of explaining how private property arose from the primitive commons and how inequality in property arose – both in accordance with natural law. His theory of property is an apology, in the strictest sense, for the privatization of the commons. Property ownership begins in an individual's reflexive relationship to their own person: one's first item of property is one's person. From this basis Locke moves to the activity of appropriation: nature offers many goods for human use, but to be used they must be gathered and in some cases transformed. The individual's ownership of their person is then transferred to their activity: I own my labour. Ownership then undergoes one more transfer to the product of my labour. I own my person, I own my labour of gathering berries, and then I own the basket of berries. It is the addition of my labour that distinguishes my berries from what still lies in common. This activity of appropriation through labour is not organized through the accord of other individuals: 'the taking of this or this part, does not depend upon the express consent of all the Commoners' (*ST*, §28). If it did, Locke claims, 'man had starved, notwithstanding the Plenty God had gave him' (*ST*, §28). The existence of plenty in the primitive commons is an important premise. Given that appropriation by labour is carried out in the absence of consent, any scarcity would quickly give rise to a Hobbesian war of all against all, and no property could be accumulated.

From the produce of one's labour Locke then transfers ownership to land itself: 'as much *Land* as a Man Tills, Plants, Improves, Cultivates, and can use the product of, so much is his *Property*' (*ST*, §32). Again, it is the premise of plenty that prevents instantaneous conflict arising from such land-grabbing: 'there was still enough [land], and as good left; and more than the yet unprovided could use' (*ST*, §33). Locke continues by providing in no uncertain terms an apology for one of the most deeply divisive practices of the seventeenth century: enclosure. Enclosure involved the fencing in of formerly common or shared land. One ostensive reason for this act of privatization was to encourage efficiency in agriculture. Locke uses the very term in his theory: 'He by his Labour does, as it were, inclose it from the Common' (*ST*, §32). He later reinforces the apology, and anticipates Adam Smith's invisible hand doctrine on the way, by arguing that private appropriation contributes to the common stock. It does so through bringing about massively increased productivity compared to that of waste land lying in common (*ST*, §37).

Locke finally sets out to explain differing rates of accumulation of property. Here his object is none other than justifying the vast inequalities in property ownership between individuals who belong to the same political society, and who are thus equal before the law. To the objection that his doctrine of appropriation by labour will lead to individuals seizing as much land as impossible and 'ingrossing', he replies that nature sets bounds to property in the form of the perishability of goods. God has awarded us the plenty of the earth to be enjoyed and used, not to lie rotting in a storehouse. Hence nature itself sets the measure to property: every individual should possess as much as she or he can make use of (*ST*, §36). This rule of utility is infringed if goods in an individual's possession perish or rot. In such a case, the individual is said to have invaded her neighbour's share, regardless of scarcity or plenty (*ST*, §37). At this stage, it is possible that there be small differences in the amounts of property. Some individuals possess more land and goods than others because they are more industrious. Trade gives them the opportunity to exchange their surplus goods for other goods they might need, but always within the bounds of what they can use. Everything changes, however, with the introduction of money: in Marx's terms with the emergence of exchange value. It is agreed that a small piece of gold is worth 'a great piece of Flesh, or a whole heap of Corn' (*ST*, §37). It is also the case that gold keeps, it does not perish and so it retains its use-value over time. Once money is invented, an individual may justifiably possess more land and goods than he can use, since he can sell his surplus product and receive money in exchange. This money will not rot, its utility is maintained, and so hoarding it does no injury to the proprietor's fellow man (*ST*, §50). This claim involves an odd confusion of use-value with exchange value, but to analyse it would take us too far afield. Locke rounds off his theory of property by grounding inequality in property in the people's consent, just like government. Once money 'has its *value* only from the consent of Men, whereof Labour yet makes, in great part, the measure, it is plain, that Men have agreed to the disproportionate and unequal Possession of the Earth' (*ST*, §50).

Locke's model of the political system is not indifferent to the acquisition of property, and to inequalities in the amount of property: property is the very presupposition of citizenship. In his argument against arbitrary taxation, Locke explains that the end of government is to preserve property. This is the very reason for which an individual enters society. But this stipulation 'necessarily supposes and requires, that people should *have Property*' (*ST*, §138). He explains further '*Men* therefore *in Society having Property*, they have such a right to the goods, which by the Law of the Community are theirs' (*ST*, §138). Indeed it is the integrity of one's property that is the true measure of the arbitrariness of governmental power. As remarked above, property is the bulwark against absolute power (*ST*, §193). It sounds as though Locke is close to Ireton's position in the *Putney Debates* when Ireton argues against any extension of the franchise on the grounds that only those who have fixed property have a genuine anchored interest in public affairs.

Locke, as James Tully remarks, uses an expanded seventeenth-century sense of property in the *Second Treatise*.[17] It covers not just land and material goods but an individual's own person, his labour and the produce thereof, his civil and religious liberties. But this does not change the fundamental point: the model of contractual action is designed to facilitate the disposition of property, whatever form that property might take. Whatever the subject's property consists of, it has a value for the subject, it can be changed or transformed, and it has been the result of a choice. Moreover, the crucial passages in Locke's argument that refer to property seem to refer to material property. For instance, tacit consent to the social compact does not involve reference to one's own person as one's property, but rather to the act of inheriting material property (*ST*, §120-1). As revealed in the critique of conquest, the Lockean subject wields two fundamental rights, to personal freedom and to inherit property. But these two rights are intertwined: the subject is free inasmuch as it can dispose of both its person and its property as it sees fit. Even the act of joining another commonwealth or creating a new commonwealth is modeled after the act of investing one's property elsewhere. In Locke's model of contractual action the subject materializes its freedom through its placement and use of property. The content of liberty is flexibility and dynamism in the ordering and disposing of one's possessions. This is the form of the subject's existence in the state of nature, and under the social compact: switch and disposer.

## *Contractual action as a frame for social action: Punishing offenders*

In the natural state, each individual has the power to punish those who violate the laws of nature. A large part of Locke's initial description of the state of nature is consecrated to such punishment. To violate the laws of nature is to harm other human beings and invade their rights. Such an act declares its agent to be living 'by another rule, than that of *reason* and common Equity' (*ST*, §8). Such an act immediately casts its agent out of any proto-community that may have formed in the state of nature. He does not belong to the community of rational individuals who could agree to form a political society. This agent is thus not just a criminal but a non-subject: a *barbarian*. Indeed by committing a crime, a man 'declares himself to quit the Principles of Human Nature, and to become a noxious Creature' (*ST*, §10).

In the state of nature, any private individual may judge another individual to be violating the laws of nature, and then punish that individual. In the state of nature, every individual is both judge and executioner (*ST*, §90, §125). The basis for such action is nothing other than private judgement. The crucial question is whether there remains a place for this privileged natural action of punishment within the commonwealth. Does contractual action facilitate the punishment of barbarians?

It is certainly the case that natural law continues in a political society. Consequently, the category of violation of natural law also continues in political society. At a more concrete level, the functions of punishment in society are grounded in its three functions in the state of nature: prevention of further crimes through example, restraint of the perpetrator, and reparation of damages

(ST, §7–8, 11–12). Natural law achieves force of obligation through the fear of penalty attached to its violation: 'Each Transgression may be *punished* to that *degree*, and with so much *Severity* as will suffice to make it an ill Bargain to the Offender, give him cause to repent, and terrifie others from doing like' (ST, §12). This is the first preventative function of punishment. Locke identifies its second function when he says the 'power to execute that Law . . . preserve[s] the innocent and restrain[s] offenders' (ST, §6). The third function of reparation is also present in the state of nature: Locke states that it is the injured party alone who may appropriate 'the Goods or Service of the Offender' (ST, §11). Locke directly grounds the activity of the civil magistrate in society in these functions of punishment at work in the state of nature.

If this is the case, the place of the barbarian, the object of punishment, remains an active one within the category of criminals. The barbarian is an extreme criminal. The Lockean commonwealth retains the right to punish, and if necessary, to expel those individuals who show themselves incapable of keeping the civil laws. Through the chiasmus of agency, whenever a magistrate passes a sentence on an offender I also pass sentence, I authorize his punishment, I police the commonwealth.

The Lockean subject, proprietor of its own person, free disposer of its property, is engaged in two proto-political actions in the state of nature: the acquisition of property and the punishment of barbarians. Through labour and industry he increases his property, and though he owes a duty of love to fellow citizens, he is also continually on the look out for infractions of the law of nature, ready to punish offenders; the sole case in which it is rational and legitimate to harm other human beings. Accumulation and punishment, these are the two activities that are framed, facilitated and rendered free of conflict by the contractual model of political action. Under a Lockean government we are free to dispose of our property, and free from the infractions of law committed by barbarians.

## *Frames for action and their multiplication*

Locke's doctrine of tacit consent to government includes an opt out clause: upon 'quit[ting] the said Possession, [the subject] is at liberty to go and incorporate himself into any other Commonwealth'

(*ST*, §121). This freedom may be exercised in the absence of any need for resistance. It is merely a matter of choice and convenience for the property-owner. 'In the beginning, all the world is America' and each subject is free to begin their own commonwealth, to start anew. Hobbes, on the contrary, stipulates that no subject may set up a new commonwealth once already obliged (*L*, 122).

Hobbes' stipulation is quite understandable. Locke's position seems extreme since it could lead to the balkanization of all commonwealths – the very danger Cromwell fears in the Putney Debates, England being *switzerlanded* into cantons by means of the multiplication of radical manifestos. Locke is well aware of this risk when he lays out his doctrine of the right to resistance. He assures the reader that he has not laid a 'ferment for frequent rebellion' (*ST*, §224). Against the objection that '*no Government will be able long to subsist*, if the People may set up a new Legislative, whenever they take offence at the old one', Locke counters that the people are slow to stir, and that not every little mistake is occasion for resistance, only outright and continued abuse of power (*ST*, §223). Finally he distinguishes between resistance and rebellion, where rebellion takes up arms against authority and law per se, whereas resistance takes a narrower aim, targeting a particular government's abuse of authority. He claims that the doctrine of legitimate resistance is a bulwark against rebellion, since resistance always aims at setting up a new legislative authority (*ST*, §226).

But the fear of the commonwealth being pulverized and fractioned into bits through its subjects leaving haunts the *Second Treatise*. It is precisely the same fear of pulverization that haunts Locke's account of a tolerant church. If each individual is free to leave and join an alternative church, or establish a new church, then surely the splintering of Christianity, of Protestantism, and then of the dissident protestant churches will only continue ad infinitum till we end up with churches of one, or indeed, of less than one if religious beliefs are only part of person's property.

In the *Second Treatise*, the spectre of the splitting and incessant multiplication of commonwealths is not conjured away once and for all by Locke's qualifications of the right to resistance. Indeed he fields an objection about the multiplication of governments with regard to the very hypothesis of the social compact: if all individuals are born under a government, no one in right was ever free to set up a new government (*ST*, §100). To grant such a right is by implication to open the door to an endless multiplication of commonwealths. Locke turns the tables on his opponents, identified as theorists of patriarchal sovereignty, and asks how, if the formation of new governments is prohibited, one can explain the historical existence of a multitude of 'lawful monarchies' (*ST*, §113). Either all men, even if born under government, are free to create a new government, or there could only ever have been one lawful government throughout the whole history of the world, which is absurd. He then argues from historical precedent:

> For there are no Examples so frequent in History, both Sacred and prophane, as those of Men withdrawing themselves, and their Obedience, from the Jurisdiction they were born under . . . and setting up new Governments in other places; from whence sprang up all that number of petty Common-wealths in the beginning of Ages, and which always multiplied, as long as there was room enough, till the stronger, or more fortunate swallowed the weaker; and those great ones again breaking into pieces, dissolved into lesser Dominions. (*ST*, §115)

Here Locke turns the multiplication of commonwealths into the very process of history. He exorcizes the fear of pulverization by naturalizing the process of creation and dissolution of governments. He installs a cyclical rhythm of multiplication and reduction, with the factor of strength alone determining patterns of growth and decrease at a macro-level. This passage echoes the ontological description of the domain of executive prerogative, cited above, in which circumstances continually vary and accidents steer fortune's wheel. Even if political bodies split and splinter into 'petty Common-wealths', the multitude will be reabsorbed into the few in time, and then the cycle will begin again. This is his first historical safeguard against pulverization.

The second safeguard is normative: each and every commonwealth is constituted through the operation of the same mechanism, that of natural law. However many new commonwealths may be established, their civil laws must conform to the natural measure of equity. Locke stipulates: 'The *Rules* that [Legislator's] make for other mens' actions, must, as well as their own and other Mens Actions, be conformable to the Law of Nature' (*ST*, §135). But it is natural law, incarnate in the right to resistance and the doctrine of consent to government, that also leads to the proliferation of commonwealths. Once established, a wide range of different systems of civil law may claim to be in accordance with natural law.

Whether the shape of history is cyclical and the many always reabsorbed by the few over time, whether each multiplying government must conform to the laws of nature, nevertheless there is a risk present in the proliferation of commonwealths. The risk is that this differentiation of political bodies will throw up an instance of what Alain Badiou, in *Theorie du sujet*, calls 'strong difference' or 'disjunction' in the relationships between such political bodies. In other words, the multiplication of commonwealths could lead to a multiplication of conflicts. This is precisely what Locke recognizes when he states that each 'community is one Body in the State of Nature, in respect of all other States or Persons out of its Community' (*ST*, §145). Each community is integrally exclusive of other communities: this is the metaphysical postulate. Consequently their relationship takes place within an 'ill condition' with no higher authority to adjudicate conflicts. A special organ of government, termed federative power, is required to manage such international relations, the declaration of war and peace, the creation and dissolution of alliances. Federative power is the site of the strongest exercise of prudential action within Locke's entire model. The risk of disjunctions between proliferating commonwealths corresponds to an intensification of the role of prudential action. The proper name of this risk is thus arbitrariness: the expansion of arbitrary power, of action without a rule. Locke constructs a counter-model of despotic action and condemns its arbitrariness – and yet this critique conceals a problem in his own atomized conception of popular sovereignty, the problem of the arbitrary multiplication of frames for social action.

## Conclusion: Sovereign and contractual action

Recall the five queries of political action that emerge from the Leveller-agitator experience in the New Model Army:

- Who can act?
- Who can act on what grounds?

- Who is right about what is to be done?
- Why do we succeed or fail?
- If you and I split, were we ever united, and to what end?

To apply these questions to Hobbes' *Leviathan* and *On the Citizen* is to carve out the model of sovereign action. The Lockean model of contractual action has already been sketched in detail. Nevertheless, application of the five questions not only brings into relief its difference from sovereign action, but also reveals crucial tensions in both models.

Who can act? In neither Hobbes nor Locke does the collective act. For Hobbes it is explicit: the multitude cannot act save as resumed in one, in the sovereign, by means of the chiasmus of agency. The sovereign alone acts, and all subjects act through the sovereign. For Locke it is more complicated. In appearance a collective acts: the executive in concert with the legislative. Yet the relationship between these two organs of government is ruled by accountability and transparency – by judgement. As such, they remain fundamentally separate in their responsibilities, and also in the temporality and mode of their action. In Locke, there is another potential site of collective action, and that is the right to resistance. As in Hobbes, citizens act *through* the actions of their government, but they are not subsumed within their representative institutions. As active parties to the social contract, each citizen is on the watch for a breach of trust on the part of the government, ready to exercise his or her right to resistance. However, this too does not give rise to a collective act: each individual makes his or her individual judgement alone. At certain moments many individuals may coincide in their judgement and thus initiate a movement of resistance. Yet at any moment each individual is free to change his mind and defend the government or leave the commonwealth altogether. In the end, the form of the collective in Locke's philosophy remains that of the contract. A contract joins two actions together; it collectivizes action between two parties. The government will seek to preserve the property of all, and the individual will aid the government in the execution of the civil law. The collective articulation of action thus takes the form of one individual joined to one government, each time, giving rise to a bundle of parallel contracts between individuals and government, any of which could be dissolved at any moment on the basis of private judgement.

This situation gives rise to a strong tension in Locke's model. When he identifies the end of government he says the 'first fundamental natural law' governing the activity of the legislative is 'the preservation of the society, *and* (as far as will consist with the publick good) of every person in it' (*ST*, §134; my italics). This difficult formulation attempts to unite both a holistic and an individualistic definition of the end of government. In Hobbes, the rights of the whole are clearly privileged over the rights of any individual. Locke, in contrast, tries to balance the preservation of society with the preservation of every individual of that society. In granting the right to resistance, he clearly puts a primacy on the individual, and the price to pay is the stability of the commonwealth and the risk of its fracturing and multiplication. Let us call this a tension in Locke's model, *the tension of the multiple*.

Both Locke and Hobbes criticize a model of action they call 'enthusiasm' in which private men pretend divine inspiration and act on their conscience outside any institution or rules. It is in the name of legitimate consent-grounded institutions that both Locke and Hobbes disqualify enthusiasm. Hobbes condemns enthusiasm as a seditious doctrine that weakens the commonwealth, defining it as the position *'that Faith and Sanctity, are not to be attained by Study and Reason, but by Supernatural Inspiration, or Infusion'* (*L*, 222; Hobbes' italics). He flatly declares that there is no such thing as inspiration (*L*, 268, 278, 295). He stipulates that it is unlawful for a private man to oppose his spirit to the laws of the commonwealth (*L*, 323). Locke too does not hold himself back on the subject of enthusiasm, spending an entire chapter of the *Essay* on its critique. He defines it not only as revelation without reason, but as fancy rather than revelation, the overcooked conceits of a strained constitution imposing themselves as the word of God. This would be of little concern to the commonwealth if it were not for these supposed revelations being taken as grounds for action, and 'odd action' at that (*EHU*, IV, 19, §6). For both of our authors, the subject fails to apply his own reasoning to the matter at hand, and claims to be illuminated from above. The enthused subject places himself as a passive instrument in the hands of God – albeit a special, chosen instrument. In short, the enthused subject abandons his agency to an outside source.

There is a problem with the critique of enthusiasm. In both Locke and Hobbes, the institution acts by following rules. In doing so, it too functions through displaced and potentially external agency. This is the inverse implication of the chiasmus of agency: when the sovereign acts, it is the subject who has authorized the sovereign to act, and thus it is the subject who acts. The subject as atomic switch is fundamentally external to the institution. Thus in a certain sense the sovereign also abandons his agency to an outside source. Note that this does not undo the distinction between enthusiasm and institutional action. Unlike the inspired individual, institutions establish procedures and require independent reasoning at various stages of those procedures, such as a magistrate's application of precedent to a singular case. Yet it remains the case that in Hobbes and Locke an institution's agency is *not all its own* – institutions are not entirely self-contained, being activated by a multiplicity of opaque individual consciences. The structural problem here is simple: one cannot, especially under the influence of mechanism, exclusively place agency inside or outside a given body. A more spatially sophisticated concept of agency is required, according to which it can be relayed, accumulated, and shared. Let us call this *the tension of agency*.

Who can act, and on what grounds? In both Locke and Hobbes, the answer is simple: the ground for all political action is natural law and the consent of the people. The difference between the our two philosophers emerges in the third query: who is right about what is to be done? For Locke, each private individual may judge and thus be right about what is to be done: this is one sense of the right to resistance. Each individual, acting as a switch, may withdraw her assent from the institutions of government. In Hobbes, the sovereign alone is right about what to be done, and there is no purchase for an independent viewpoint on the matter since the very possibility of private judgement is condemned as a seditious doctrine.

Why do we succeed or fail? For Hobbes there is no standpoint to judge success of failure save that of the government's hierarchy of command. Each decree or command on the part of the sovereign must lead to a local and verifiable change that occurs at another level of government. The weak point in this articulation lies in the people's consciences, which lie beyond the scope of the law. These consciences become active only in the case of a global failure of political action, which may occur in the case of invasion leading to the dissolution of government. For Locke, government fails if it begins to exercise arbitrary power and invades its subjects property. We, whether subjects to a government, or ministers and magistrates of that government, succeed or fail in so far as we keep the terms of the original contract. Each individual is free to judge whether those terms have been kept. But again, the criteria for judging success and failure are blunt and global: either the government is acting contractually or not, either it is exercising arbitrary power or not. Whoever happens to be the judge of success, subject or sovereign, the assumption is that an action's fate is not primarily determined by circumstance, but by decision and through judgement on the part of an institution, whether terrestrial or celestial. We are given solely a glimpse of a properly ontological approach to the question of success in Locke's inverse-model of prudential action, but the dominant schema is juridical.

If you and I split, were we ever united, and to what end? This is the historical query, since it opens a time for change, change in the relationships between actors, change in their understanding of each other, and change in their political identities. In Hobbes' holistic conception of the commonwealth, where the sovereign stands above the law and decides everything, you and I were simply his subjects while he guaranteed our preservation. For Locke, you and I were subjects of a particular legislative and a particular executive. If we ever joined together in resistance, then we were united, as always, for mutual preservation in whatever form that may have taken. Yet there was forever a tension in our alliance since we both, in our own corners, watched out for any conflict between the common good and our individual interests. For neither of us did our collective hold absolute priority over us as individuals, even within the zone of resistance. As long as the balance between the common good and the good of each individual lasted, so the alliance lasted. But there was always the possibility that the balance might fail, and the opt-out clause be invoked.

We were united in a commonwealth. If you and I have split something happened to that unity. If something happened, then we are in the register of history, with a strong differentiation between past and present. But what place for history in Locke's and Hobbes' models of political action? Perhaps this is entirely the wrong question to ask of seventeenth-century philosophers. After all it is clearly at the turn of the eighteenth century in Hegel's philosophy that the historicization of political action takes flight. Hobbes flatly dismisses the republican model according to which history furnishes examples of great actions to be imitated, exemplars: 'we cannot derive any argument of right from historical examples, only examples of fact' (B, 91). Yet there is a small place for history in these models. Locke engages in whig history *avant la lettre* by telling a story of humanity's progress from primitive patriarchal regimes towards the political system he advocates. He historicizes the state of nature by means of an odd fusion of biblical history and a colonial understanding of the American Indian peoples (ST, §101–12, 162). Yet this is global history conceived of as a single orientated process: there is also a place for history as singular event. A Hobbesian subject's obligation is purely based on the present, on the rational calculation of present protection. There is no place for loyalty nor for a historical sequence of actions in grounding obligation. Yet the present can be a moment of differentiation, it can contain an event. And the only possible event in Hobbes' model is that of the dissolution of the commonwealth under invasion by a foreign power. In this case the subject, robbed of any protection, is free of any obligation to the former sovereign and may switch their consent to the occupying sovereign. Locke recognizes exactly this form of historical event: 'Indeed [conquest] often makes way for a new Frame of a Common-wealth, by destroying the former; but, without the consent of the people, can never erect a new one' (ST, §175). To use a contemporary euphemism, history as an event occurs in these models as *regime change*. The micro-event is the subject's switch of consent from one commonwealth to another. The macro-event is the change of frame, the constitution of a new commonwealth.

This conception of history as punctual event creates a little problem for both Locke and Hobbes. In the very moment of frame-changing, when organized resistance or conquest has dissolved the former government, there is no higher power to adjudicate conflict. The sovereign has been dethroned and a new sovereign has not yet been consecrated. In Locke's words, the people can only appeal to heaven to justify their actions. And heaven's judgement is extremely difficult to decipher in the mouth of the event, as Locke insists in the *Essay* in his critique of enthusiasm. In both Locke and Hobbes the outcome and nature of actions are decided by judgement. Yet in the event of frame-changing no one is judge and no one decides the nature nor outcomes of actions. The nominalist metaphysics of action is interrupted by the event. Let's term this *the tension of history*.

Finally, to tighten the screw one more turn, let us recall Locke's pragmatist semantics of action from Chapter three. In Locke's terminology an idea of an action is a 'mixed mode', a combination of simple ideas that has its origin in the mind rather than nature. Since mixed modes are 'archetypes made by the mind to rank and denominate things by', there should never arise any problem over their adequacy with regard to the things they represent (*EHU*, II, 31, §3). The problem arises in the transmission of mixed modes: different people may employ slightly different combinations of simple ideas in their understanding of the same mixed mode. There is no objective standard against which to measure these divergences. Moreover, certain cases arise in society wherein it is difficult to know which mixed mode to apply. Should it be called 'murder' or 'collateral damage' when a drone misses its target and kills civilians in the Pakistani hinterland? These epistemological conditions are ripe for the emergence of conflict over the naming of actions. Locke finds a solution in practice: it is the community's normal use of names that fixes what name should be used for a certain kind of action. But then a further problem arises: given variations amidst a community, how does one know who is making the correct use of a name for action? Perhaps the usage of terms could be ranked according to their statistical frequency, but Locke does not take this path. His solution at this crux is exactly the same as Aristotle's faced with the problem of defining prudence – Locke supposes a master. The proper use of names for action must be supposed to be that of those people, those authorities who *appear* to use them correctly.

In a moment of frame-changing or in a zone of resistance in which some subjects are resisting the government, and others not, it is difficult to presume that there would be one homogeneous community of language-users.[18] The very exercise of resistance begins in naming the government's actions as arbitrary and despotic. Those subjects who continue to support the government would name its actions in different terms. The very act of resistance creates disjunct regions within a political body, regions that eventually become separate bodies. Amidst disjoint and opaque regions of a people, there can be no presumed master who knows how to correctly name actions. The consequence is simple: in situations of absolute civil conflict – such as the English revolution – *there is no rule for right action*. Even in ordinary situations, in which people may quarrel over the nature of actions, the practical indeterminacy of use is such that the supposition of a master is always a shortcut, a stopgap measure. Let us term this *the tension of use*.

The models of sovereign and contractual action are subject to four tensions: the tension of *multiplicity*, the tension of *agency*, the tension of *history* and the tension of *use*. Nevertheless these models survive and go on to enjoy a long legacy in European political thinking. If I today, activist or politician, act as sovereign or act contractually, if I take decisions or make deals, if I initiate change or fulfil promises, I do so as an avatar of Hobbes or Locke. Between the seventeenth century and today, there are many models of political action to inherit and translate into contemporary contexts: such is the subject of the sequel to this work. Yet the Lockean and Hobbesian models form an important substrate, a significant geological layer of our political imaginary.

Perhaps, ideologically, an individual could dream of being a pure Hobbist or Lockean, efficaciously deciding all matters or remaining transparently accountable for all actions. But no one can be a pure Lockean or Hobbist because the models are impure and presuppose each other: there where they are not entirely themselves they depend upon another. It has been shown how sovereign action includes a basement of contractual action, and how contractual action includes an inverse-model of prudential action. These kinds of inclusions and overlaps are familiar from the traditional merry-go-round between liberalism and authoritarianism. But these are not the only inclusions, overlaps and supplements possible for sovereign and contractual action. Both models are inhabited by tensions, and in so far as they do not resolve these tensions they leave room for other models to be created. To ensure a legacy any model of political action must engage with these tensions just as it must answer the five fundamental queries. In the final chapter, the Leveller-agitator model will be subjected to this test.

In the relatively calm pages of this book, these models of political action are compared and contrasted without fire or fury. This was not the case when Hobbes wrote in the days of the English revolution, nor was it the case in the lead-up to the Glorious Revolution, when Locke wrote. When describing how an executive may abuse the people's trust, Locke yields us one damning reference: 'Thus to regulate Candidates and Electors, and *new model* the ways of Election, what is it but to cut up the Government by the Roots, and poison the very Fountain of publick security?' (*ST*, §222; my italics). Even if Locke is referring to James II, as Laslett surmises, he condemns the latter's actions by using a very peculiar adverbial phrase: to 'new model'. The hostile reference is clear. On 6 December 1648, the New Model Army reformed the Presbyterian-dominated parliament by force, expelling all members who had been in favour of renewing negotiations with the king. 'Colonel Pride's purge' most thoroughly regulated candidates and electors, generating the Rump parliament that saw through Charles's execution and the beginning of the republic. To *new model* – is it to cut up government by the roots, or is it to forge a new alliance?

# CHAPTER SIX

# Unveiling the forgotten model: The Leveller-agitators on joint action

This final chapter takes a different form to that of the other chapters. It is not a matter of narrative history and philosophical extraction of concepts as in Chapter two, nor of philosophical interpretation and the extrapolation of models of action, as in Chapters three, four and five. Here the task is the conceptual construction of a Leveller-agitator model of joint action.

This construction will necessarily remain incomplete. To outline a model of political action is also to identify its legacy. Locke's and Hobbes' legacies are more than evident: their twin influences stretch across entire traditions of liberalism and authoritarianism. But it is not so clear where the legacy of the Leveller-agitator model lies, at least not yet. So here it will be a matter of extracting what ideas we can from the story told in the second chapter, and extrapolating on their basis.

As I type these words I hear Thrasymachus laughing behind me: one more fool philosopher who thinks to turn away from the reality of politics, who would bypass the ruling authorities to dream new histories and play with ideas. 'How long did the Leveller-agitator alliance last?' he demands, 'Seven months at best! What basis this for a theory of political action? The Levellers *failed*! The *Agreement of the People* was not adopted as a blueprint for a constituent assembly, the social revolution never happened, Cromwell seized power and the republic sounded democracy's deathknell – the House of Commons withered away from long, to rump, to barebones parliament. You, the philosopher, in love with truth, you are idealizing failure.'

And yet there is truth in failure. This book begins in an embrace of failure: the failure of philosophy to think political action without falling into the bind of angelism or apology; the failure of political action to ever realize the ends it sets itself. When have the people, each and all of them, ever been secure? What city-state has ever been just? What city on earth has ever overlapped with the city of God? What revolution ever led to a classless society? What austerity cure ever convinced the markets to lend money at manageable rates to European governments?

Amidst general failure and widespread dysfunction one short sequence of political history has been examined here: the experience of the Leveller-agitators in the English Revolution, allied with the grandees and with the rank and file of the New Model Army. In the analysis of the difficulties of the Leveller-agitator experiment, five queries are shown to make up the question of political action:

- Who can act?
- Who can act on what grounds?
- Who is right about what is to be done?
- Why do we succeed or fail?
- If we split, were we ever united, and to what end?

Each of these queries marks a site where political conflict can explode and an alliance dissolve. The eventual dissolution of the Leveller-agitator alliance was brought about by irreconcilable conflicts occurring around these five points. These are the points of failure. They draw an anatomy of the shape of the Leveller-agitator action, an anatomy of failure.

Any coherent model of political action must provide answers to the five queries. Locke and Hobbes provide such answers. It is from their philosophies that the models of contractual and sovereign action emerge. But answering the five queries is no guarantee of success for any political action performed in accordance with these models. Every model has its opacities, limits and impurities: this has been shown in detail for sovereign and contractual action. No model guarantees success – indeed, this is one way to counter

Thrasymachus' charge of idealizing failure. What is called 'success' and what is called 'failure' depends on the model one adopts. To even accept that there is such a thing as a 'ruling authority' in a city is to embrace an entire metaphysics.

For centuries, the success and failure of political action has been understood according to the model of sovereign commands and their execution. For nearly as long, action has been measured as the government's transparent and accountable fulfillment of obligations. Both of these models determine success and failure through the lens of judgement and decision. It is time to think action and its fate in a different manner. What do the Leveller-agitators have to offer?

## Regional contexts: Where do we act?

We are already familiar with Hobbes' aetiology of the English Civil War, identifying Greek and Roman philosophy as responsible for seeding many of the seditious doctrines that led to the dissolution of the commonwealth. In the first dialogue of the *Behemoth*, his partisan history of the war, Hobbes is more concerned with the insidious influence of Catholicism in English public affairs. In the *Leviathan* the doctrine subordinating spiritual to temporal authority is designed to curb any ambition on the part of Rome to exert political authority across national borders. Back in the *Behemoth*, if it is not the Catholics it is the Presbyterians that Hobbes accuses of discontent and trouble.

In each case, Catholics and Presbyterians, Hobbes identifies a faction at work within the commonwealth. In the *Politics* Aristotle identifies faction as the first originating cause of the destruction or change of regimes.[1] Factions begin, in most cases, over an error with regard to proportionate equality. That is, some parts of the people believe that they do not have a fair share in the profit and honours accruing to the city, that other people receive more than their fair share. In Aristotle's diagnosis, the error lies either in believing that if one is equal in a single respect, then one is equal in all respects, and this kind of error leads to a democratic faction; or one believes that if one is unequal in a single respect, one is unequal in all respects – this kind of error leads to an oligarchic faction. Both kinds of factions pursue distributive justice, but on the basis of errors. As such, their actions do not contribute to the common good, but only to the good of the faction. A faction, such as an industry lobby, pursues private interests at the expense of the public interest. A faction is opaque, and it obeys an internal logic that is independent of that of government. Hobbes devotes the twenty-second chapter of the *Leviathan* to a classification of all those parts of a commonwealth termed 'subject systems', political or private assemblies of men 'joyned in One Interest or One Businesse', that are or should be 'subordinate . . . to a Soveraign Power' (*L*, 155, 158). Among all the systems he classifies, the problem lies with 'irregular' private systems that are constituted not by the authority of the sovereign, but 'by Subjects amongst themselves, or by the authoritie from a stranger' (*L*, 155). He immediately explains that 'no authority derived from forraign power, within the Dominion of another, is Publique there, but Private' (*L*, 155). A faction is a part that appears to belong to a commonwealth, yet it actually belongs to another external and foreign political body. It forms a kind of intrusion within the body of the commonwealth, an outpost of a foreign authority, a fifth column.

Philosophy classically condemns factionalism in the name of the integrity of the whole, whether city-state or commonwealth. But what if we no longer have a concept of the political body as a whole? What if the commonwealth were plural, as Aristotle recognizes of the city-state, but so plural and so impure that it could never form a whole?[2] All we are left with is a patchwork of foreign intrusions, an assemblage of parts none of which originally belong to one commonwealth.

The fear of factionalism is not quite the same as the risk of atomization, which also haunts Locke's and Hobbes' commonwealths (*L*, 199). The risk of atomization raises the spectre of inconsistent multiplicity, which figures so prominently in Hobbes' writings in the shape of the crowd or the state of nature. Locke chooses to explicitly assume atomization, activating it in the right to resistance, and in the right to quit a commonwealth and join another at the moment of cessation of property ownership. Both philosophers embrace mechanism, and it is mechanism that opens up an ontology of infinite unbounded contexts – it relegates the concentric wholes of the Aristotelian cosmos to the dusty shelves of a university library, one more curio for the scholars. The ontological question that divides the models of political action is thus whether these infinite contexts are to be divided up into wholes, parts or atoms.

My hypothesis: the Leveller-agitator model of action constructs a positive account of factionalism. It embraces the inexistence of the whole, and affirms the patchwork of foreign parts as making up the infinite context of action. For the agitators the city is irreducibly plural.

The New Model Army was composed of regiments that originated in different counties and different social classes. To belong to a cavalry regiment one needed more resources at one's disposal than to belong to regiment of foot soldiers. That the army was segmented in line with English society's own segmentations is predictable and needs no demonstration. What is unique to the New Model experience, however, is the upsetting of that social stratification through the work initiated by the Self-Denying Ordinance, passed by the House of Commons on 3 April 1645. This bill, originally proposed by Cromwell, was designed to reform the command structure of the army by preventing any member of the House of Commons or the House of Lords from enjoying automatic leadership of their county's regiment. The previous structure, maintained through tradition, assigned leadership of the parliamentary army to aristocrats, such as the earl of Essex and the earl of Manchester, neither of whom appeared to be particularly enthusiastic about defeating the royalist forces. The ordinance affected Cromwell, being a member of the House of Commons. However, the committee overseeing the war decided to make an immediate exception and reinstate him as lieutenant-general, due to his evident military skill. Whatever the *realpolitik* behind the Self-Denying Ordinance it installed a principle of meritocracy whereby command at all levels was assigned according to demonstrated ability in the field. Rank and file soldiers, whatever their social origins, could now rise through the ranks on the basis of their military performance. One could engage and initiate the workings of distributive justice. A soldier, a commoner, no longer had to wait and perhaps in vain for his just deserts; now he could publically earn them on the field and in the eyes of his peers. The principle of meritocracy does not overturn the social order, but rather installs individual mobility and changeability within that order; no longer can one assume that a military rank simply equates with a social rank. Meritocracy, if it is actually at work, democratizes the workings of distributive justice. In doing so, it allowed soldiers to reach organizational levels that were traditionally reserved to inaccessible social strata, and were still dominated by members of higher social classes. As such a soldier could traverse entirely different social contexts to that in which he originated, and in so doing be exposed to many different discourses and perspectives on the army experience.

One way to travel through many different contexts in the New Model Army was through merit. Another way was geographical. The regiments of the army marched through, sought quarter, and pursued and engaged royalist forces in parts of the country that soldiers had never seen before. And the rank and file did not remain indifferent to the local populace, not least in demanding quarter, lodging, food and even sequestering horses. Some engaged in lay-preaching, interrupting the sermons of local preachers from the back of the church, giving the congregation something different to think about. Others even took it upon themselves to extend the work of the reformation by smashing all icons that smacked of Catholicism: the iconoclasts. These soldiers had occasions to measure the local reception of their actions, and to compare the reactions and sympathies of different counties. They took their own in-depth opinion polls across many sectors of the population, using no questionnaire but provocation and the proselytization of the parliamentary cause. To gauge reactions to the same actions across different counties was to gain a wide experience of society and its political leanings.

In the midst of the civil war, which some would turn into a revolution, there was no agreement between different sides as to the shape the government should take in the settlement of that war, nor was there agreement over the shape the kingdom had taken under Charles I and the Presbyterian-dominated long parliament. Diverse political agents fought for political power and their vision of justice in the same country, England, but no one agreed on the signification and status of that commonwealth: 'England' was but a name. Surrounding countries entered into the conflict, first among which was Scotland, then Ireland and Wales, to the point that some historians now feel more comfortable speaking about the 'British civil war', or even 'the wars of three kingdoms'. At the level of historical analysis the entity undergoing a war – England, or Great Britain, or the three kingdoms, or a set of amalgamated counties – can be subject to ever further division and particularization.[3]

This may appear to be a merely semantic or at best epistemological argument for the inexistence of any whole, of any unified commonwealth. And one might feel short-changed, given the promise to have done with models of action based on decision and judgement and in its place to think action in ontological terms. But to develop an ontological approach is not to directly theorize the inexistence of a global entity, the absence of a unified political body called 'England' or even 'Britain'. In the field of politics the only beings that count are actions; everything else is an epiphenomenon. As part of their being actions vehicle names, they construct and magnify symbolic identities. The existence or inexistence of the English commonwealth, or Stuart Kingdom, takes place through multiple actions at a symbolic level. So a semantic approach is not inconsistent with an ontological approach: symbols and meanings have their own type of existence, and their own efficacy.

This is not to say that we are about to embark, at this late stage, on an ontology of the sign. No, all we need do is draw some further consequences from the argument of Chapter one concerning the relation between actions and their contexts.

What did the agitators disingenuously claim that the New Model Army was not doing? As cited in Chapter one in the *Solemn Engagement* their abnegation is total: 'neither would we (if we might and could) set up any particular party or interest in the Kingdom' (*SE*, 10). Yet on the very same page they admit that the army seeks to 'study and promote such an establishment of common and equal right and freedom to the whole' (*SE*, 10). What flagrant ambition! The agitators would most definitely set up the army as a particular party, and its interest would not be private but that of the entire kingdom: they would rival parliament. The agitator's answer to the second query – who can act and on what grounds? – is revealed in *The Case of the Army Truly Stated*. The army is not one particular faction amidst others; rather, it exercises a more genuine claim to represent the English people than the parliament, especially given the narrowness of the franchise. The army gave new meaning to what it could mean to be a 'commoner of England'. And in return how do other political agents react? With declarations of dislike and refusals to negotiate. The agitators register such hostility, noting with amusement 'we find many strange things suggested or suspected to our great prejudice concerning dangerous principles, interests and designs in this

Army' (*SE*, 10). In the opening session of the Putney Debates, Edmond Sexby castigates Cromwell and Ireton for misrepresenting the voice of the army to parliament: 'your credit and reputation have been much blasted . . . for seeking to settle the kingdom in a way wherein we thought to see satisfied all men, and we have dissatified them – I mean in relation to the King' (*PL*, 2). Cromwell and Ireton, stung, return that they may say what they will in their capacity as private members of parliament, and that in their capacity as officers of the army they did not misrepresent the army's voice.

What is happening in cases like these?

No one action is capable of generating its entire context and thus guaranteeing its correct reception and success. Only classical republicanism dreams of such a Baron Munchausen trick with its encomium for the founders of cities, Solon of Athens, and Lycurgus of Sparta, authors of not just the constitution but the city itself. Rather, each action presupposes and projects a certain context. Each context in turn is composed of nothing but other actions. If there are multiple agents on the political field, then there are multiple actions, and diverse presuppositions concerning contexts. To project a context is to project a particular reception for an action. Multiple contexts mean multiple receptions of one and the same action, or rather a multiplication of the being of that action. In the English revolution there is no single point from which one all-encompassing context would be presupposed. Rather there are multiple points from which agents claim to encompass, critique and refute other agents' presuppositions about the context of their own actions. This is what happens between parliament, agitators and grandees. We all think we know the name of the whole. We all dismiss the other side's names. This is precisely why we fail in everything we do – and so do they. In such a situation, no one is right about what is to be done.

The New Model Army travels through many different contexts, and in its experience these contexts do not add up to one whole. Not only that, but each context itself is neither pure nor whole but intersects and overlaps with other contexts, containing opacities and blindspots. In November 1647, in the face of conflicting imperatives, regiments split. In Robert Lilburne's foot regiment, some soldiers obeyed their officers and respected Fairfax's call to march to a separate rendezvous at Newcastle, other soldiers, following the agitators, seized their company's colours from their officer and urged each other to join fellow regiments in a general rendezvous at Ware.[4] Even one regiment could not constitute a uniform context for action. How could it be otherwise if a context is made up not of institutional routines or standard procedures, but of actions, and micro-actions, all the way down, every action complete with its partial projection of a context? Overlapping and incomplete contexts, in sufficient number, generate a *zone of indeterminacy* in which actions go every which way.[5] The practical indeterminacy of usage becomes the norm rather than the exception to a norm. Predictions of success become inaccurate and ever new forms of failure emerge. In each context an action receives a different name, to the point that it is transformed beyond recognition. All actions necessarily fail if they take place across plural contexts. There is no stable ground for politics at any level, global, regional, local, individual *or* pre-individual.

In the absence of a whole, of a unified total political body with a single order of parts, and in the presence of multiple intersecting and incomplete contexts, what hope for political action, what measure for success?

A political action is a construction of an alliance across diverse contexts. A political action bridges factions. To succeed in acting amidst multiplicity is to create sameness. This is the great teaching of the Leveller-agitator model.

## Alliances: Who or what acts?

To act politically is to build an alliance.

The construction of an alliance is an action, in the properly Aristotelian sense, because it changes the agents of that action. They become members of a new collective, but a collective that exists solely through its actions. An alliance is not a community, nor a group, but a collective action.

The construction of an alliance is an action, in a properly New Model Army sense, because in creating a new collective it changes the greater context, it changes the alignment of actors within the political domain. When grandees join with soldier-agitators, the parliament can no longer predict either party's direction. Cromwell's political identity has multiplied, beyond his status as member of parliament, and the soldier-agitators have created an unprecedented political identity.

An alliance is a joint action. I do not act alongside you, in parallel, in a separate but coordinated manner; rather, we act together. There is no longer any distinction between your action and mine.

In a contract between two parties both act in unison yet both remain separate. Each judges the other's fulfillment of obligations. Each party retains its own minimal identity apart from the contract. A party may enter, intact, into new contracts, being fundamentally indifferent to the historical content of any contract. Each individual party judges the contractual political body for its efficacy in preserving that party's property, and in punishing other parties who do not respect property law. A party to a contract is an atomic switch.

An alliance, in contrast, changes each subject of the alliance. Joint action means that one acts only in concert *with* others, not by the other's measure, nor by the other's command. Without partners, one cannot act as a member of an alliance. An alliance thus creates a new dependency: I am no longer myself as political agent without my partners. So to act is no longer to initiate, or to separate, or to gain and express autonomy. To act is to share, and not in the sense of distributing one' property or communicating one's ideas to others, but in the sense of learning to own what is not one's own. As the authors of *An Agreement of the People* put it, 'we now do hold ourselves bound in mutual duty to each other' (*AP*, 1). I am responsible for the alliance's actions, yet on my own I would never have acted in the same way that the alliance acts. Within an alliance, as Rimbaud says, *I is someone else*. That is to say, an alliance incompletes each agent. I am only an agent in acting together with my partners, and yet I cannot see myself in my partners: they come from different contexts. No soldier-agitator identifies with a grandee, and yet they act in concert. An alliance is a joint action by virtue of the different contexts and agents it joins. Although you cannot see yourself in me, together we become something different, which I do not yet understand, though I know it will eventually find a name.

For these reasons, an alliance is always an alliance of inconvenience. This is the condition of *co-implication*. It introduces constraints on individual action, because if one attempts to act on one's own, or as part of another opposed alliance, then one runs the risk of dissolving one's place in the original alliance. Cromwell, who would enjoy more than one political identity, more than one arena of manoeuvre as both member of parliament and grandee, marks the difficulty and constraint inherent in an alliance when he reputedly thundered behind closed doors at Westminster: 'I tell you, if you do not break these men [the Leveller-agitators], they will break you.'[6]

At the same time, through repeated collective action, the differences diminish and the sameness increases. In a healthy alliance, each individual member will become more and more indistinct from the others by virtue of shared activity. We have been at this so long, I no longer know where I end and you begin. This is the sense of socialization through action. Aristotle condemns 'mere alliances', comparing them unfavourably to the city-state. One can join an alliance for economic exchange, for the punishment of evil-doers and one can even share a common place, yet for Aristotle this is a 'mere society' and does not yet make up a city-state.[7] A 'mere alliance' exists between 'distinct places' whereas in a city-state, all exist 'for the sake of noble actions', and 'for the sake of a perfect and self-sufficing life'.[8] My hypothesis is that in the absence of self-sufficiency, in the absence of a whole political body, an alliance will exist 'for the sake of' its own 'noble action' precisely when formerly distinct places become indistinct.

Our shared exposition to the fortune of the alliance, to its ups and downs, to its expansion and contraction, gives us common experience. It also removes any certainties about who we will become by means of this alliance. Yet in an alliance we become who we are.

To act jointly is to share agency, but not with a transcendent God as in Luther's conception of faith, nor at the very limits of the commonwealth, as in Hobbes' conception of dissident religious conscience. I share agency with other mortals – just as Hobbes glimpsed in his thinking of teaching and conversion under the primitive church.

The first criterion of success and failure in the model of shared action is that of very existence of the alliance. The alliance does not exist separately from the actions it undertakes, nor from the actions that construct it, yet its stability and solidity may be estimated, on the fly, and they provide a measure of success. For an alliance to be stable in a particular locality, an agent must understand who she is for her partner, however different that might be from her original political identity. Each partner must be able to encompass and maintain its relation to other partners. If what I am for my partner makes me break away from her, then the alliance, at least on a local level, collapses. To encompass one's partners' relationships to oneself is to accept to become other in an alliance, and at the same time to accept that one acts solely as member of the alliance.

How can we share agency if we cannot agree on what is to be done? What can be done if opinions are divided on the direction of the alliance? In Locke's *Second Treatise* this problem arises in the question 'who shall judge?'. In the *Essay* it emerges as conflict over the names of action. The solution of *Second Treatise* is to institutionalize and multiply standpoints for judgement in a contractual model: the executive judges what to do in situations beyond the letter of the law; in turn the legislative judges and holds the executive accountable. The government as a whole is then judged by every individual as switch, creating an atomized multiplicity of potential deciders. This dissolves any notion of the collective save as temporary aggregate. In the *Essay*, if no norms are available, the solution of mastery is invoked. Yet when action traverses disjoint contexts, the solutions of norms or mastery are ruined. When actors are dependent on their partners, and eventually rendered indistinct through the work of the alliance, the solution of atomic switches is obsolete.

Each criterion we identify for success or failure in an alliance generates a response to the query of who is right about what is to be done. The first criterion for success is the simple stability and existence of the alliance. As such, we are right and have been right, if the alliance remains stable and continues to exist, on local, regional and global levels. We are wrong and have been wrong, if the alliance dissolves and breaks apart, on local, regional or global levels. Success and failure can only be measured at a collective level. Between the multiple contexts joined by alliance, there is no sovereign, there is no single point from which to globally judge; nor are there multiple separate points from which individuals may be right or wrong about what is to be done. Nevertheless from the ground of any locality it is possible to assess the health of the alliance. A locality is not a single partner; rather it is constituted from a minimal articulation of partners, a small set of active relationships.

The second criterion of success in the model of shared action grows out of the first. An alliance will not only gain stability and solidity, but also expand if it is able to construct regional envelopes. To construct an envelope is to dissolve, through the experience of joint action, established distinctions between formerly disjoint contexts or actors. Former identities and distinctions are not erased, but they become far less important in comparison to a new regional identity that emerges as result of repeated joint action between localities. It is thus possible, over time, for actions to change their context.

I dismiss above, as a republican fantasy, the notion of an action that entirely generates its own context: *creatio ex nihilo*. But this is but one extreme case among a whole range of relationships between actions and their contexts. Machiavelli speaks approvingly of one particular action on the part of Cesare Borgia.[9] Having acquired dominion over the province of Romagna he put a 'cruel and efficient' deputy in power to install law and order. Once the population was subdued, Borgia then won them over by placating their hostility to his cruel deputy. One morning, the people of the town of Cesena discovered this deputy's cadaver quartered in the town square, accompanied with a bloody sword and an executioner's block. Machiavelli celebrates this action for its spectacular and punctual effect: the people are seized with fear and amazement – henceforth they will relate to their new governor in a different manner. In this case, the action does not generate but profoundly modifies its context.

At the other extreme, when a bureaucratic procedure results in the rejection of a refugee's application for asylum, an action has most definitely has occurred, and its effects are devastating for the applicant. But within the context of the bureaucracy, nothing changes. The standard procedure was followed, and its results are aggregated and compared to those of previous years. In routine institutional procedures, where norms do apply, and a restricted mastery is possible, actions do very little to modify their institutional context. Between these two extremes, there is a great variety of relations between actions and contexts, an entire range of degrees to which actions can affect contexts.

Each context is composed of actions. At the most minimal level, if an alliance acts within a context, it adds an element to that context. If an alliance repeatedly acts within a context, then it adds a set of elements to that context. But the degree to which an action modifies a context depends not just on frequency and repetition, but on the quality and homogeneity of the reactions it provokes. If reactions display a sufficient homogeneity with the action that provoked them, then a new regional envelope is created inside that context. In other words, an extremely successful action intervenes in the internal order of a context and rearticulates that order. Richard Overton, Leveller, condemned to the Tower by the House of Lords in 1646, dreams of just such a rearticulation in his pamphlet 'A Defiance against all Usurpations and Encroachments'.[10] The people have been duped by the royalists, bishops and lords, and even the 'newly re-royalized' presbyters, into forgetting their own birthrights; they are ignorant of their own 'immunities and strength'. They do not recognize these usurpers for who they are. In their delusion the people take their own vassalage for freedom, and 'esteem tyranny' sweeter than property. The real friends of the people, who fight against such usurpers, are taken to be enemies. In short, the entire situation is topsy-turvy and must be righted. Overton's strident pamphlet, one action in a series of many, will not right the order of government on its own. One pamphlet will not transform its global context. Nevertheless, if it was part of a coherent series of actions, and if it expanded the alliance in different localities, then it just might have contributed to the very movement of ideas that was more forcefully incarnated by the agitators of the New Model Army.

Actions can contribute to the texture of contexts, even to the point of changing their internal order, if and only if a sufficiently homogeneous set of reactions occur. But what determines the homogeneity of reactions? A political action can meet with affirmative reactions, reactions that materialize sympathy and thus homogeneity with the first action, if it expresses a principle.

## Principles, consequences, accidents

A political action is an alliance if it declares a principle and unfolds its consequences.

A political action is an alliance if it extends and takes part in a larger, unfinished action. 'The settlement of the war' was the agitator's name for the greater action they were engaged in. Each of their individual actions was a concretization of the principle at work in the longer action: the principle of popular sovereignty, to be embodied in a reformed House of Commons acting as the sole seat of government, shorn of the House of Lords and the monarchy as unrepresentative and usurping powers. Each action in a particular context was conceived of as unfolding the local consequences of that longer action. It is in this manner that a political action declares its principle, over and over again. A political action propagates itself through exemplars.

In the Leveller-agitator counter-model of instrumentalism, the means are always subordinate to the ends, and the ends are often opaque or concealed. This can result in partial and compromised efforts. In *Putney Projects* Wildman accuses Cromwell and Ireton of only wanting 'partial justice' with their purge of parliament: 'had single simple justice been the object of their desires, then they could have known no bounds or limits, no respects or relations' (PP, 8). Wildman understands neither delay, nor expediency nor compromise. Perhaps this is why he and his ilk got a reputation for enthusiasm. But to insist on full commitment to principles is not to ignore context, but rather to attempt to realize and unfold principles within different contexts. In instrumentalism means are subordinate to ends. In action driven by principle, means are employed to realize ends, but each means can also be understood as an end in itself. This is the true sense of any millenarianism found in Leveller-agitator writings: heaven and hell are not the ends our actions lead to, but the very milieu in which they take place. Heaven and hell are right here on earth, and they are created by the means we use in our actions. If each means is understood an end for the realization of principle, then the end is always nigh.

This book has many origins, but one important origin was an idea I had while reading Quentin Meillassoux's *After Finitude*. He criticizes neo-Kantian philosophy under the name of 'correlationism'. A correlationist holds that there is no access in thought to the absolute, to the thing-in-itself, but solely access to what exists in relation to us, to our categories, to our conceptual schemas. Perhaps, I thought, one could think of the thing-in-itself not as substance but as action. What would it mean for thought to access action as absolute? One hundred and fifty years before *The Critique of Pure Reason* I found a nominalist or proto-correlationist approach to action in the writings of Hobbes and Locke. Actions do exist outside institutions, and they may be thought in the terms of natural law, but in society our sole access to action is by way of the names imposed by institutions. And yet beyond those names, and even beyond the rules of natural law, Locke and Hobbes also opened up the possibility of a mechanist ontology of action, as we saw in Chapter three. Still my problem remained, late into the research. It is all very well to pinpoint the blind spots and limits of a nominalist metaphysics of action, but what would it mean to speak of access, in thought, to the absolute of action?

One day on the train, I was taking notes on *Moby Dick* for a conference in Lisbon and just before my stop I stumbled upon the very passage that answers my question, an answer that had been staring me in the face, an answer in the very title of my book, *Anatomy of Failure,* and I scribbled notes into the novel and tumbled out of the train into the winter air. Had I caught the whale?

Melville:

How vain and foolish, then, thought I, for timid untravelled man to try to comprehend aright this wondrous whale, by merely poring over his dead attenuated skeleton, stretched in this peaceful wood. No. Only in the heart of quickest perils; only when within the eddyings of his angry flukes; only on the profound unbounded sea, can the fully invested whale be truly and livingly found out.[11]

The question is not how does *thought* access the absolute as substance, but rather how does *action access the absolute,* how does action, beyond its judgement, encounter not the thing-in-itself but the situation-in-itself. The answer is action encounters the absolute in the mouth of the event, in the heart of quickest perils. The truth of action is found out in the disaster of its occurrence. In more domestic terms, the proof lies in the pudding. Ahab acted in alliance with the whale and the shape of that joint action was 'truly and livingly found out' in the event of their encounter. An *anatomy of failure* traces the being of action in neither its intention alone, nor its consequences alone, but in its full occurrence and declaration through every context it bridges. What fit between an action and its contexts? Only the event can decide.

In the event of action, accidents do happen. Accidents, however superficial and unimportant, are what measure the gap between an action and its contexts. Accidents range from simple material mishaps, such as a loop of rope catching Ahab's leg and dragging him overboard, to the unpredictable and unknown designs and actions of other agents, such as those of the white whale. As Locke himself recognizes in the case of international relations, 'what is to be done in reference to Foreigners, depend[s] much upon their actions, and the variation of designs and interests' (*ST*, §147). The truth of action is neither the will of God nor the disclosure of self but the occurrence of accidents that interrupt purpose as they also incarnate and realize it. The absolute, understood in a properly Hegelian sense as the unfolding of the concrete, consists of a series of accidents.

If political action is understood as an alliance across diverse contexts, and if it aims to declare a principle in each of those contexts, then how can it cope with accidents? The more disjoint the contexts that an alliance bridges, the more likely it is for unforeseen accidents to affect the unfolding of action. The very being of an action consists not only of its principle but also of its consequences, of the reactions it sets off across different contexts. If the alliance is mature, and many regional envelopes have been created, blurring the distinctions between formerly disjoint contexts, then clearer and more uniform reactions will occur. The principle behind the action will become more transparent, it will gain flesh, and the capacity of the alliance to absorb accidents will be increased. Furthermore, the clearer the principles declared in the action, the more accidents can be accommodated. This is why people sometimes say, when an action misfires, 'oh well, it's the intention that counts'. The pronunciation of such a phrase is precisely a consequence of the botched action, and it occurs because the declaration of principle within the action was clear, however clumsy its realization.

If, on the other hand, an alliance is immature and it bridges radically disjoint contexts, then accidents could go so far as to block and dissolve the alliance.

The degree to which an alliance can render regional contexts indistinct, and thus increase homogeneity in the reception of actions, and thus accommodate accidents, is a measure of the alliance's *power*. An alliance wields power in direct proportion to its capacity to bridge and join further contexts while maintaining its declarations of principle.

On the one hand, an immature alliance is one that struggles to stretch across just two contexts. A mature alliance, on the other hand, inhabits a number of stable regional envelopes created across many contexts. Yet no alliance will ever reach a point of saturating its contexts. Parts of those contexts will always remain outside the alliance. There is a limit to the homogeneity that can be constructed through action. The fit between an alliance and the contexts it inhabits also depends on the existence and configuration of other alliances. The Leveller-agitators were faced with royalists and Presbyterians, each of whom entertained their own alliances, with varying degrees of success.

To understand the success and failure of actions, generations of metaphysicians have modelled actions as productions, measuring them by their external results, all the way up to game theory. Actions are subsumed under the concept of production. But there is a counter-history within the metaphysics of action, and it is not particularly marginal – no great effort is required to rescue it from oblivion. Luther critiqued ossified institutions and ceremonial rites as seedbeds of hypocrisy and false piety. In their place, he offered faith as a gift from God and its spontaneous works that breathe faith: *emanating works*. An emanating work is not an external end product of faith where faith is understood as an inner attitude or set of mental beliefs. Rather, the work lives in so far as it is an ongoing act of faith – this is how to subsume production under a concept of action. In turn, faith does not exist apart from works but exists in and through works. Otherwise faith would be disjoint from action, as in Hobbes' figure of the Christian immigrant in a pagan country, or the dissenting Christian in England. For Luther, conscience must fully inform action; works inspired by faith themselves inspire faith: they are exemplars. An emanating work shares agency by communicating faith, which itself is nothing but a sharing of agency between God and an individual.

A long incomplete action directed by a principle is something like an emanating work. It too subsumes any production under the concept of action. Productions are evidently deficient if they are not complete. Yet an action can take effect while remaining incomplete. The war had not been settled, its action was incomplete, and yet petitions were drawn up, a solemn engagement taken and a new political voice made itself heard. In the Aristotelian conception, the end of a production is a separate substance that remains external to the actual process of production. In the case of virtuous action, however, the end is not the separate existence of some external substance but rather the carrying out of further virtuous actions. This is the difference between *poiesis* and praxis. The end of action is happiness, and happiness consists in the performance of virtuous actions. So it is with political action understood as an alliance driven by principle: its end is identical with its own existence.

Finally the answer emerges for the fifth and most difficult query of political action. If you and I split, were we ever united, and to what end? It encompasses the four other queries.

To what end did the Levellers join with the agitators who joined with the rank and file soldiers to join with the grandees? They united to bring about the settlement of the war. And the name of that settlement for the Leveller-agitators was *An Agreement of the People*. When the Levellers alone entered into a second, far more problematic alliance with the grandees in the Autumn of 1649, their goal remained the constitutional arrangements set out in the Agreement, as recorded in the Whitehall debates (*PL*, 125–78). 'Agreement' is neither a local nor a regional but a global name. It could quite easily be the case that there is no whole, no integrated political body, but rather a series of disjoint and incomplete contexts. It may also be the case that a significant part of the Leveller-agitator struggle consisted in critiquing and undermining the parliament's and the royalist's global visions of the commonwealth. However, this does not prevent the existence of a one integrated and rearticulated political body from being the end, the goal of political action. An alliance acts to embrace ever further contexts for action. The whole exists as an ideal, as a maximum alliance.

To what end were the Levellers, rank and file soldiers, agitators and grandees ever united, if they split? The ground of their action was the prosecution of the war, fighting for a representative assembly for the people, for the commoners, for all those who risked their lives in 'the common bottom'. The ultimate motor of their action was literally the repeated experience, in agitating, in meeting, in composing petitions and collecting signatures, of forming an agreement of the people. Unlike many of the other Leveller-agitator pamphlets, the *Agreement* is not a petition addressed to parliament. The authors explain that it is addressed to the people and not to the parliament since any act of parliament can be undone by another parliament (*AP*, 9). They then restate the theory of popular sovereignty: parliament receives its power from the people so the people can determine its powers. Rather than positing the people as existing solely as a hypothesis or chaotic multitude, as in Hobbes, or as an aggregate of atomic switches, as in Locke, the people are addressed as an historical body that can act by 'joining them [the authors] in this agreement'. The *Agreement* is the opposite of a petition: its destination is not an already constituted and corrupt institution but an institution to be constituted.

An extension of the franchise, government democratized in the House of Commons alone, government decentralized and limited in its powers, religious toleration: these were the ends for which the alliance held. The name for these ends was *An Agreement of the People*. If actions bring new signifiers into the world, as Lacan argues, then this was the new signifier in 1647.

—§—

Thrasymachus will not let me go. He chides me, he gently reminds me that it is not the philosopher but the ruling authority who decides the nature of justice. It is futile to criticize established models of political action in the name of some ideal of cooperative action. Angelic critique only solves problems in the philosopher's head, not reality.

Thrasymachus, you go too far. You end up in the opposite extreme, apology, another trap for philosophers. Your thesis: all that is done in a city-state is right, because it was made such by the ruling authority, and there are no other measures of right. Not even Hobbes went so far; he recognized the measure of natural law. As Socrates argued, sometimes rulers make mistakes. And if that is possible there must be at least two measures for action: what has been done, and what should have been done. The rule for action cannot be power alone. Otherwise there would be no art of politics, just what is done by rulers. And art there is, for sometimes alliances hold, and sometimes they immediately dissolve.

The anatomy of failure has only just begun. Once the anatomy is complete, and only then, there will be no place for angelic critique, nor for apology. All that will remain is Thrasymachus' question: who is and who shall be the ruling authority? Shall we become who we are?

# NOTES

## Chapter 1

1 G. R. R. Ferrari (ed.) (2000), *Plato: The Republic*, trans. Tom Griffith. Cambridge: Cambridge University Press. Bk I, 339a. All subsequent references will be to this translation and will be marked in the body of the text by the abbreviation R followed by the book number and the Stephanus pagination.

2 See Jacques Lacan (2007), *The Seminar of Jacques Lacan: Book XVII, The Other Side of Psychoanalysis*, trans. R. Grigg. New York: W.W. Norton & Co.

3 K. F. Hermann was the first commentator to argue that Book I was composed much earlier than the rest of the *Republic* in Hermann (1839), *Geschichte und System der Platonischen Philosophie*. Heidelberg: C. F. Winter, pp. 538–40. Gregory Vlastos also subscribes to this view in Vlastos (1991), *Socrates: Ironist and Moral Philosopher*. Ithaca, NY: Cornell University Press, p. 250.

4 Amartya Sen (2010), *The Idea of Justice*. London: Penguin, p. xi.

5 Niccolò Machiavelli (1988), *The Prince*, trans. R. Price. Cambridge: Cambridge University Press, p. 54.

6 Ibid., p. 54.

7 Ibid., pp. 54–5.

8 Vincent Descombes, 'Philosophie du jugement politique', republished in Descombes, et al. (2008), *Philosophie du jugement politique*. Paris: Seuil.

9 Boyer, Comte-Sponville and Descombes (2002), *Pourquoi nous ne sommes pas nietzchéens*. Paris: Livre de Poche.

10 See the interview with Philippe Raynaud titled 'L'impression d'une immense gâchis' [The impression of an immense waste] in *Philosophie Magazine*, No. 44, November, 2010.

11 Jacques Rancière (1995), *La mésentente*. Paris: Galilée.

12 Alexander Pope, 'Epistle 1', *An Essay on Man*, in Alexander Pope (2009), *The Major Works*. Pat Rogers (ed.). Oxford: Oxford University Press.
13 Ibid., p. 7. My translation.
14 Ibid., p. 8.
15 Raymond Geuss (2008), *Philosophy and Real Politics*. Princeton, NJ: Princeton University Press, pp. 69–70. Author's italics.
16 Ibid., p. 94.
17 Ibid., p. 97. Author's italics.
18 John Austin (1962), *How to Do Things with Words*. Cambridge, MA: Harvard University Press, p. 23.
19 It is true that this book makes little mention of Alain Badiou. Yet in its own way, it is a thoroughly Badiousian work.

## Chapter 2

1 Edmond Bear, *An Agreement of the People*, E.412[21]. Henceforth references to this pamphlet will be signalled in the body of the text by *AP*, then a page number. Unless otherwise stated, all contemporary tracts were consulted from the Early English Books Online Database, which includes the Thomason Tracts collection found the British Library, London. The reference given for these tracts, usually prefixed by E or 669.f in the case of broadsheets, refers to the British Library classification.
2 A. S. P. Woodhouse (1951), *Puritanism & Liberty: Being the Army Debates from the Clarke Manuscripts with Supplementary Documents*. Chicago: University of Chicago Press, pp. 127–8. Henceforth referred to in the body of the text under the abbreviation *PL* and a page number.
3 Kishlansky's hypothesis. See Mark A. Kishlansky, 'The Emergence of Adversary Politics in the Long Parliament', *Journal of Modern History*, 49:4 (1977), 617–40; and his 'Consensus Politics and the Structure of Debate at Putney', *Journal of British Studies*, 20 (1981), pp. 50–69.
4 For a brief overview of these hypotheses see Brian Manning (1992), *1649: The Crisis of the English Revolution*. London: Bookmarks, pp. 13–17.
5 Anon, *A Solemn Engagement of the Army . . .*, Wing S4436, or, 2nd edn, E.992[9]. Henceforth references to this pamphlet will be signalled in the body of the text by *SE*, then a page number.

6 Austin Woolrych (1987), *Soldiers and Statesmen: The General Council of the Army and Its Debates 1647-8*. Oxford: Clarendon Press, pp. 35-6.
7 Ian Gentles (1992), *The New Model Army in England, Ireland and Scotland, 1645-1653*. Oxford: Blackwell, pp. 149-50 and n. 70.
8 John Morrill in his argument for the fragility of the alliance between soldiers and Levellers makes precisely the same distinction between the rank and file's 'bread and butter' concerns and the Levellers' 'ideological jam'. See 'The Army Revolt of 1647' in J. Morrill (1993), *The Nature of the English Revolution*. London: Longman, pp. 307-9.
9 Cited in Woolrych, *Soldiers and Statesmen*, p. 38.
10 Ibid., p. 55.
11 E.385[18]; Gentles, *The New Model Army*, p. 158; Woolrych, *Soldiers and Statesmen*, p. 58.
12 Woolrych's summary of events in *Soldiers and Statesmen*, p. 59. Gentles, *The New Model Army*, p. 159, n. 141.
13 See Woolrych, *Soldiers and Statesmen*, pp. 63, 64, n. 7. Morrill also draws attention to the existence of different generations and groups of agitators, claiming that the radical pamphlet *The Case of the Army Truly stated* was solely the work of agitators newly elected to five regiments. See Morrill, *The Nature of the English Revolution*, pages 325 and 247 for his revisionism.
14 Morrill, *The Nature of the English Revolution*, pp. 308, 321. Woolrych, *Soldiers and Statesmen*, pp. 202-3, 218. Woolrych claims that the agitators as a whole were separate to Levellers – and thus the agitators cannot be understood as instruments of a foreign ideology. He points out that Leveller leaders like Lilburne berated and at times distrusted the agitators as being the creatures of the senior officers (Woolrych, *Soldiers and Statesmen*, pp. 190-3, 199, 202). On the other hand, Woolrych also points out that some agitators were influenced by Levellers, and some actually were Levellers. For instance, Edward Sexby, Lockyer and William Allen of the original agitators were most identified with the Levellers.
15 Morrill, *The Nature of the English Revolution*, p. 310.
16 Woolrych, *Soldiers and Statesmen*, p. 73.
17 Ibid., pp. 78-9, 81-2.
18 Gentles, *The New Model Army*, pp. 159-60, 172.
19 This pamphlet is to be found as an appendix to *A Solemn Engagement* referred to in note 5.

20 See Jacques Lacan (2007), 'The Function and Field of Speech and Language in Psychoanalysis', in Lacan, *Ecrits*, trans. Bruce Fink. New York: W.W. Norton & Co, pp. 197–268.
21 Aristotle (1999), *Nicomachean Ethics*. 2nd edn, trans. Terence Irwin. Indianapolis, IN: Hackett. VI, 5, 1140a5; Pierre Aubenque (1963), *La prudence chez Aristote*. Paris: Presses Universitaires de France.
22 G. W. F. Hegel (1991), *Elements of the Philosophy of Right*, trans. H. B. Nisbet. Cambridge: Cambridge University Press. See §75.
23 Included in the *Solemn Engagement* pamphlet, Wing S4436.
24 Woolrych, *Soldiers and Statesmen*, p. 112.
25 Gentles, *The New Model Army*, p. 171.
26 Ibid., p. 154.
27 See *The Case of the Army Truly Stated*, 3. See also Gentles, *The New Model Army*, p. 149.
28 John Wildman, *Putney Projects or the Old Serpent in a New forme*, E.421[19]. Henceforth referred to in the body of the text under the abbreviation *PP* and a page number.
29 Baron Thomas Fairfax, *The Case of the Army Truly Stated*, Wing 2168, and also E.411[9]. Henceforth referred to in the body of the text by the initials *CA* and a page number.
30 The five horse regiments and their attendant agitators are those of Lieutenant-General Cromwell (Robert Everard, George Sadler), Commissaire General Ireton (George Garret, Thomas Beverly), Colonel Fleetwood (William Priar, William Bryan), Colonel Whalley (Mathew Wealy, William Russell, Richard Seale), Colonel Rich (John Dober, William Hudson). Of the 11 agents printed on the pamphlet, Robert Everard alone is identified as being a newly elected agitator. This does not seem enough evidence to claim that it was the 'new caucus of Leveller agitators' alone that lay behind *The Case of the Army Truly Stated*. See Woolrych, *Soldiers and Statesmen*, p. 203. Cf. n.12.
31 See the 'Preface' in S. R. Gardiner (1889), *The Great Civil War Volume II*. London: Longmans, Green & Co, pp. v–vi. And again the 'Preface' in S. R. Gardiner (1891), *The Great Civil War Volume III* (London: Longmans, Green & Co.), pp. vii–viii.
32 John Morrill and Philip Baker, 'Oliver Cromwell, the Regicide and the Sons of Zeruiah', in David L. Smith (ed.) (2003), *Cromwell and the Interregnum*. Oxford: Blackwell, p. 17.
33 Christopher Hill (1972), *The World turned Upside-down: Radical Ideas during the English Revolution*. London: Penguin, p. 53. Hill claims there was a block in the English political imaginary whereby

the Grandees and other Independents were capable of limiting the king's sovereignty but not capable of envisaging full parliamentary sovereignty (p. 175). This statement should be qualified: the Leveller-agitators suffered no such block in their political imagination.

34  Morrill and Baker, 'Oliver Cromwell', p. 21.
35  Ibid., p. 25.
36  Pompey: 'It was necessary to sail, not to live'.
37  Gentles, *The New Model Army*, p. 201.
38  See Jean-François Lyotard (1989), *The Differend: Phrases in Dispute*, trans. Georges Van den Abbeele. Minneapolis: University of Minnesota Press.
39  Robert Everard, *Two Letters from the Agents of Five Regiments of Horse*, Wing T3463, E.412[6].
40  Hegel (1991), *Elements of the Philosophy of Right*, §75.
41  C. B. Macpherson (1962), *The Political Theory of Possessive Individualism*. Oxford: Oxford University Press, p. 112.
42  Macpherson, *Possessive Individualism*, p. 115. See Note K on p. 297.
43  See Rainborough at *PL*, 71, 74; Peter at *PL*, 73.
44  See Gentles, *The New Model Army*, for an entire chapter on the question of religion in the New Model Army.
45  Gentles, *The New Model Army*, p. 93.
46  J. C. Davis explains how prior to the Civil War kings were irresistible but limited in their power, however 'if one of the limitations on kings was that they should not wage war on their own people, then like artillery captains who turned their guns on their own side, they should be resisted. In civil war kings became resistible as well as limited and much of the political thought of the 1640s and 1650s was about working through the consequences of this momentous shift.' See J. C. Davis, 'Political Thought during the English Revolution', in B. Coward (ed.) (2003), *A Companion to Stuart Britain*. London: Blackwell, p. 377.
47  Gentles, *The New Model Army*, p. 216.
48  Ibid., pp. 216, 217.
49  Ibid., p. 218.

# Chapter 3

1  Thomas Hobbes (1997), *On the Citizen*. Cambridge: Cambridge University Press, p. 76. See also p. 94. All subsequent references will

be to this edition and will be marked in the body of the text by the abbreviation C followed by a page number.
2. Thomas Hobbes (1991), *Leviathan*. Cambridge: Cambridge University Press, p. 56. All subsequent references will be to this edition and will be marked in the body of the text by the abbreviation L followed by a page number.
3. Thomas Aquinas (2006), *Summa Theologiae. Prima Secundae*, Vol. 23. Cambridge: Cambridge University Press. Question 58, Article 2.
4. John Locke (1960), *Second Treatise on Government*, §222 in Peter Laslett (ed.), *Locke: Two Treatises on Government*. Cambridge: Cambridge University Press. All subsequent references will be to this edition, and marked in the body of the text by the abbreviation ST followed by the paragraph number.
5. Aristotle (1999), *Nicomachean Ethics*, III, I, 1110b2.
6. Quentin Skinner (2008), *Hobbes and Republican Liberty*. Cambridge: Cambridge University Press, p. 26.
7. Thomas Hobbes (2007), *The English Works of Thomas Hobbes of Malmesbury: Volume V*. London: Elibron Classics.
8. René Descartes (1988), *Principles of Philosophy*, AT, VIIIA, 18–21 in Cottingham, Stoothoff, Murdoch and Kenny (eds), *Selected Philosophical Writings*. Cambridge: Cambridge University Press, pp. 171–4.
9. Ibid., AT, VIIIA, 52, p. 198.
10. Ibid., AT, VII, 31–32, pp. 84–5.
11. Baruch Spinoza (2000), *Ethics*, trans. G. H. R. Parkinson. Oxford: Oxford University Press. Bk III, Preface, p. 163. All subsequent references will be to this edition and marked in the body of the text by the abbreviation E followed by the standard Book and proposition numbering.
12. Ibid., Bk III, Preface.
13. Baruch Spinoza, *Political Treatise*, in M. Morgan (ed.) (2002), *Spinoza: Complete Works*, trans. Samuel Shirley. Indianapolis, IN: Hackett, chapter 2, paragraph 6.
14. Baruch Spinoza (2007), *Theologico-Political Treatise*, trans. Michael Silverthorne and Jonathan Israel. Cambridge: Cambridge University Press, chapter VI, paragraph 14, p. 90.
15. Ibid., chapter VI, paragraph 12, p. 89.
16. Spinoza (2002), *Political Treatise*, chapter 2, paragraph 7, p. 685.
17. Ibid., chapter 2, paragraph 11, p. 686.

18  Ibid., chapter 2, paragraph 3, p. 683.
19  Baruch Spinoza, *Short Treatise*, Part II, chapter XXVI, paragraph 8 in Edwin Curley (ed. and trans.) (1985), *The Collected Works of Spinoza, Volume I*. Princeton, NJ: Princeton University Press, pp. 148–9. See also Spinoza (2002), *Short Treatise on God, Man and His Well-Being* in Morgan (ed.), *Spinoza: Complete Works*, p. 100.
20  John Locke (2008), *An Essay Concerning Human Understanding*. Oxford: Oxford University Press. Book II, chapter 21, paragraph 5. All subsequent references will be to this edition and marked in the body of the text by the abbreviation *EHU* followed by the Book, chapter and paragraph number.
21  Descartes (1988), Part I, Proposition 39, AT, VIIIA, 19, p. 172.
22  The fullest development of this idea in the *Essay* is found in the following passage. *EHU*, IV, 3, §18: '*Where there is no property, there is no injustice*, is a proposition as certain as any demonstration in Euclid: For the *Idea* of *property*, being a right to any thing; and the *Idea* to which the name injustice is given, being the invasion or violation of that right; it is evident, that these ideas being thus established, and these names being annexed to them, I can as certainly know this proposition to be true, as that a triangle has three angles equal to two right ones. Again, *no government allows absolute liberty*: the *Idea* of government being the establishment of society upon certain rules or laws, which require conformity to them; and the *idea* of absolute liberty being for any one to do as he pleases; I am as capable of being certain of the truth of this proposition, as of any in mathematics.' See also *EHU*, IV, 4, §7 and IV, 12, §8.
23  This difficulty is pursued in great detail in Jean Hampton (1986), *Hobbes and the Social Contract Tradition*. Cambridge: Cambridge University Press.
24  When Hobbes states the primary axiom of natural law he says: 'The only rule he needs is that when he is doubt whether what he proposes to *do to someone* is in accordance with natural right or not, he should think himself into the other person's place' (*C*, 53).
25  See Aubenque (1963), *La prudence chez Aristote*.
26  Thomas Hobbes (1990), *Behemoth or the Long Parliament*. London: University of Chicago Press, p. 39. All further references will be to this edition and marked in the body of the text by the abbreviation *B* followed by a page number.
27  Strictly speaking, Hobbes' doctrine is solely an ancestor of legal positivism, a position that takes on its proper form in the writings

of Bentham a century and a half later. Hobbes is not a pure example of legal positivism because he recognizes, apart from the instituted civil laws of any country, a set of universal norms called the laws of nature. See Hampden (1986), pp. 107–10 on the vexed question of Hobbes' legal positivism versus his use of natural law.

28 See also 'There are no authentic doctrines of just and unjust, good and evil, except the laws established in each commonwealth' (C, 9–10).

29 James Tully (1993), *An Approach to Political Philosophy: Locke in Contexts*. Cambridge: Cambridge University Press.

30 Quine's critique of ostension applies here: why would an observer interpret this activity as 'wrestling' and not as an erotic display?

31 Locke develops a similar account of the role of convenience in describing the genesis in experience of our ideas of substance (*EHU*, II, 23, §1).

32 Locke's oscillation between the adequacy of mixed modes for 'the Mind' in general, and their inadequacy between particular people in their transmission parallels his displacement of ontological question of unity of mixed modes in chapter 22 by the supposedly empirical question of their transmission. For a true empiricist, however, mixed modes would exist nowhere but within particular transmissions. There is no general 'Mind' that adequately invents and understands Archetypes. Consequently there is no tidy distinction between ontological and empirical questions. Moreover, at the level of the ontological question, as Frege argues against psychological accounts of the genesis of numbers, if a mixed mode is given unity by the unity of the mind's act in inventing it, from whence the unity of that mental act? Locke's solution would be to place unity in the name alone.

33 A comparison with Donald Davidson's employment of the principle of charity would be of no little interest.

# Chapter 4

1 See Gentles (1992), *The New Model Army in England*.

2 Spinoza (2007), *Theologico-Political Treatise*, trans. Michael Silverthorne and Jonathan Israel. Cambridge: Cambridge University Press, chapter 6, paragraph 1, p. 68.

3 Luther, M., 'Preface to the Complete Edition of Luther's Latin Writings', in J. Dillenger (ed.) (1962), *Martin Luther: Selections from His Writings*. New York: Anchor Books, p. 11. All subsequent

references to Luther will refer to this edition, and will be marked in the body of the text by the abbreviation *ML* and a page number.

4  As self-referential as Aristotle's definition in the *Nicomachean Ethics* of the goal of virtuous action: to continually perform further virtuous actions.

5  Size is not everything, but chapter 42 on 'Ecclesiastical Power' is the longest chapter in the *Leviathan*, 64 pages long in the Cambridge Student Edition, quadruple the average chapter.

6  Hobbes also clearly takes aim at the Catholic church in chapter 12 on religion, pp. 85–6.

7  Further investigation of this question evidently leads to a confrontation with Carl Schmitt (2002), *Le léviathan dans la doctrine de l'état de Thomas Hobbes*. Paris: Seuil. The French edition is to be preferred to the English edition on account of the excellent introductory essay by Etienne Balibar.

8  See Quentin Skinner (2001), 'Conquest and Consent: Hobbes and the Engagement Controversy', in *Visions of Politics Vol.III: Hobbes and Civil Science*. Cambridge: Cambridge University Press, pp. 287–307.

9  For a detailed analysis of Locke's change of heart see Richard Ashcraft (1986), *Revolutionary Politics and Locke's Two Treatise on Government*. Princeton, NJ: Princeton University Press. In particular chapter 3. See also James Tully (1983), 'Introduction', in Locke, *A Letter Concerning Toleration*. Indiana: Hackett, pp. 3–6. Raymond Klibansky (1965), 'Préface' in Locke, *Lettre sur la tolerance*, trans. R. Polin (from the Latin). Paris: Quadrige, pp. vii–xcix. Jean-Fabien Spitz (1992), 'Introduction' in Locke, *Lettre sur la tolerance et autres texts*, trans. Jean le Clerc. Paris: Flammarion, pp. 11–97.

10  John Locke (1976), 'Locke to S. H. [Henry Stubbe]' 1659–61, in E. S. Beer (ed.), *The Correspondence of John Locke Vol. I*. Oxford: Clarendon Press, pp. 109–12. John Locke (1967), *Two Tracts on Government*, ed. Philip Adams. Cambridge: Cambridge University Press.

11  John Locke (2010), *An Essay concerning Toleration: And Other Writings on Law and Politics, 1667–1683*, ed. J. R. Milton and Philip Milton. Oxford: Oxford University Press.

12  For Smith, the mechanisms of supply and demand have an immediate affect on prices, whether it be the price of grain or of labour. But there are compensatory mechanisms that assure that market prices will gravitate around a natural price, reaching a

long-term equilibrium. If the rate of profit in one industry vastly outdistanced the rates of profit in other industries, investment would flood the lucky industry and desert others – to the evident detriment of the economy as a whole. Yet once the number of companies operating in the superprofitable industry increases, there will be an immediate intensification of competition. Higher competition means increased costs and lower revenue: for instance, the price of labour could increase under increasing demand for labour, or a price war could occur on the end-product. The rate of profit will thus decrease over time, and inefficient firms will be eliminated by competition. Investment will thus flow out of this industry into another new superprofitable industry. What these mechanisms presuppose are aggregated consequences of individuals making rational calculations as to the investment of their capital. Smith's economic man invests and withdraws his or her capital according to one exclusive criterion: the best rate of return. Locke's subject of toleration switches his preference from one church to another according to one exclusive criterion: the best chances of eternal life.

# Chapter 5

1 On this issue, see Q. Skinner 'Hobbes' Theory of Political Obligation' and 'Hobbes and the Engagement Controversy' in Skinner (2001), pp. 264–307.
2 Ibid., p. 284.
3 Cited in ibid., p. 280.
4 Rousseau (1964), *Du contrat social*, Book I, chapter 5 in *Oeuvres Complètes III*. Paris: Pleiade, 359. My translation.
5 See Skinner (2001), 'Conquest and Consent', p. 294.
6 Beyond the scope of this book, to be examined in a sequel, the eighteenth and nineteenth century saw the emergence of disciplines that positioned themselves as inheritors of the mantle 'science of action', not least among which was economics. Still today economics assumes the title 'science of action' via game theory, decision theory and rational choice theory.
7 Distilled from chapter 18 on the Rights and Marks of Sovereignty by Institution and chapter 23 on the Public Ministers of Sovereign Power. See also Hobbes (1997), *On the Citizen*. chapter 6, p. 88.

**8** See Hobbes (1990), *Behemoth or the Long Parliament*, p. 52 on the Apostles, and their exceptional status as having direct experience of Jesus as God. See the previous chapter on the exception Hobbes has to make for the primitive church.

**9** '[A]ll Lawes, written, and unwritten, have their Authority and force, from the Will of the Common-wealth' (*L*, 186).

**10** Aristotle identifies this vulnerability in the *Politics* when he debates the rule of law versus the rule of a king: 'laws speak only of the universal and do not give commands relative to the actual circumstances'. See Aristotle (1996), *Politics*, trans. Phillips Simpson. Chapel Hill: University of North Carolina Press. See III, 15, 1286a9. Aristotle, in turn, is recalling Plato's arguments in the *Statesman*, 294a–b in Plato (2005), *The Collected Works of Plato*. Princeton, NJ: Princeton University Press.

**11** See the first dialogue of Hobbes' *Behemoth*.

**12** In his introduction to his edition of the *Two Treatises on Government*, Peter Laslett argues that it is misleading to speak of 'the relation between government and governed' as contractual since it is rather a matter of trust, and contracts imply that each party gets something out of the exchange which Locke is anxious to avoid on the part of government. See Locke (1960), *Second Treatise on Government*, p. 114. This is to anthropomorphize the government: as an institution it does not gain economically but receives obedience from subjects through the contract. Furthermore, the relation between subjects and the government may well go under the name 'trust', but that trust takes the general form of a contract.

**13** See Laslett's note to §168 on p. 379.

**14** These arguments may be found in nine of its 19 chapters: 2, 3, 4, 7, 9, 13, 15, 18 and 19.

**15** This argument may be found at *ST*, §§6, 8, 23, 149, 168 and 172.

**16** Peter Laslett, 'Introduction', in *Locke*, p. 116.

**17** Tully (1993), *An Approach to Political Philosophy*, pp. 77, 96, 120–1.

**18** Here I owe a debt to Jacques Derrida's critique of John Austin's presumption of 'saturated contexts'. See Jacques Derrida (1982), 'Signature, Event, Context', in *Margins of Philosophy*, trans. A. Bass. Chicago: University of Chicago Press, pp. 307–30.

## Chapter 6

1. Aristotle (1996), *Politics*, 1301a3, 1301b27. Phillips Simpson rearranges the books of the *Politics* so as to assign these sections to VII, 1; they are normally found in V, 1.
2. Ibid., II, 2, 1261a16, 1261a22.
3. The existence of multiple contexts is precisely what revisionist and then post-revisionist historiography of the English civil war has explored by moving ever further away from Christopher Hill, Lawrence Stone and C. B. Macpherson's grand synthetic visions into particularism. We are now treated not just to a social class or even a county's experience of the war, but a particular family's perspective on the war. See Mary Fulbrook on the 'proliferation of local studies' in 'The English Revolution and the Revisionist Revolt', in P. Gaunt (2000), *The English Civil War: The Essential Readings*. London: Blackwell, pp. 59–78, specifically p. 61.
4. See Gentles, *The New Model Army*, pp. 221–2.
5. See Thomas Pynchon's conception of Berlin as a 'zone' under the allies occupation in Part 3 of Thomas Pynchon (1973), *Gravity's Rainbow*. New York: Viking Press.
6. Gentles, *The New Model Army*, p. 322. Based on John Lilburne's testimony to the arrest and questioning of the Leveller leaders in late March 1649 in *The Picture of the Councel of State* in W. Haller and Davies, G (eds) (1944), *The Leveller Tracts 1647–1653*. New York: Columbia University Press.
7. Aristotle, *Politics* III, 9, 1280b30–33.
8. Ibid., 1281a2, 1280b35.
9. See Machiavelli (1988), p. 26.
10. Richard Overton (1646), 'A Defiance against all Usurpations and Encroachments'. Thomason E.353[17].
11. Hermann Melville (2002), *Moby Dick*, 2nd edn, ed. H. Parker and H. Hayford. New York: W.W. Norton & Co., chapter 103.

# BIBLIOGRAPHY

Aristotle (1996), *Politics*, trans. Phillips Simpson. Chapel Hill: University of North Carolina Press.
— (1999), *Nicomachean Ethics*, 2nd edn, trans. Terence Irwin. Indianapolis, IN: Hackett.
Ashcraft, Richard (1986), *Revolutionary Politics and Locke's Two Treatises on Government*. Princeton: Princeton University Press.
Aspe, Bernard (2011), *Les mots et les actes*. Paris: Nous.
Aubenque, P. (1963), *La prudence chez Aristote*. Paris: Presses Universitaires de France.
Austin, J. (1962), *How to Do Things with Words*. Cambridge, MA: Harvard University Press.
Carvallo, Sarah (2006), 'Les dilemmes leibnitiens de l'action', in *L'action: délibérer, decider, accomplir*, ed. Hervé Guineret. Paris: Ellipses. pp. 9–30.
Coward, Barry (2003), *A Companion to Stuart Britain*. London: Blackwell.
Derrida, Jacques (1982), *Margins of Philosophy*, trans. A. Bass. Chicago: University of Chicago Press.
Descartes, René (1988), *Selected Philosophical Writings*, eds, Cottingham, Stoothoff, Murdoch and Kenny. Cambridge: Cambridge University Press.
Descombes, Vincent (2008), 'Philosophie du jugement politique', in *Philosophie du jugement politique*, eds, Vincent Descombes, Thomas Pavel and Alain Boyer. Paris: Seuil.
Ferrari, G. R. R. (ed.) (2000), *Plato: The Republic*, trans. Tom Griffith. Cambridge: Cambridge University Press.
Frank, Joseph (1969), *The Levellers: A History of the Writings of Three Seventeenth-Century Social Democrats: John Lilburne, Richard Overton, William Walwyn*. New York: Russell and Russell.
Gardiner, S. W. (1889), *The Great Civil War Volume II*. London: Longmans, Green & Co.
— (1891), *The Great Civil War Volume III*. London: Longmans, Green & Co.
Gaunt, P. (2000), *The English Civil War: The Essential Readings*. London: Blackwell.

Gentles, Ian (1992), *The New Model Army in England, Ireland and Scotland, 1645–1653*. Oxford: Blackwell.
Geuss, Raymond (2008), *Philosophy and Real Politics*. Princeton: Princeton University Press.
Gurney, John (2007), *Brave Community: The Digger Movement in the English Revolution*. Manchester: Manchester University Press.
Hampton, Jean (1986), *Hobbes and the Social Contract Tradition*. Cambridge: Cambridge University Press.
Hill, Christopher (1966), *The Century of Revolution, 1603–1714*. New York: Norton.
— (1972), *The World Turned Upside-down: Radical Ideas during the English Revolution*. London: Penguin.
— (1997), *Intellectual Origins of the English Revolution Revisited*. Oxford: Clarendon Press.
Hobbes, Thomas (1990), *Behemoth or the Long Parliament*. London: University of Chicago Press.
— (1991), *Leviathan*. Cambridge: Cambridge University Press.
— (1997), *On the Citizen*. Cambridge: Cambridge University Press.
Locke, John (1960), *Second Treatise on Government in Locke: Two Treatises on Government*, ed. Peter Laslett. Cambridge: Cambridge University Press.
— (1965), *Lettre sur la tolerance*, trans. R. Polin (from the Latin). Paris: Quadrige.
— (1967), *Two Tracts on Government*, ed. Philip Adams. Cambridge: Cambridge University Press.
— (1976), *The Correspondence of John Locke Vol. I*, ed. E. S. Beer. Oxford: Clarendon Press.
— (1983), *A Letter Concerning Toleration*. Indiana: Hackett.
— (1992), *Lettre sur la tolerance et autres texts*, trans. Jean le Clerc. Paris: Flammarion.
— (2008), *An Essay Concerning Human Understanding*, ed. Pauline Phemister. Oxford: Oxford University Press.
— (2010), *An Essay Concerning Toleration: And Other Writings on Law and Politics, 1667–1683*, eds, J. R. Milton and Philip Milton. Oxford: Oxford University Press.
Luther, Martin (1962), *Martin Luther: Selections from His Writings*, ed. J. Dillenger. New York: Anchor Books.
Machiavelli, Niccolò (1988), *The Prince*, trans. R. Price. Cambridge: Cambridge University Press.
Macpherson, Crawford B. (1962), *The Political Theory of Possessive Individualism*. Oxford: Oxford University Press.
Manning, Brian (1992), *1649: The Crisis of the English Revolution*. London: Bookmarks.

Melville, Herman (2002), *Moby Dick*, 2nd edn, eds, H. Parker and H. Hayford. New York: W.W. Norton & Co.
Mendle, Michael (ed.) (2001), *The Putney Debates of 1647: The Army, the Levellers and the English State*. Cambridge: Cambridge University Press.
Milton, John (2004), *Paradise Lost*, 3rd edn. London: W.W.Norton & Co.
Morrill, John (1993), *The Nature of the English Revolution*. London: Longman.
Pocock, John (1975), *The Machiavellian Moment*. Princeton, NJ: Princeton University Press.
Pynchon, Thomas (1973), *Gravity's Rainbow*. New York: Viking Press.
Rancière, Jacques (1995), *La mésentente*. Paris: Galilée.
Rousseau, Jean-Jacques (1964), *Oeuvres Complètes III*. Paris: Pleiade.
Schmitt, Carl (2002), *Le léviathan dans la doctrine de l'état de Thomas Hobbes*. Paris: Seuil.
Scott, Jonathan (2004), *Commonwealth Principles: Republican Writing of the English Revolution*. Cambridge: Cambridge University Press.
Sen, Amartya (2010), *The Idea of Justice*. London: Penguin.
Skinner, Quentin (2001), *Visions of Politics Vol. III: Hobbes and Civil Science*. Cambridge: Cambridge University Press.
— (2008), *Hobbes and Republican Liberty*. Cambridge: Cambridge University Press.
Smith, David L. (ed.) (2003), *Cromwell and the Interregnum*. Oxford: Blackwell.
Spinoza, Baruch (1985), *The Collected Works of Spinoza, Volume I*, ed. and trans. Edwin Curley. Princeton, NJ: Princeton University Press.
— (2000), *Ethics*, trans. G. H. R. Parkinson. Oxford: Oxford University Press.
— (2002), *Spinoza: Complete Works*, ed. M. Morgan and trans. Samuel Shirley. Indianapolis, IN: Hackett.
— (2005), *Oeuvres Tome V, Tractatus Politicus Traité Politique*, trans. C. Ramond. Paris: Presses Universitaires de France.
— (2007), *Theologico-Political Treatise*, trans. Michael Silverthorne and Jonathan Israel. Cambridge: Cambridge University Press.
Tully, James (1993), *An Approach to Political Philosophy: Locke in Contexts*. Cambridge: Cambridge University Press.
Woodhouse, A. S. P. (1951), *Puritanism & Liberty: Being the Army Debates from the Clarke Manuscripts with Supplementary Documents*. Chicago: University of Chicago Press.
Woolrych, Austin (1987), *Soldiers and Statesmen: The General Council of the Army and Its Debates 1647–8*. Oxford: Clarendon Press.
Zagorin, Perez (1998), *The English Revolution: Politics, Events, Ideas*. London: Ashgate.

# INDEX

accidents 88, 94, 198, 226, 227, 241, 266–7
agency 16–17, 41, 88, 98–9, 118–21, 129, 130, 155, 177, 202, 244–5, 249
  chiasmus 196, 214, 219, 239, 243, 245
  sharing 135, 148, 156, 164, 177, 180, 261–2, 268
agent 7, 9, 30, 34–6, 40–1, 83, 87, 91–4, 102–4, 106–9, 118–20, 128–9, 135, 168–71, 173, 187, 192–3, 198, 209, 219, 228, 238, 260–1
*An Agreement of the People* 29, 37, 49, 51, 59–60, 62, 64–5, 70, 76, 81, 84, 188, 251, 260, 269–70
anatomy of failure 22, 25–6, 104, 111, 181, 252, 266
angelism, angelic critique 10–11, 14, 16–19, 22, 25–6, 252, 270
apology 10–12, 14–18, 21–2, 25–6, 34, 184, 188, 229, 235–6, 252, 270
arbitrariness 125, 218, 234, 237, 242
arbitrary 38, 42, 61, 63, 71, 143–4, 212–13, 216, 221, 223–6, 228–9, 233–4, 237, 242, 246, 248

arguments against religious persecution (Locke's) 166–73
  argument from charity 166–7
  argument from dominion 166, 168
  argument from hypocrisy 166–7
  argument from uncertainty 166–7, 171
arguments against Thrasymachus (Socrates') 6
  argument from collective enterprise 6, 8, 10
  argument from error 6, 199
  argument from technique 6–8
Aristotle 8, 16, 18, 24, 40, 91–2, 95, 103, 111, 127, 152, 205, 227, 253–4, 261

Badiou, Alain 13, 242

*Case of the Army Truly Stated* 31, 33, 48–51, 56, 58, 69–70, 158, 257
civil law 66–7, 84, 119, 129, 142, 156, 186–7, 195, 197–202, 204–5, 207, 210, 215–16, 222, 232, 242–3
conditions of the law's successful operation (Hobbes) 199–206
  condition of exclusive authority 200, 205, 213

condition of exclusive
  interpretation 202, 203, 205
condition of
  perfectibility 204–5
condition of verification 202–3,
  205
conscience 61, 71, 89, 132–3, 139,
  144, 156–60, 162–5, 167,
  172–5, 177, 180, 207–9, 244,
  261, 268
context 24, 26, 30, 40–1, 94, 120,
  125, 127, 190, 209, 222, 226,
  255, 258–9, 263–6
contractual model of political
  action 26, 32, 55, 62–4, 66,
  71, 85, 102, 181–3, 197, 210,
  214–20, 222–3, 225, 227,
  230–4, 237–9, 242, 249, 252,
  260, 262
conversion 139, 150–2, 180, 209,
  261
counter-models of political action
  counter-model of despotic
    action 223, 225, 233, 235,
    242
  counter-model of imperial
    action 97–8, 102, 128
  counter-model of
    instrumentalism 63–4, 70–1,
    74, 265
critique of inspiration 75, 87,
  148–9, 206, 244

decision 21, 43, 69, 113, 115, 137,
  151–2, 186, 189, 218, 220–1,
  246, 253, 257
Descartes 88, 92, 95, 98, 105,
  107, 109, 168
Descombes, Vincent 12–14,
  18–20
disjoint action 139, 153–5, 157,
  165, 169, 174, 178–80, 208,
  268

dissent 155–6, 208

emanating work 138–9, 154, 165,
  173–4, 180, 268
empty work 134–6, 138, 154,
  166, 168
enthusiasm 9, 26, 35, 75, 87, 149,
  181, 244–5, 247, 265
excommunication 139, 150–1,
  158, 170, 175

faction 8–9, 48, 50, 53, 131, 193,
  253, 259
faith 58, 132, 134–9, 152–61,
  165–7, 169, 172–80, 261, 268
freedom 61, 72, 90, 93, 100, 105,
  129, 158, 176, 179, 212, 215,
  218, 224, 231–3, 237–40,
  257, 264
freedom of conscience 132, 144

Geuss, Raymond 18, 20–1

idea of action 102–9
identity 85, 88, 109, 117–21, 129,
  162, 169, 177–8, 185, 203,
  215, 217, 259–63
indeterminacy (of use, usage,
  practice) 128, 179, 182, 205,
  226–7, 249, 259
inverse models of political
  action 190
  inverse model of
    prudence 226–34, 246, 249

judgement 7, 13–15, 19, 45–6,
  61, 80, 109, 112–13, 119–21,
  125, 130, 134, 167–8, 175,
  183, 186–90, 196–9, 205,
  210, 219–20, 228, 230, 238,
  243–8, 253, 257, 262, 266
juridical institutions 89, 119–21,
  129–30, 246

INDEX

Lacan, Jacques 2, 40, 270
law 40, 42, 52, 66, 71, 78, 80, 83,
  93–4, 101, 119–20, 134–40,
  142, 144, 146, 153–7, 165,
  172, 180, 181–3, 186, 193,
  209, 220–3, 226, 232, 236,
  240, 246, 262–3
  civil law 66–7, 84, 114, 119,
    129, 142, 156–7, 186–7, 189,
    195, 197–208, 215–16, 218,
    222, 232, 242–3, 260
  divine law 66–7, 119–20,
    132–3, 141–2, 145–6, 149,
    153, 156–7, 164, 201
  natural law 61, 65, 66, 110–12,
    142, 145, 161, 164, 182–6,
    189–90, 195, 200–1, 204,
    208, 210–11, 213–14, 216,
    218, 224, 233, 235, 238–42,
    244–5, 266, 270
Leveller-agitator model of joint
  action 26, 85, 90, 251–70
liberalism 82, 174, 249, 251
Luther, Martin 133–9, 165, 173,
  268

Machiavelli, Niccolò 11, 263
mechanism 89–97, 101–2, 108–9,
  112–13, 117, 128–9, 132,
  152, 190, 245, 254
Meillassoux, Quentin 265
mixed modes 122–8, 248

Nietzsche, Friedrich 13, 15–16, 20
nominalism 109, 113–14, 117,
  119–21, 124, 128–9, 152,
  180, 182, 187, 190, 199, 227,
  248, 265–6

ontology, ontological
  description 22, 73–4, 88,
  91, 93–5, 102–5, 108–9, 116,
  121, 128, 179, 182, 188–90,
  199, 208, 218, 226, 241, 246,
  254, 257, 266

parts 90, 95, 121, 192, 253–6,
  259, 268
personhood 87–9, 117–20,
  129–30, 177
Plato 1–10, 12, 17–18, 20, 22, 95,
  159, 229
polis (city-state) 23, 94, 227
popular sovereignty 29, 52, 64,
  66, 79, 84, 242, 265, 270
pragmatism, pragmatist 124–5,
  128, 130, 227, 248
primitive Christians 159–60
primitive / early church 149–53,
  159–62, 167, 180, 209, 261
problems with mixed modes
  (Locke) 121–7, 130
  problem of application 125–7,
    130
  problem of transmission 122,
    124, 130
property 142, 170, 183–4, 186–7,
  198, 206, 211, 213–17, 221,
  224, 231–40, 243, 246, 254,
  260, 264
prudence 92, 111–12, 190,
  204–5, 209, 222, 226–32,
  234, 242, 246, 248–9
Putney debates 26, 31, 37, 48,
  51–6, 58–85, 158, 237, 240,
  258

queries (the five queries of political
  action) 31, 36, 38, 47, 51, 59,
  73, 83–5, 116, 155, 181, 190,
  198, 206, 242–6, 252, 257,
  262, 269

region, regional 41–2, 55, 94–5,
  179, 201, 248, 253–9, 262–4,
  267–9

religious persecution 153, 166–9, 173, 175
religious toleration 131–2, 134, 139, 148, 165–6, 170, 173–5, 177–9, 270
right to resistance 61, 90, 183, 185, 187, 214, 217–19, 229, 240–1, 243–6, 254

salvation 132, 156, 161, 166, 170–2, 176–8
Socrates 1–11, 17, 20, 23, 113, 124, 163, 199, 270
*A Solemn Engagement* 30, 32, 37–53, 61–2, 70, 158, 257, 268
sovereign model of political action 26, 32, 42, 85, 88, 102, 113–17, 139–41, 182, 190–210, 220, 223, 242–50, 252–3
Spinoza, Baruch 89–90, 97–102, 105–6, 108–9, 128, 132–3
state of nature 110–11, 129, 142, 156, 161, 181–90, 197, 199, 206, 211–15, 218–20, 224, 227, 230, 232–5, 238–9, 242, 247, 254
subject
 subject as atomic switch 178–80, 185–6, 197, 208, 216, 229, 232–3, 245, 260, 262, 270

subject of state of nature 161–2, 238
subject of toleration 177–80

teaching (apostles' practice of) 150–2, 160–1, 166–7, 180, 209, 261
tension of agency 249
tension of history 248–9
tension of the multiple 244
tension of use 249
Thrasymachus 1–10, 17, 32, 44, 113–14, 142, 163, 199, 251, 253, 270
truth 1, 7, 9, 13, 137, 252, 266–7
 truth as adequation of mixed modes 124–8

vulnerabilities of the law (in Hobbes) 199–204
vulnerability of the law's agents 203
vulnerability of the law's generality 204
vulnerability of the meaning of the law 203
vulnerability of the source of law 200–1

whole 43, 48, 50, 83–4, 94–6, 102, 121, 227, 244, 254–9, 261, 269

zone of resistance 229–34, 248

www.ingramcontent.com/pod-product-compliance
Lightning Source LLC
Chambersburg PA
CBHW052153300426
44115CB00011B/1646